DRUPAL 7: THE ESSENTIALS

Johan Falk

ISBN-13: 978-1463659714
ISBN-10: 1463659717

Drupal is a registered trademark of Dries Buytaert.

Cover design: Matts Hildén
Cover photography: Eva Hildén Smith

Printed in the United States of America 2011.

CONTENTS

Part B: Information structure in Drupal 75

CHAPTER 6 Fields 77

CHAPTER 7 Taxonomy 97

CHAPTER 10 Advanced Views configuration 155

Part C: Other essential modules 187

CHAPTER 13   Basic Page manager and Panels configuration   231

Appendix 1: Installation and code base management   273

Appendix 2: Language management in Drupal   305

INTRODUCTION

Congratulations! The fact that you have started reading this book means that you are interested in learning more about the web publishing system Drupal. Drupal is a powerful, flexible, easy-to-manage, and inspiring tool. You will have many fun and rewarding experiences ahead of you. And if you use Drupal right, the administrators and visitors of the sites you build will also have fun and rewarding experiences.

When starting to learn Drupal it might seem like there are an infinite amount of things that you can learn. And as far as I know this might actually be true. During the years I've worked with Drupal I have constantly learned new things, and yet I still have never gotten the feeling that I have learned it all.

But over the years I have also become more and more convinced that there is a way to *start* learning Drupal that is better than most (if not all). When you start learning Drupal I think it is important to begin by learning how to use several important modules. If you are not skilled in using these crucial modules you will reinvent the wheel, and miss many of the advantages that Drupal's framework offers. On the other hand if you learn to master these modules, you will not only have a the tools to quickly and efficiently build the structure for practically all types of websites, you will also be equipped to deepen your knowledge in web development with Drupal, regardless if you want to code, build interfaces, lead projects, or niche your skills in some other way.

This book covers the core skills you need to learn as new Drupal developer (and a bit more). It is by no means a complete description of everything you need or can use, but the book is designed to give you a solid foundation to continue to learn.

I hope you will have as much fun as I did when I started to learn Drupal, and I look forward to learn from the unique knowledge you will bring into the Drupal community.

Welcome.

//Johan Falk

WHAT IS DRUPAL?

The simple answer to the question, "What is Drupal ?" is, Drupal is a *web publishing system*. Drupal is a program, or a web application, used to manage content on a website.

But this is only one part of the real answer, Drupal is not only a tool for managing content on a website, but a tool *to build tools* to manage content on websites. It is a meta tool, used by web developers to build customized web publishing tools. In some respects you may even call Drupal a programming language.

But even this is not the full answer. Most people who have used Drupal for a while will tell you that Drupal is a *community*. A group of people spread out over the world, sharing a common goal or interest, and feeling that they have something connecting them. At the time of writing this book this community has more than half a million members, in one way or another contributing to the project called Drupal. Some put their efforts into making Drupal look better (an appreciated contribution). Quite a few people code and build new functionality. Some work with documentation, translations, or with answering questions from people new to Drupal. Some people in the community are so well-known that they almost could be compared to rock stars. But the vast majority of the community consists of people who mostly just use Drupal as a publishing tool. They help the project every once in a while by posing new questions, reporting a bug or bringing feature requests to developers.

Several of the people who will be most important to Drupal's growth and development in the future have just started using it.

Free software

Drupal is distributed with a license usually called *open source*. It means that in contrast to nearly all other publishing systems of the same magnitude, Drupal is free of charge. There is no fee for download or starting to use Drupal, and no yearly license payment to continue to use it.

More fundamental than the price, though, is what you are allowed and not allowed to do with Drupal. If you have taken the time to read the fine print of end-user licence agreements for software you have often seen that they require that you agree to not install the program on more than a certain number of computers, that you won't hack or reverse-engineer the software, and that you don't violate any of the patents the software includes.

Open source licenses were created as a reaction against the limits that closed-source software creates. Open source software have licenses that explicitly say that you *may* use the program as much as you like, you *may* fiddle with its code to find out how it is built, you may share copies of the software to your friends, and you *may* use the software (or parts of it) to make new and better software. If you use Drupal to build a website you can be sure that you can write plugins to help your site to work with other systems you use, without being sued.

The philosophy behind open source is really quite simple: It is better if we work together.

For quite long time open source software was pretty insignificant in comparison to other paid software systems, It was only used by computer nerds with weird beards. Today one of the top-ten websites in the world (Wikipedia) is run on open source software, and is filled with information that is also governed by open source licenses. Also, one of the top web publishing systems in the world is shared as open source. We call it Drupal.

What you will learn with this book

Drupal may be free and used by lots of hobbyists, but it is not a toy tool. It is a software system so massive that even its most bright and devoted developers can *(and sometimes do)* spend many years understanding *parts* of Drupal. Most Drupal developers have a hard time even keeping pace with development of the system, to avoid coming to work one day and knowing less than they did the day before.

Roughly half of this book explains concepts that Drupal developers of every specialization should know; coders and module developers, designers and interface experts, server managers and database optimizers, as well as site builders.

The other half of this book is primarily targeted towards you. Someone who wants to be a great Drupal site builder. Building website functionality by clicking in the Drupal interface and making different modules work together well. But if you're aspiring to become a great Drupal coder you will also find this book's second half usefull.

The content of this book deals almost exclusively with *functionality* and *information structure* – things that could be called "the skeleton structure" of how a website works. Relatively little focus it put on topics like user interface or modifying the presentation of websites – there is, for example, no chapter explaining how to install a wysiwyg editor in Drupal. This choice is very deliberate – building the right information structure for a website is the foundation for making them useful, and learning other Drupal skills first would be a mistake. When you feel that you grasp most things presented in this book, you will have no problems installing a wysiwyg editor of your choice – but if you had been using wysiwyg editor to upload images, without taking your information structure into account, you would risk serious problems when trying to reuse the images on other parts of your website.

The Drupal Way

Nothing covered by this book requires that you know how to code – the most advanced "code" mentioned is HTML links, and even HTML coding is only mentioned in some exceptions. Yet the topics in this book are essential to anyone who wants to code and build Drupal modules. Why?

One of the strongest merits of Drupal is that it allows you to build professional websites with very little coding. This is possibly thanks to some very general and extremely flexible modules (plugins) available to extend Drupal's capacity. These modules not only make it possible to assemble amazing web applications without a single line of coding, they also provide coders with powerful libraries that can make every line of custom-written code a hundred or even thousand times more useful.

A coder who doesn't know the ecosystem of Drupal modules well, might reinvent the wheel over and over again. She might write code that to a large extent is unnoticed, unused – and unnecessary. On the other hand if you as a coder know the most common Drupal modules well, you have the chance to extend them with small, efficient pieces of code. The result is much less code to maintain and update, better opportunities to reuse your code in other settings, and surprisingly often, other Drupal developers find new and unexpected use cases for the functionality you have added.

The philosophy of using the ecosystem of modules when building sites by clicking and configuring in addition to coding your own modules has by some been called *the Drupal Way*. The Drupal Way includes:

- Using common and well-used Drupal modules to solve tasks, when possible.
- Using modules that extend the common and well-used Drupal modules, rather than modules that are relatively isolated islands in the ecosystem.
- Focusing problem solving around how you can use and re-use the common and well-used Drupal modules, even when writing new code is required.
- Sharing your solutions with the Drupal community, if at all possible.

The philosophy behind the Drupal Way is the same for open source in general - things are better when we work together.

The advantages of building sites the Drupal Way is not only that the ecosystem of modules grows and the community is strengthened – the direct economic advantages are equally appealing. One example of this is the work often put into maintaining and eventually upgrading websites. Drupal sites based on common and well-used modules will have the help of thousands of other website maintainers when it comes to finding and fixing bugs, getting one-click upgrade paths, developing new features – It also has the advantage that all Drupal developers will understand how the site works. A site owner on the opposite end of the scale – with a site largely based on custom code – will have to find and solve bugs themselves, develop all new features alone, and will most likely not be able to port the site to the next version of Drupal when the time comes. In worst case he won't even be able to apply security updates provided by Drupal's security team, since custom hacks in the Drupal source code might be overwritten. On top of all this, there is only a handful people in the world who know how the site works – making it unpleasantly vulnerable. In effect, the site owner could just as well have ignored Drupal all together and built a custom publishing system, like web developers used to do in the previous millennium. This is not a situation you want to be in.

This book is completely based on the Drupal Way. All modules mentioned in this book are among the most used and tested modules in Drupal's ecosystem. The four modules given a closer presentation – *Views*, *Flag*, *Rules* and *Page manager/Panels* – are the foundation of uncountable websites over the world and are by many considered the most important modules for Drupal.

How should I read this book?

This book is divided into a few separate parts:

- Part A covers basic concepts and skills you need to have when using Drupal. Each chapter in part A ends with a number of exercises or tasks you can use to put the concepts into practice.
- Part B covers some of the more challenging aspects of the functionality provided by Drupal. It also covers the Views module – an important step in understanding and leveraging the power of Drupal. The chapters in part B ends with more extensive exercises, requiring more time than the tasks in part A.
- Part C is a sequel you should use when you are comfortable with the concepts in part B. Three new modules are presented, each of them an important key when building Drupal sites. The point of part C is more of a reference and less of a narrative, but examples of use cases are provided in separate boxes as well as in the exercises at the end of each chapter.
- Appendix 1 covers how to install Drupal, modules and themes. It also presents an approach for how to version control your configuration in Drupal.
- Appendix 2 covers how to use Drupal in other languages than English.

> **TIP**
>
> Throughout this book there are comments written in boxes like this. They contain some more advanced tips that you may appreciate the second or third time you read a section – you could safely skip them on your first read.

The exercise suites

This book contains a large number of exercises and tasks which you can use to practice your new Drupal skills. All tasks and exercises belong to an *exercise suite*. There are three suites:

- The *Boss suite* is used in part A, where a fictive boss provides you with comparatively straight-forward tasks. The purpose of these tasks is to make you try out Drupal's administrative and editorial interface – not to build complete websites.

- The *Documentation site suite* spans over both part B and C, building up a website used by a community for online documentation. Though exercises fit together in both functionality and theme, most of the exercises only require that you have the very basics on the site built up – you are not forced to do all exercises in sequence, nor to do them at all.

- The *News site suite* also spans both part B and C, building a website used for publishing news. These exercises are suitable for anyone who wants to spend more time on exploring and trying different solutions in Drupal – while each exercise is described with a user story and how-to-demo instructions, there are no suggested solutions and only a few comments.

> **TIP**
>
> All exercises in the Documentation site suite are available as screen recordings – video clips demonstrating the desired functionality as well as how to build it in Drupal. Visit nodeone.se/learn-drupal to watch them!

Exercises and user stories

The exercises in the *Documentation site* and *News site* suites (in part B and C) are presented as *user stories*. A user story is a way of describing development tasks that is increasingly common in web development – and software development in general. The core of a user story is a short description of what a particular type of site user *wants to do* on the website. Describing functionality as user stories helps focus on the actual point of the functionality, rather than technical solutions.

User stories are an important part of *agile development methods*, a central concept in modern software development. You can find a quick introduction to agile development on Wikipedia: http://en.wikipedia.org/wiki/Agile_software_development.

The News site suite only contains a bare minimum of user story information, while the Documentation site has rich descriptions to help you get going:

- A short but descriptive title, hopefully making it easier to find and remember the exercise.
- The actual user story for the exercise is a statement about *who* should be able to do something, *what* they should do, and *why* the functionality is desired. The why part is considered important in agile development, since it for example may help developers choose among different solutions.
- A screenshot, displaying an example end result.
- Each exercise also has a *how to demo* section. These are steps that you should carry out to ultimately deciding if the user story has been completed or not. Often these steps include details about the task not mentioned in the short user story – make sure to read these sections!
- The exercises also have any *required preparations* listed. These are limited to short and easy tasks, and no extra preparations are necessary if all tasks are carried out in sequence. (See below for details about the suites of exercises.)
- Each exercise is followed by a suggested solution, intended to be the most natural way of solving the task. Each step in the solution points to relevant sections in the book, where you can read more about how this step works and is carried out.
- Finally, exercises have comments pointing out details that may have been easily missed or they may mention alternative approaches for a solution.

The suggested solutions are intended to be the most natural ones, but it is quite possible that there are other solutions that are better from a certain perspective – there are even cases where the exercises intentionally are written this way.

"At the time of writing"

The first words of this book were written just a few days before Drupal 7 was released in it's first stable version. At that point there were many modules (plugins) available in more or less stable versions, and many more were waiting in the starting blocks for their Drupal 7 versions. The examples in this book are based on what was available when the book was written, but a few cases also describe functionality expected to be available at the time of the release of this book.

You will find the expression "at the time of writing" throughout this book, accompanying descriptions of bugs or lacking functionality. It is likely that most of these issues will be solved when you read this book.

Places to learn more

This book will hopefully give you a solid start in how to use Drupal, but it only covers a small fraction of everything there is to know. Here are some tips on where to find more Drupal knowledge:

- drupal.org: This is the main website for Drupal, and a hub for everything related to Drupal. The site contains global forums, project pages for modules and themes, and powerful search functionality that will help you to find just about anything Drupal.
- The Drupal Documentation, http://drupal.org/documentation: This is the official Drupal documentation, with loads of guides and how to's for everyone – from absolute newbies to experienced developers.
- groups.drupal.org, http://groups.drupal.org/: This is a place where like-minded Drupalists get together to discuss Drupal. It is likely that you will find a Drupal group for your country or city, as well as a group for your particular interest – be it newspapers on Drupal or designing with grid systems.
- Internet Relay Chat (IRC): Drupal has many channels for chatting, often with several hundred users present. Live chatting with people is an excel-

lent way of getting urgent help, as well as getting to know people in the Drupal community. You will find more information about IRC where you find the chat rooms and how to access them.

- Planet Drupal, http://drupal.org/planet: This page contains an aggregated river of news about Drupal, collected from all over the Drupal world.

Acknowledgements

When writing this book I have received invaluable help from by awesome colleagues at NodeOne. I would especially like to thank the CEO Thomas Barregren for his encouragement and most importantly for convincing me that writing a book was not complete madness. I would also like to thank my colleague Rustan Håkansson who's ideas have made a substantial contribution to improving this book, and my colleague BJ Wilson for helping out with language issues even when in extreme time constraints. Any language issues remaining in the book are entirely my fault – while any brilliant wordings surely are the work of BJ. A big thank-you also goes to Matts Hildén, for invaluable help in getting the digital manuscript into an actual printed book.

Part A:
Drupal core basics

This part covers the most important functionality and concepts in Drupal core – Drupal without any additional modules. These concepts are used at virtually all Drupal sites, and they are essential for understanding how to use Drupal.

Nodes

It is a strange but never-failing effect that people who know a lot about a subject start building their own language; words that are obvious to everyone initiated in the language, but sheer nonsense for those who aren't.

Surgeons may use *stents*, carpenters have *sharpening jigs* and sailors know how to raise and lower a *jib*. Drupalistas, too, have their share of strange terms – some of which you will learn in this book. The most important of them is probably *node*.

A node is, to say it out loud, a piece of content on a Drupal site. It can be a information page, a blog post or a press release, but also things you don't usually read as separate web pages can be nodes – for example an image with associated information, an uploaded video, or a container to collect pages that can have restricted access for certain users.

Understanding how to use nodes to build information structure on a website is one of the most important things you will learn as a Drupal developer. This chapter explains how to use the basic features of nodes.

> **TIP**
>
> The term *node* has in Drupal 7 almost completely been replaced with *content*. But the term *node* is still widely used by many modules (plugins) and in documentation. This makes it important to know and recognize. In this book the terms *node* and *content* are used interchangeably if not otherwise stated.

Creating nodes

On the first page you see as an administrator on a new Drupal site there is no less than three links to create new content – one in the sidebar, one in the shortcuts at the top of the page, and one right in the middle of the page. (See figure 1.1.) They all open the administrative overlay, allowing you to create either an *Article* or a *Basic page*. (See figure 1.2.)

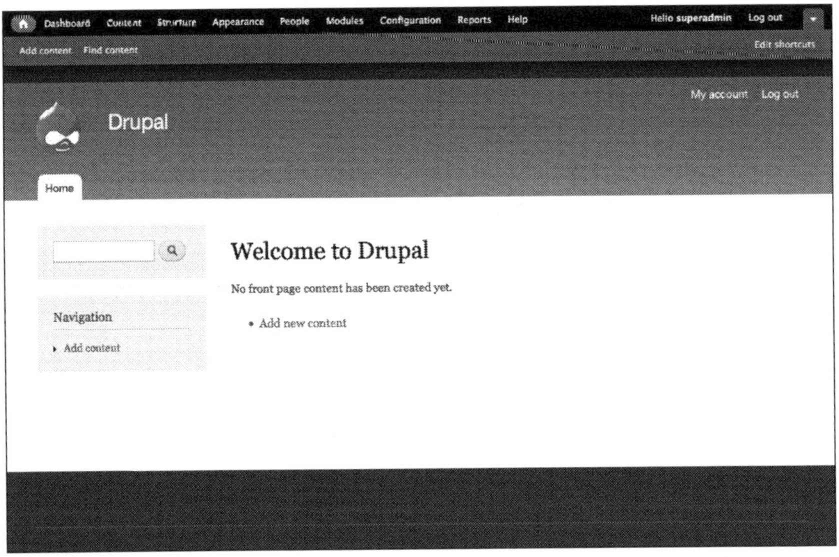

FIGURE 1.1 A Drupal standard installation without any content – click create content to create your first node!

FIGURE 1.2 Nodes – content – by default come in two flavors: Articles and Basic pages.

Articles and Basic pages are two *node types* – types of content – and by clicking on any of the type names will give you a form used to build a content of that type – the node form. The forms used for Articles and Basic pages are different, but they work the same way: you get a number of fields where you can input information in one way or another, and you have buttons for previewing or saving the piece of content. (See figure 1.3.)

Below is a description for the fields available in the Article node form.

- Title: This is the headline for the article, and will be shown at the top of the article's page on the website (it will also be used for the HTML title shown in the web browser's top bar).
- Tags: This is an opportunity to assign your article one or more keywords, used to categorize the content. Drupal will suggest any matching existing keywords while you write, but you can also provide new ones. If you want several keywords, separate them with commas. Keywords are usually displayed as links to lists of all nodes with the same keyword.
- Body: This field is used for the main text of the article.
- Edit summary/hide summary: When clicking *edit summary* you get a box where you can write a summary of the article. Summaries are often used when articles are listed, as a so called *teaser* (see separate section). The link *hide summary* hides the box again. If no explicit summary is written, Drupal will create one from the first part of the body.
- Text format: Usually the body field only contains plain text, but it can interpret some HTML markup. The settings in the text format field decide which markup should be allowed, which is important from a security point of view. See separate section for details.
- Image: This gives you the opportunity to upload an image to be displayed along with the article. Uploaded images can by default be provided with alt texts – text shown if the image isn't loaded (This is important for screen-readers used by visually impaired as well as for search engine robots).
- At the bottom of the node form there is a number of settings for menus, comments and some other things. These are described later.
- Finally there are buttons to save or preview the article. A click on the save button brings you to a new web page, showing the article you just created. (See figure 1.4.)

Title *

Hello world!

Tags

alpha, beta, gamma

Enter a comma-separated list of words to describe your content.

Summary (Hide summary)

This is a special summary, created by clicking the 'edit summary' link.

Leave blank to use trimmed value of full text as the summary.

Body

Proin in velit libero, vitae sodales lectus. Aenean posuere interdum magna ut imperdiet. In mollis velit et ante posuere ut ullamcorper augue ultricies. Fusce eu sem ut lectus scelerisque dignissim. Pellentesque egestas orci suscipit elit tincidunt a egestas magna malesuada. Praesent sollicitudin nulla ac metus semper auctor! Donec in arcu arcu, eget faucibus lectus. Suspendisse ut metus erat, at ultrices risus. Praesent non ipsum vitae ante facilisis sollicitudin in et ante. Fusce hendrerit rhoncus elit, vel venenatis tortor pretium vel. Proin a lectus velit. Pellentesque eget massa tortor. Maecenas a tellus libero. Aliquam venenatis dui sit amet tellus interdum in porta libero elementum. Proin malesuada massa a lectus eleifend ut viverra felis auctor! Cras sit amet tellus magna. Donec diam mauris, vulputate id volutpat ut, commodo in leo. Vestibulum ante ipsum primis in faucibus orci luctus et ultrices posuere cubilia Curae; Curabitur faucibus, sem gravida accumsan lacinia, sem nibh tincidunt magna, ut euismod metus mi quis urna.

Nullam ut leo orci. Duis sed placerat sapien? Etiam aliquet ultricies dui; vitae rutrum risus sollicitudin ac. Vestibulum consectetur dolor orci aliquam.

More information about text formats

Text format Filtered HTML

- Web page addresses and e-mail addresses turn into links automatically.
- Allowed HTML tags: <a> <em> <strong> <cite> <blockquote> <code> <ul> <ol> <li> <dl> <dt> <dd>
- Lines and paragraphs break automatically.

Image

DSCN4861.JPG (589.13 KB)   Remove

Alternate text

This is a pinecone.

This text will be used by screen readers, search engines, or when the image cannot be loaded.

Upload an image to go with this article.

Menu settings
Not in menu

☐ **Provide a menu link**

Revision information
No revision

URL path settings
No alias

Comment settings
Open

Authoring information
By superadmin

Publishing options
Published, Promoted to front page

Save   Preview

FIGURE 1.3 The form used to create new articles has room for different sorts of information.

FIGURE 1.4 A saved article page, in it's default layout.

> **TIP**
>
> Node types are also called *content types.*

Editing nodes and managing revisions

An article page – as well as other node pages – have two tabs; *view* and *edit.* By clicking the edit tab you will re-open the node edit form, identical to the one you just used except for two things: The form is pre-populated with the content of your article, and there is a button to delete the node next to the save and preview buttons.

Among the settings at the bottom of the node form you will find *revision information.* (See figure 1.5.) Checking the option *create new revision* tells Drupal to archive the present version of the node when a new version is created – a pretty useful feature if you want version control of your content. A node that has archived revisions will be displayed with an additional tab – *revisions* or *log.* A click on the tab gives you an overview of all available revisions, with links to view them, revert the node to a selected revision, and also deleting revisions if necessary. (See figure 1.6.) Reverting a node doesn't delete any revisions – it merely places a copy of the selected revision on top as the current revision.

> **TIP**
>
> As a rule, links and settings are only visible if you are allowed to use them. Thus, the tab for editing a node is only displayed for users who are allowed to edit it, and the option for changing text formats are only displayed if you are allowed to switch format. When logged in with user account 1 you will usually see all settings, for better and for worse.

> **TIP**
>
> The module *Diff* allows you to compare node revisions to see what is changed between them. It also allows you to preview changes in a node before saving.

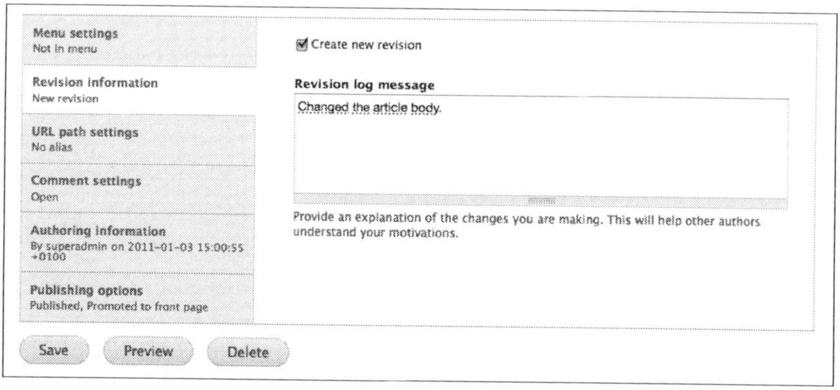

FIGURE 1.5 Drupal has built in functionality for node revisions.

FIGURE 1.6 The tab revisions (or *log*) shows all previous versions of a node, along with any log messages for revisions.

Other node settings

Apart from *revision information* there are usually five other tabs with settings at the bottom of the node form.

- Menu settings: This gives you the chance to add a menu item linking to the node. Read more about menu management in the menu chapter.
- URL path settings: This allows you to give the node a URL path in parallel to the path used internally by Drupal. The internal path for nodes is always on the form 'node/NN', where NN is a unique ID number for the node.

- Comment settings: This allows you turn on or off commenting on each node. If the node already has comments, you can choose to hide these.
- Authoring information: This shows which user account was used to create the node, and when it was created. Both fields can be changed, if necessary.
- Publishing options: This gives you three settings deciding how and where the node should be displayed on the site.
  - Published: By default only administrators may view unpublished content, while published content is accessible for anyone.
  - Promoted to front page: With this option checked, the node will be included in the list by default used as Drupal's home page. (Most larger sites have customized home pages, and this option is hidden.)
  - Sticky at top of lists: This option make the node show up above other nodes on the front page, as well as some other lists.

> **TIP**
>
> The *Pathauto module* will give your nodes (and some other pages on your site) automatically created URL aliases. These are based on customizable patterns, such as 'news/2011/may/title-of-article'.

View modes for nodes

When visiting the page for a node, you will usually see all of it's content. But when listed on the front page, only parts of it are displayed – for articles the body is replaced by a summary, and any images are displayed in a smaller format. This represents to view modes for nodes: *full node* and *teaser*.

Nodes may be configured to be displayed in different ways in each display mode. More details about this can be found in the chapter about view modes and displaying fields.

Node types and node administration

Articles and basic pages are two different node types – two different templates used to create and manage the nodes. These differences are reflected in some different ways, such as:

- There are separate links for creating each node type.

- Each node type has room for different sets of information. Details about this can be found in the fields chapter.
- You may set separate permissions for which users may create, edit and delete each node type. Details about this can be found in the chapter about users and permissions.
- Each node type may have different defaults settings for comment handling, publishing options, menu links, and more. Details about this are found below.

Home » Administration » Structure

✦ Add content type

NAME	OPERATIONS			
Article (Machine name: article) Use *articles* for time-sensitive content like news, press releases or blog posts.	edit	manage fields	manage display	delete
Basic page (Machine name: page) Use *basic pages* for your static content, such as an 'About us' page.	edit	manage fields	manage display	delete

FIGURE 1.7 The administration link structure, content types in the administration toolbar provide an overview of all node types on your website.

DEFAULT SETTINGS FOR NODE TYPES

The administration menu – the black list at the top of the page in a standard installation – There is an item called *structure*. It leads to a page with some of the most interesting settings when building a Drupal site – such as *content types*. A click on this link leads to an overview of all node types available on the website, along with links to manage each content type. There is also a link to create new content types, above the list. (See figure 1.7.)

The links named *manage fields* and *manage display* are so interesting that they have their very own chapters, and are not discussed further here. (See the chapters on fields, view modes, and field display.) You won't be surprised to learn that the *delete* link is used to delete the node type. The *edit* link is used to set the most basic properties for a node type (see figure 1.8):

- Name: This is the name of the node type. Based on the plain-text name, Drupal suggests a *machine name*, among other things used to identify the node type in Drupal's database.

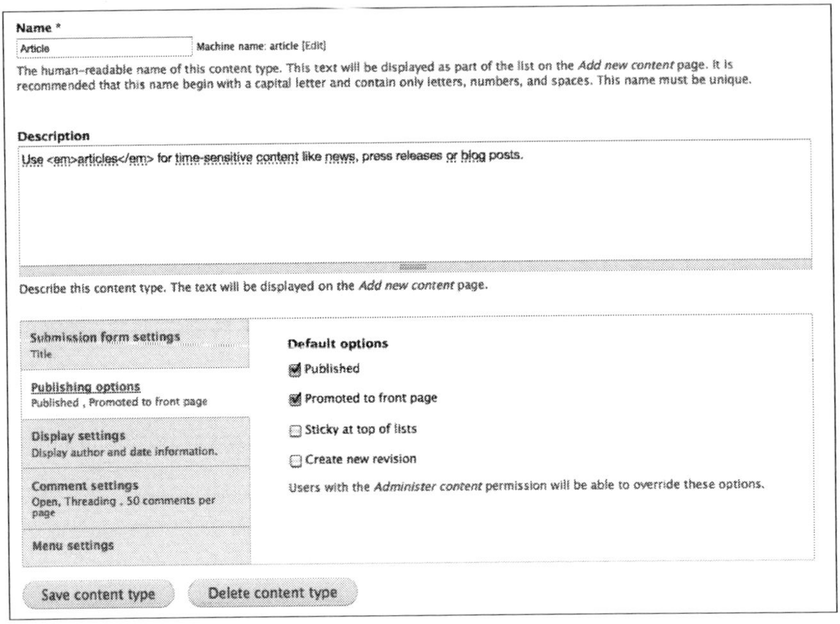

FIGURE 1.8 It is possible to set a number of default settings per content type, such as node revisioning.

- Description: This text is shown in some lists of node types, such as the list provided when you click *add content*.
- Submission form settings: This gives you the opportunity to change the label used for the title of the node type – if you have a node type for contacts, setting the label to 'name' makes more sense than 'title'. There are also options for changing the node preview settings, and providing the node form with help text.
- Publishing options: This is used to set the default settings for the nodes' publishing states – This includes the option to create new revisions by default when editing content. Changing these settings will not affect any existing nodes (with the exception of revisioning, which is returned to default every time a node is edited).
- Display settings: This gives you the opportunity to show or hide the information about who created the node, and when.
- Comment settings: This allows a number of settings for comments, such as: commenting can be allowed by default or not, and comments can be listed as a straight list or in a tree structure.

- Menu settings: These options dictate which menus (usually) should be able to link to nodes of this type, and if by default nodes should be placed under a particular menu item. More details about menus are found in a separate chapter.

More modules – plugins – may provide new options on the page for editing node type settings.

NODE ADMINISTRATION

Nodes may be scattered all over a Drupal site, and it is not always easy to find the very node you are looking for. The administration toolbar's option *content* provides a list of all nodes on the website, along with some useful tools (see figure 1.9):

- Filters to limit the node list to only selected content types or nodes with selected publishing options.
- Links to see, edit and delete each node.
- Options to perform mass updates on nodes, for example to publish, unpublish or delete several nodes at once.

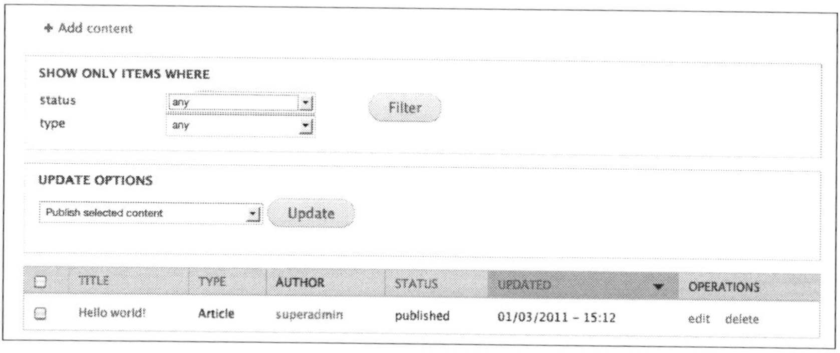

FIGURE 1.9 The administration page to manage content has tools for performing mass updates on nodes.

> **TIP**
>
> Larger Drupal sites usually have custom tailored administration pages to manage content according to workflows relevant for that site. The *Views Bulk Operations* module offers an alternative administration page for content, with more options and greater flexibility.

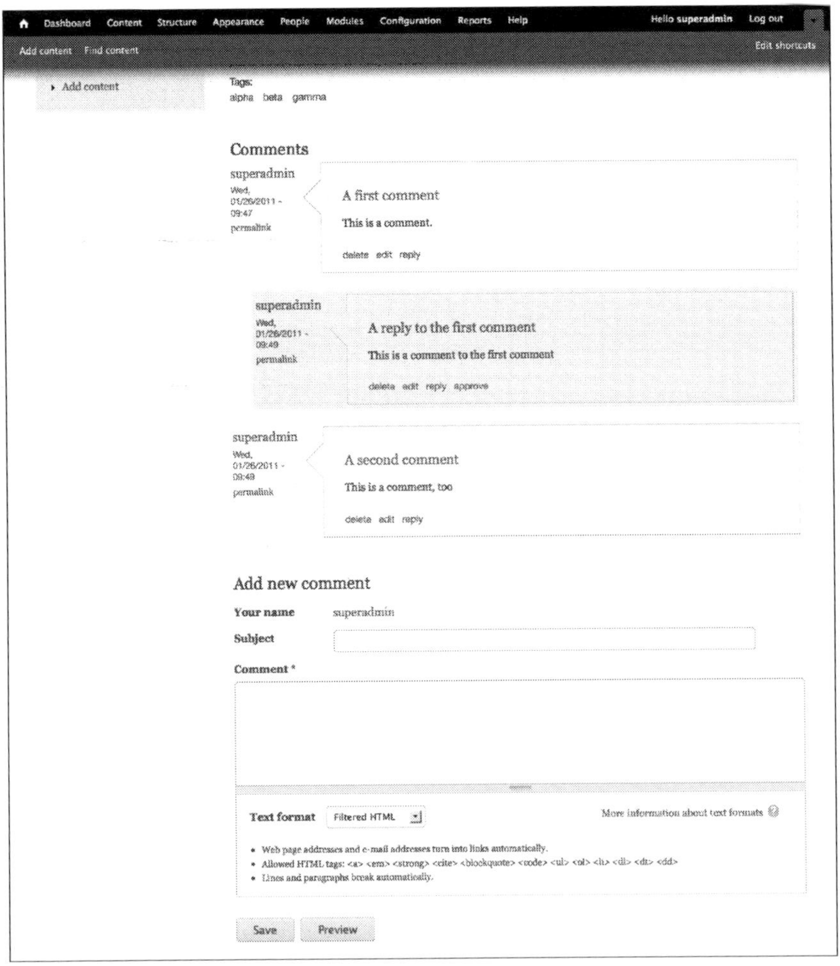

FIGURE 1.10 Nodes may have comments, and comments may be ordered in a tree structure.

Node comments

When the module *Comment* is enabled – which is the case for a standard installation – users may post comments to nodes. (See figure 1.10.) As previously mentioned it is possible to turn on and off the comment settings for each node, and it is also possible to change the default setting for each node type.

Administrators can manage comments in two different ways:

- Each comment has an *edit* link, allowing administrators to edit the content of each comments, including changing posting information and optionally publishing/unpublishing the comment. (See figure 1.11.)
- At the content overview page there is a tab *comments*, leading to a list of all published comments on the website. There are also sub tabs available to switch between viewing published and unpublished comments, and each list has tools for publishing, unpublishing and deleting comments. (See figure 1.12 and 1.13.)

Comments are similar to nodes in their structure, but from a technical point of view they are not nodes.

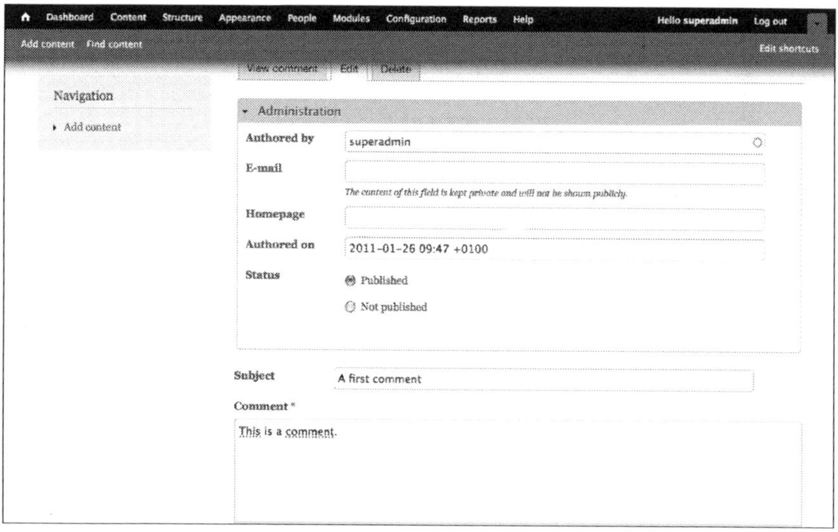

FIGURE 1.11 Administrators can, if necessary, edit each individual comment.

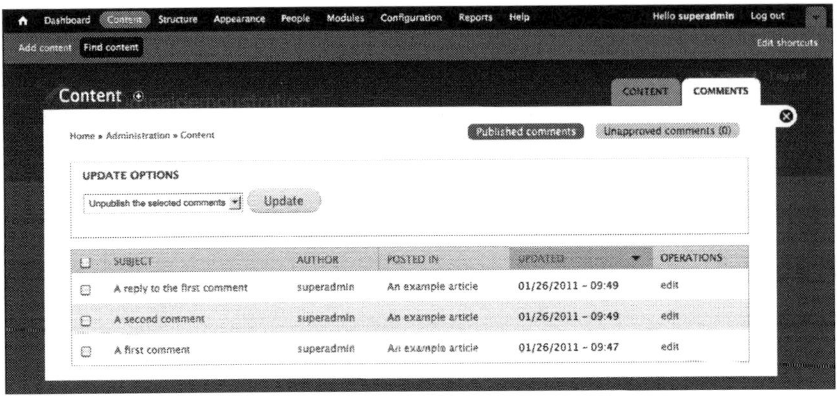

FIGURE 1.12 The administration list for published comments has tools for unpublish several comments at once.

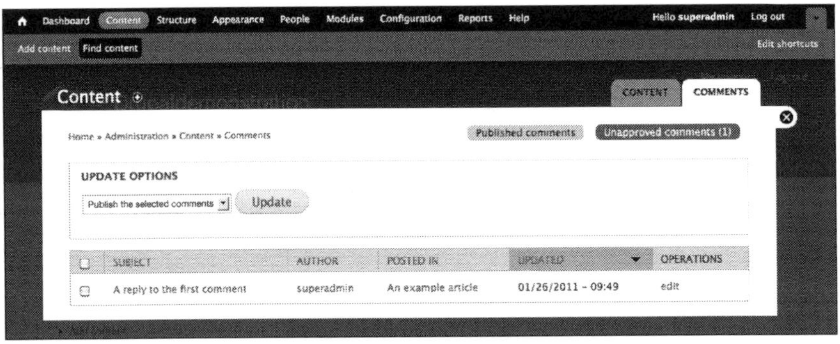

FIGURE 1.13 The list of unpublished comments has tools similar to the list of published comments.

Try your skills

The tasks described below are the first in a set of tasks being issued by a fictive Boss, and later also involving an intern. They are not full user stories – as used in exercises in part B and C in this book – but rather quick tasks with a clear goal. These exercises are also available at nodeone.se/learn-drupal.

CREATE AN ARTICLE

Hi, it's Boss

I've written a news story that I would like to have published on our new website. I called our web consultants, but they say we can post news ourselves to the site now and that they have showed you how to do it.

The story I've written can be found at lipsum.com. Will you put that up on our site? I'd like it to be right on top on our front page. Thanks.
//Boss

CREATING REVISIONS

Hi, it's Boss again

It seems the Lorem Ipsum guy has changed his name, and now wants to spell it Lorem Epsum. Could you update the article? I'd like to have the old version available in some kind of log, in case Lorem changes his mind again. Thanks.
//Boss

EDITING ARTICLE SUMMARY

Hi, it's Boss

I've been thinking more about the Lorem article, and it doesn't look excellent on our front page. I called our web consultants to ask them to use a special text for the front page only – and apparently this is something we are able to do ourselves. I prepared an introduction text at lipsum.com for the front page. Will you take care of it? Thanks.
//Boss

39

NICE URL FOR A PAGE

It's Boss

The website is coming together nicely, but I think we should have an about us page available at example.com/about-us. I called our web consultants, and they say you can fix this. Unfortunately I have no time to write up the text myself, so you'll have to do it. Thanks.

//Boss

WRITING ARTICLES WITHOUT PUBLISHING THEM

Hi, it's me again

You know the news story we've been working for a few days? I know it's finished, but I'd like to think a bit more before we publish it. I called the web consultants, and they say that we can actually put it on our website, but make it so that visitors can't see the article. Can you do this? I might get back to you during the weekend with some more changes to the article. Thanks.

//Boss

PUBLISHING AND UPDATING POST DATE

Hi, it's Boss

I had a great weekend golfing and then taking a small tour with the boat in the archipelago. I hope yours was good too. About that article – I have no further changes so you can publish it now. By the way: The web provider said that you have to do something to the post date to make it look as it was written today Monday. Thanks.

//Boss

MASS UPDATE NODES

Before starting this task you should create a number of basic pages and published them to the site front page.

Hi, it's Boss

I know I said that I wanted a number of basic pages published on our

front page, but some things have changed now. Could you remove all of them from the front page? Ok, thanks.
//Boss.

> **TIP**
>
> A swift tool for mass generating test content is the *Devel generate* module, found in the Devel project at drupal.org – see the chapter on installing and enabling modules in appendix 1. Once enabled, test content can be created by clicking *configuration* in the toolbar and selecting *generate content*.

CHANGE NODE DEFAULT SETTINGS

Hi, it's Boss

This revisioning thing is actually quite useful, but I'm getting irritated of having to check the "create new revision" checkbox every time. I called our web consultants, and they say that you can fix this too. (I'm beginning to wonder if we really need the consultants.) Can you make it so that all the articles and basic pages are revision controlled by default? Thanks.
//Boss

COMMENT ADMINISTRATION

Before starting this task you should post a number of comments on the site. (Use Devel generate if you have it installed!)

Hi, it's Boss

I noticed there are some weird comments on our site. I called our web consultants, and they say that you know how to hide or delete comments. (I was this close to telling them that they can't just direct every task back at us, but then I realized that you're much cheaper labour than those consultants.) They also said that it's possible to add "shortcut links" to administration pages that you use often, but I don't know. Anyway – can you have a look at the comments and remove any that look bad? Thanks.
//Boss

Users and permissions

Next to content, users are probably the most important component of a website – They might even be more important than content. This chapter will show you how to manage users, divide them into groups, and decide the things that each group of users will be allowed to do on your website.

Adding and managing users

The administration toolbar's link *people* provides you with a list of all user accounts registered on your website. (See figure 2.1.) The list of users share many features with the content list – there are links to view and edit each account, and there are tools for filtering and mass updating accounts.

On top of the list is a link *add user,* used to add new accounts to the site. The form for adding new accounts is very similar to the form you get when

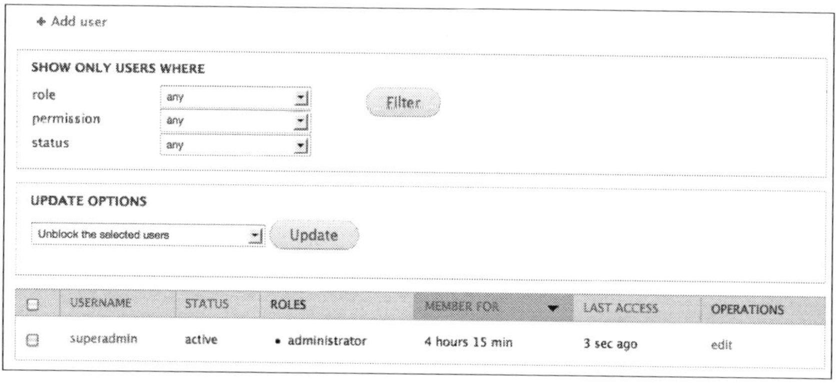

FIGURE 2.2 The list of user accounts contains shortcuts to edit each account, as well as tools for mass updates.

editing an existing account. (See figure 2.2.) Below is a a description of the settings in the forms.

- Username: This is the user's name on the website, used when logging in. It must be unique.
- Current password (only when editing your own account): To change your e-mail address or password, you must usually give your current password.
- E-mail address: The e-mail address must, as the username, be unique. The reason for this is that the e-mail address should be able to use if password or username is forgotten.
- Password/confirm password: This is the user's password, repeated to avoid misspellings. Note that Drupal *cannot* show the current password – all passwords are encrypted before they are stored, and Drupal has no way of decrypting them. If you enter a short or simple passwords you will get a warning, but Drupal won't prevent you from using it.
- Status: User accounts that are *blocked* cannot be used for logging in.
- Roles: This shows, or sets which *permission roles* the user has. (See next section for details.) All users automatically have the role *authenticated* user as soon as they have logged in.
- Picture (only on editing): This allows users to upload an image, associated with their account.
- Administrative overlay (only on editing): This setting makes it possible to disable the administrative overlay for selected users, displaying the administration pages without the overlay.
- Locale settings (only on editing): This setting is used to change time zone for a user.
- Notify user of new account (only on creation): This option makes Drupal send out an e-mail to the new user with the account information. This is the only time Drupal sends out a password – if users lose their passwords they will get a one-time login rather than their existing password.

> **TIP**
>
> Best practice dictates that you should not use the user 1 account as a personal account. The first user account bypasses all access controls in Drupal, and should be available to pass on to new site managers.

Username *

superadmin

Spaces are allowed; punctuation is not allowed except for periods, hyphens, apostrophes, and underscores.

Current password

Enter your current password to change the *E-mail address* or *Password*. Request new password.

E-mail address *

johan.falk@nodeone.se

A valid e-mail address. All e-mails from the system will be sent to this address. The e-mail address is not made public and will only be used if you wish to receive a new password or wish to receive certain news or notifications by e-mail.

Password

Password strength:

Confirm password

To change the current user password, enter the new password in both fields.

Status

○ Blocked

◉ Active

Roles

☑ authenticated user

☑ administrator

PICTURE

Upload picture

[   ] (Bläddra...)

Your virtual face or picture. Pictures larger than 1024x1024 pixels will be scaled down.

▾ ADMINISTRATIVE OVERLAY

☑ Use the overlay for administrative pages.

Show administrative pages on top of the page you started from.

▾ LOCALE SETTINGS

Your time zone setting will be automatically detected if possible. Confirm the selection and click save.

Time zone

Europe/Stockholm: Monday, January 3, 2011 - 17:04 +0100   ▾

Select the desired local time and time zone. Dates and times throughout this site will be displayed using this time zone.

(Save)

FIGURE 2.3 The page used to edit user accounts contains a number of settings, such as which permission/roles the user has.

45

TIP

The picture upload in a standard Drupal installation is a remnant of previous Drupal versions – images are handled much better as fields in Drupal 7. (See the fields chapter for more information.) You can turn off the obsolete picture functionality from the toolbar, configuration, account settings.

Permissions and roles

The first account created on a Drupal site – user 1 – has permissions to do *everything* on the site. But what about other users?

To see which permissions different types of users have – and change these settings – you use the tab *permissions* under the *people* link in the toolbar. The resulting page contains a long list of permissions, and one column for each *permission role* on your site – anonymous users, authenticated users and administrators. (See figure 2.3.)

By checking or unchecking the different permissions it is possible to do things like, give authenticated users permission to create articles, or anonymous users to use the site search. The permissions are grouped by the *module* that is responsible for them, and with more modules installed more permissions are sure to turn up. (See the chapter about modules in appendix 1 for details about how to add modules.)

A sub tab *roles*, visible on the permissions list, brings you a list of all permission roles available on the website. (See figure 2.4.) If your site needs more permission levels than the three included in a standard installation – which is very likely – this is the place to add more. Each new role will be represented by a new column in the permissions matrix, and you may set permissions for each role independent of the others. (See figure 2.5.) Quick and slick!

FIGURE 2.1 Assigning roles to users is done in one of two ways – you can either edit each user account you want to change, or you can make mass updates from the user list.

TIP

If a user has more than one role – which is quite possible – she will get permissions based on *all* these roles. The rule is that roles decide what you *can* do, not what you can't.

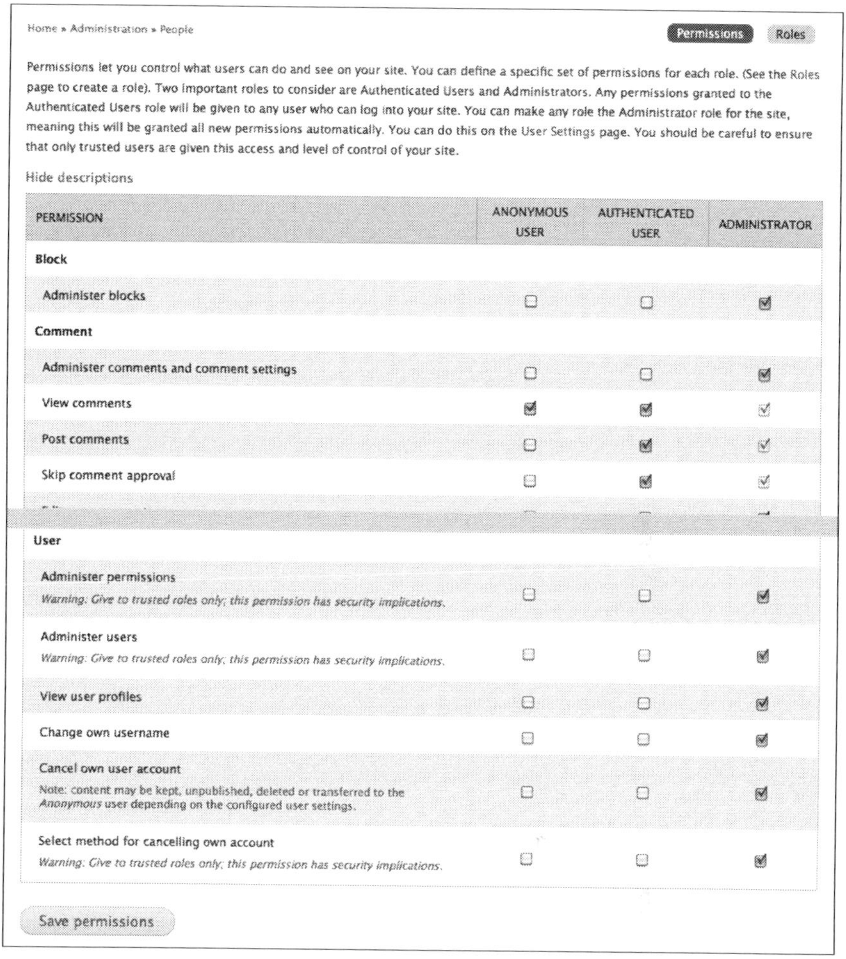

Home » Administration » People

Permissions Roles

Permissions let you control what users can do and see on your site. You can define a specific set of permissions for each role. (See the Roles page to create a role). Two important roles to consider are Authenticated Users and Administrators. Any permissions granted to the Authenticated Users role will be given to any user who can log into your site. You can make any role the Administrator role for the site, meaning this will be granted all new permissions automatically. You can do this on the User Settings page. You should be careful to ensure that only trusted users are given this access and level of control of your site.

Hide descriptions

PERMISSION	ANONYMOUS USER	AUTHENTICATED USER	ADMINISTRATOR
Block			
Administer blocks	☐	☐	☑
Comment			
Administer comments and comment settings	☐	☐	☑
View comments	☑	☑	☑
Post comments	☐	☑	☑
Skip comment approval	☐	☑	☑
User			
Administer permissions *Warning: Give to trusted roles only; this permission has security implications.*	☐	☐	☑
Administer users *Warning: Give to trusted roles only; this permission has security implications.*	☐	☐	☑
View user profiles	☐	☐	☑
Change own username	☐	☐	☑
Cancel own user account *Note: content may be kept, unpublished, deleted or transferred to the Anonymous user depending on the configured user settings.*	☐	☐	☑
Select method for cancelling own account *Warning: Give to trusted roles only; this permission has security implications.*	☐	☐	☑

Save permissions

FIGURE 2.4 The permissions list contains a large matrix of settings.

TIP

The permissions matrix is one of the most packed settings pages in Drupal, but fortunately each permission is more or less self-explanatory. Since new modules often add new permissions it is common to wait until a project is nearly finished before setting all permissions – thus avoiding having to go through the whole list more times than necessary.

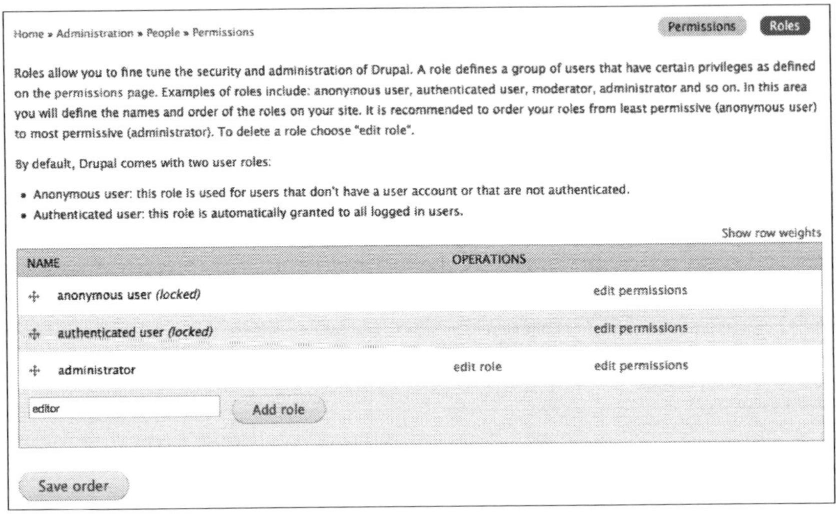

FIGURE 2.5 You may add more permission roles at the roles list.

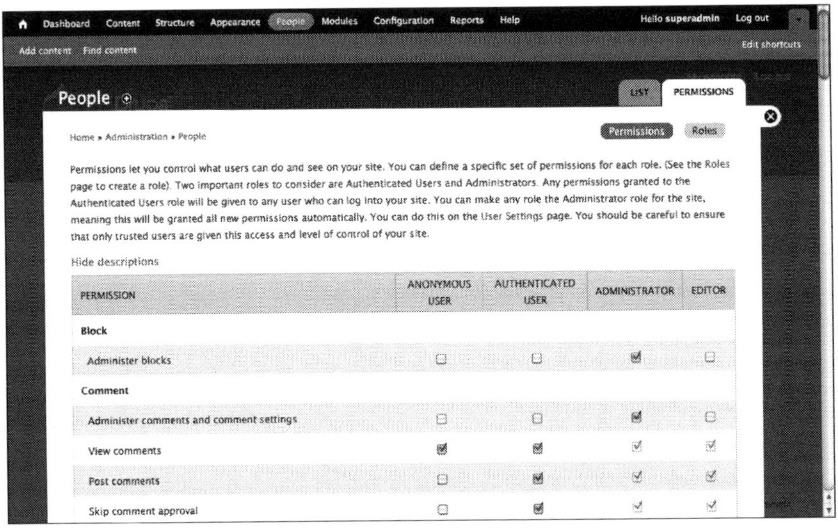

FIGURE 2.6 Each new role can have their separate permission settings.

Other user account settings

The toolbar's item *configuration* and *account settings* brings you a few more user settings that a Drupal developer should know. The most important are described below.

- Administrator role: The role set here will automatically have all permissions set in the permissions matrix.
- Registration and cancellation: This setting determines how new accounts should be created – for example if visitors should be allowed to sign up – and also how content and accounts should be treated upon cancellation.
- Personalization – signatures: If signatures are enabled, users will be allowed to set a signature that will be added to all their comments (but not to other content). If a user changes her signature, signatures on existing comments are affected.
- E-mails: This setting contains a number of e-mail templates, used when users register, lose their passwords, and some other cases. Note that there are some *tokens* available for dynamic replacements, such as [user:name] and [user:one-time-login-url]..

> TIP
>
> Like the user pictures, signatures is a remnant of old Drupal versions. By using some our wits and a few tricks, it is also possible to replace them with fields. (See separate chapter for details.)

49

Try your skills

The tasks described below continues the suite in the previous chapter – with a fictive Boss issuing orders about changes to a standard Drupal installation. The tasks are not full user stories – as used in exercises in part B and C in this book – but rather quick tasks with a clear goal. These exercises can also be found at nodeone.se/learn-drupal.

CREATE USER ACCOUNTS

Hi, it's boss

We're getting an intern to our company today, and she's going to stay a few weeks. I thought she should have a user account on our website, but I don't know if she can handle all these technology stuff. Could you create an account for her? The username "Intern" should do.

Thanks.

//Boss

UPDATE USER ACCOUNT INFORMATION

Before starting this task you should create a few user accounts on your site, at least one with the username "Dries Buytaert". (Use the Devel generate module to mass generate users, if you got it installed!)

Hi, it's Boss

I got a call from one of our site members, who had forgotten his password. I called our web provider, who says that passwords can't be recovered – only new ones set. Apparently it is some kind of security thing. Anyway, the fellow who phoned called himself "Dries Buytaert" and wants his password to be "drupal123". The web guys said that Dries could order a one-time login and do this himself, but I thought it is just as well that you go in and update his information to save him the problem.

Ok, thanks.

//Boss

CREATING AND ASSIGNING ROLES

Hi, it's Boss

I know you've had a lot to do with the website, working weekends and such, so I thought you should get some help. Our intern will help you with this the two weeks she is here. I called the web provider to give her an administration account, but apparently you can do this. (It turned out you can use her ordinary account on the site for this – I had no idea that the site was administered in the online interface!)

When talking to our consultants, they said it is possible to introduce new levels of permissions somehow – they particularly stressed that it would be a bad idea to give an intern access to settings on the site.

Anyways – if you could create an editor permission level and make our intern an editor it'd be great. (It trust your judgement when it comes to what editors should and shouldn't be allowed to do.) I hope you like getting some help!

//Boss

Blocks

Regions and blocks

When visiting a node page in Drupal – or any other page – Drupal pulls out the content corresponding to the current URL and formats it to make it possible for a web browser to display. On the URL node/1, for example, Drupal displays the content for the node with ID 1. But it is not just the content of node one that is displayed – distributed over the page there may be elements like menus, search forms, related content, latest comments on the site, and much more.

Both the main content and the other elements are displayed as *blocks*, placed in one of the *regions* of the website. These blocks can be moved around, and there are basic as well as more sophisticated ways of adding new blocks to your website.

There is a list of all available blocks on the site, which you can reach from the administration toolbar, *structure, blocks*. (See figure 3.2.) The blocks are grouped by the region where they are placed – which could for example be *sidebar first* or *content*. There is also a list of blocks under the sub heading *disabled*, meaning that they don't show up at all. You can move blocks to a new region by using the select list of region names, or by simply clicking on a block's sorting arrow and dragging it to another region sub header.

Above the list of blocks is a link *demonstrate block* regions. It leads to a page where all regions are printed clearly on an empty site template, making it easy to get an overview of the available regions. (See figure 3.1.) Don't miss the *exit block demonstration* link to return to the block list.

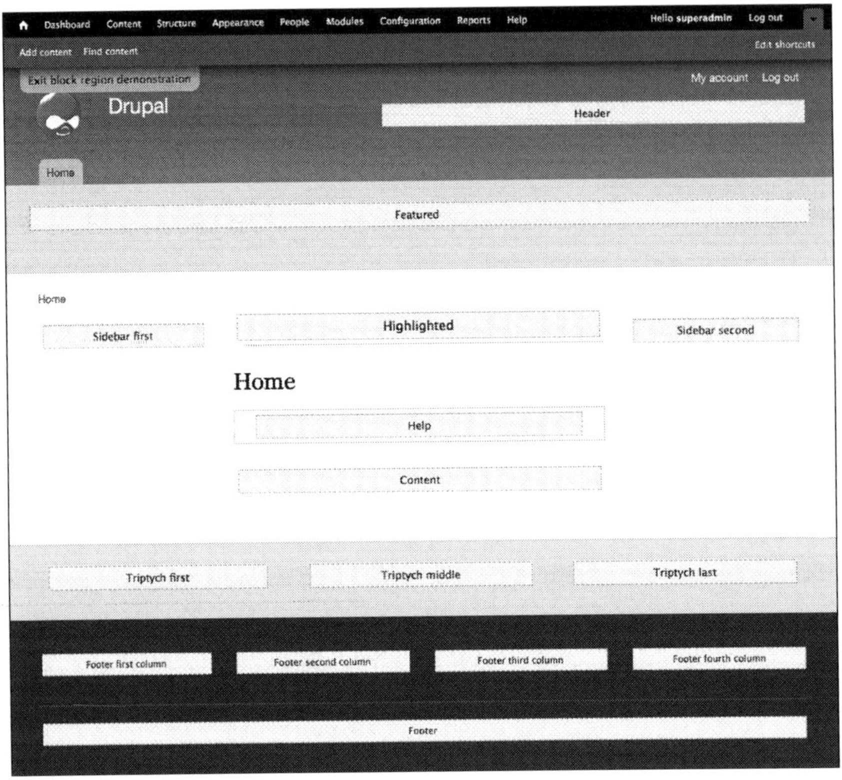

FIGURE 3.1 Blocks are placed in one of the regions of the website. The link *demonstrate block regions* on the administration page for blocks gives an overview of the regions available in your current theme.

> **TIP**
>
> Which regions are available varies with the *theme* your site uses. (Themes dictate the presentation of Drupal sites – see appendix 1 for some more details.) You may use the tabs on the block administration page to distribute your blocks for every enabled theme. On a standard installation the Seven theme is used on administration pages, while Bartik is used for all other pages.

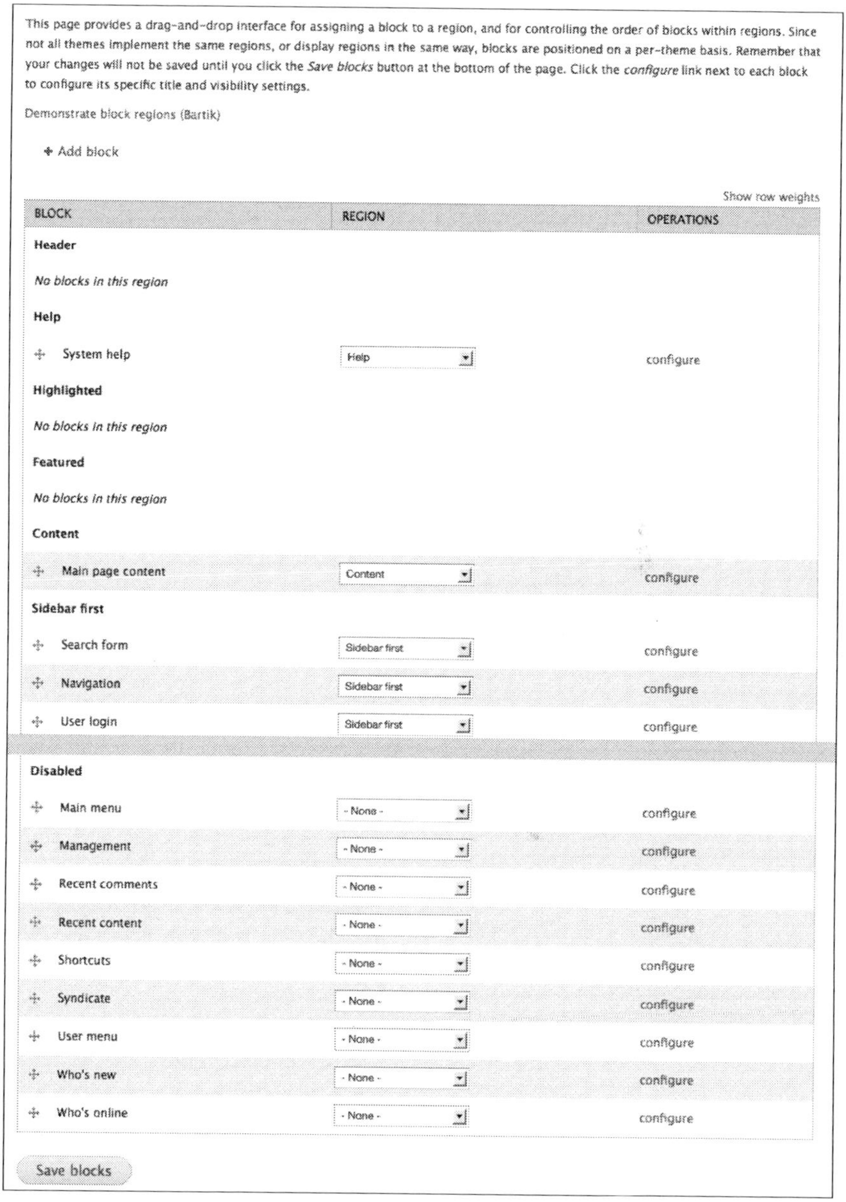

This page provides a drag-and-drop interface for assigning a block to a region, and for controlling the order of blocks within regions. Since not all themes implement the same regions, or display regions in the same way, blocks are positioned on a per-theme basis. Remember that your changes will not be saved until you click the *Save blocks* button at the bottom of the page. Click the *configure* link next to each block to configure its specific title and visibility settings.

Demonstrate block regions (Bartik)

✦ Add block

Show row weights

BLOCK	REGION	OPERATIONS
Header		
No blocks in this region		
Help		
✛ System help	Help ▾	configure
Highlighted		
No blocks in this region		
Featured		
No blocks in this region		
Content		
✛ Main page content	Content ▾	configure
Sidebar first		
✛ Search form	Sidebar first ▾	configure
✛ Navigation	Sidebar first ▾	configure
✛ User login	Sidebar first ▾	configure
Disabled		
✛ Main menu	- None - ▾	configure
✛ Management	- None - ▾	configure
✛ Recent comments	- None - ▾	configure
✛ Recent content	- None - ▾	configure
✛ Shortcuts	- None - ▾	configure
✛ Syndicate	- None - ▾	configure
✛ User menu	- None - ▾	configure
✛ Who's new	- None - ▾	configure
✛ Who's online	- None - ▾	configure

(Save blocks)

FIGURE 3.2 The administration page for blocks shows all the blocks available on the site, grouped by the regions they are placed in.

Block settings

In the block list there is a link *configure* available for each block. Each leads to a page where you may change a number of settings for the block (see figure 3.3).

- Block title: This can be used for overriding the title of the block, as shown to users. To hide the title, enter *<none>*.
- Region settings: This is an alternative way of moving the block between regions, similar to the select lists in the block overview list.
- Visibility settings: These settings provide some basic options for determining when the block should be visible or not:

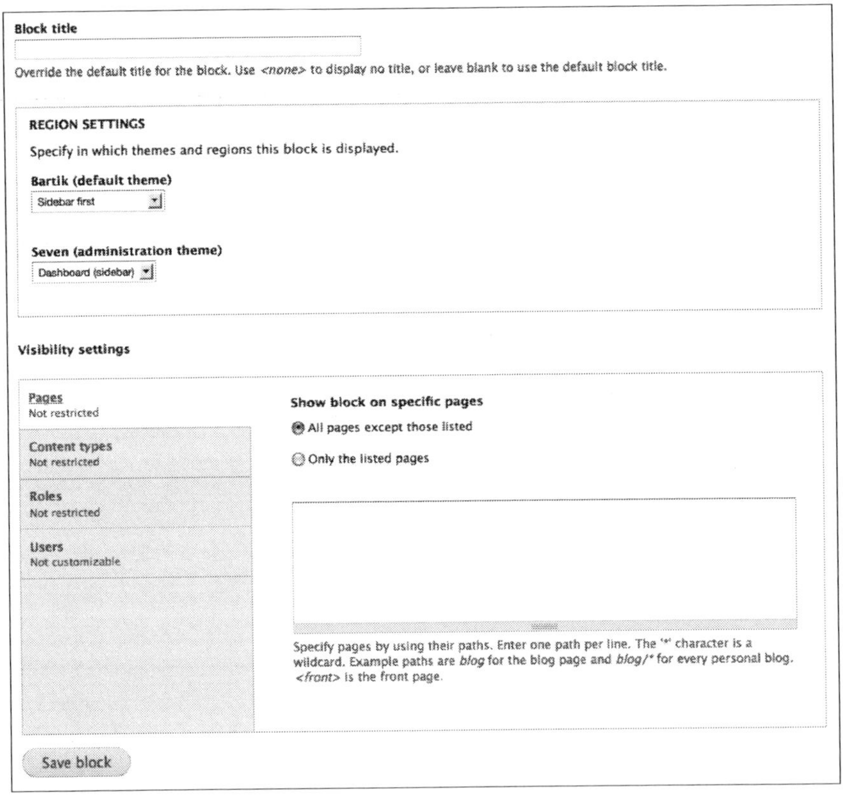

Block title

Override the default title for the block. Use *<none>* to display no title, or leave blank to use the default block title.

REGION SETTINGS

Specify in which themes and regions this block is displayed.

Bartik (default theme)

Sidebar first

Seven (administration theme)

Dashboard (sidebar)

Visibility settings

Pages Not restricted	Show block on specific pages
Content types Not restricted	⦿ All pages except those listed
Roles Not restricted	○ Only the listed pages
Users Not customizable	

Specify pages by using their paths. Enter one path per line. The '*' character is a wildcard. Example paths are *blog* for the blog page and *blog/** for every personal blog. *<front>* is the front page.

Save block

FIGURE 3.3 Every block has it's own settings, for example: settings used to determine which context the block should be shown or hidden.

○ Pages: This allows for showing or hiding the block based on the URL of the viewed page. You may use * as a wildcard to replace the entire URL or just parts of it. Any pattern will be compared with both the internal paths ('node/1') and URL aliases ('information/about-us').

○ Content types: This can be used to show the block only when selected node types are viewed.

○ Roles: This can be used to only show the block to users with the selected roles.

○ Users: Enabling this setting allows users to determine themselves if the block should be visible or not. (These then become available on each user account edit page.)

• Apart from these settings, many blocks also have their own particular settings – the block with most recent comments, for example, has settings for how many comments should be displayed.

ADDING BLOCKS

Many modules provide the block list with new blocks, and there are also a lot of modules who let you as an administrator create new blocks by configuration. (For example the *Views* module, described in two chapters of its own.) To create the most basic blocks, though, you only need the Block module itself – and the link *add block* right above the block list. This leads to a page where you can create a block with static content.

Complements and alternatives to blocks

Block management can quickly become a mess on large and complex Drupal sites. In response to this a number of modules have been created. The two most important to know are:

• Context: Among other things, this module help set visibility rules for blocks in a more flexible way.

• Panels and Page manager (part of *Chaos tools suite*): These modules replace the regular block system with *panel panes*. Compared to blocks, these panes make it far easier to access and use contextual information.

Both these modules provide more functionality by complementing or replacing the block system. Panels and Page manager are described in a little more detail in a chapter of their own. The Context module will not be discussed further in this book.

Try your skills

The tasks described below continues the suite in the previous chapters – with a fictive Boss issuing orders about changes to a standard Drupal installation, and an equally fictive Intern coming up with new ideas. The tasks are not full user stories – as used in exercises in part B and C in this book – but rather quick tasks with a clear goal. These exercises are also available at nodeone.se/learn-drupal

ENABLING BLOCKS

Hi, it's Boss

The traffic on our site is going well! I noticed there are new comments all the time, so I thought we should make this visible to our visitors. Could you make a list of newest comments appear at the top of the left sidebar? Call the web consultant if you get problems, or make use of Intern if you want to. Thanks.

//Boss

BLOCK VISIBILITY SETTINGS

Hi, it's Intern

I'm trying to keep track of how much the website is actually used, and thought it would be a good idea to see how many are logged in at any moment. I know there's a block for this, but I thought it might be a good idea to only show this block for administrators and editors, and try it out for a week before making it public. I'm not sure of how to do this – could you do it?

//Intern

CUSTOM BLOCKS AND MORE BLOCK VISIBILITY

Hi, it's Boss

The site is going splendid! I've written a welcome message that I would like all visitors to see in big style on top of the front page. The web consultants says that you could use the "featured" region for this – you maybe

understand what they mean, but it's all gibberish to me. The welcome message is included below. Remember: It should only show on the front page! Thanks.

//Boss

PS: The message is "Welcome to our successful site!"

CHANGING BLOCK TITLES

Hi, it's Boss

I think the title "Navigation" for the left-hand menu is bad. Could you remove it? Thanks.

//Boss

MOVING BLOCKS

Hi, it's Intern

Two friends of mine have independently of each other suggested that we move the search box to the site header – a suggestion that makes sense to me. Let me know if you agree, and I'll move it (or you can just move it yourself).

//Intern

Menus

By default, content on a Drupal site is not automatically placed in any particular structure. When creating a node, you don't choose "where" on the site it should be – you create it, and then other parts of Drupal can make it appear as a sub page to a particular menu item, in a list in a particular section, and in many other ways.

The most direct way of bringing structure to your Drupal site it to use menus – links collected in a tree structure.

Displaying menus

A standard installation of Drupal has four *menus: main menu, management, navigation* and *user menu*. More menus can be added via Drupal's interface, and you can also choose where and how they should be displayed.

There are, in principle, two ways of displaying menus:
- Each menu on the site has its own block, which can be placed in a region just like any block.
- The theme on the site can (but does not always have) two places where menus are displayed in a special format – *main links* and *secondary links*. In a standard Drupal installation the main links are displayed as large white tabs against the blue header, while the secondary links are displayed as quite discrete links in the upper-right corner of the site.

Which menus should be used for *main links* and *secondary links* can be changed at the toolbar's link structure, then menu and finally the tab *settings*.

> **TIP**
>
> The display of main links and secondary links only hold one level of menu links – any sub menu items are not shown. It is possible to use secondary links to display sub items of the primary menu, by configuring them to fetch links from the same menu. The module *Menu block* provides further possibilities to display selected levels and parts of a menu.

Creating and editing menu links

As with many other administration tasks, there is an overview for managing menus. It can be found from the toolbar, *structure, menus,* and displays all the menus available on your site. (See figure 4.1.) Each menu is presented with three options.

- List links: This gives you a list of all items in this menu, and is usually what you want to do when managing a menu.
- Edit menu: This allows you to change the name and description of the menu itself (not the links it contains). You may also delete any menus you have created yourself.
- Add link: This leads to a page for adding another link in the menu – see details below.

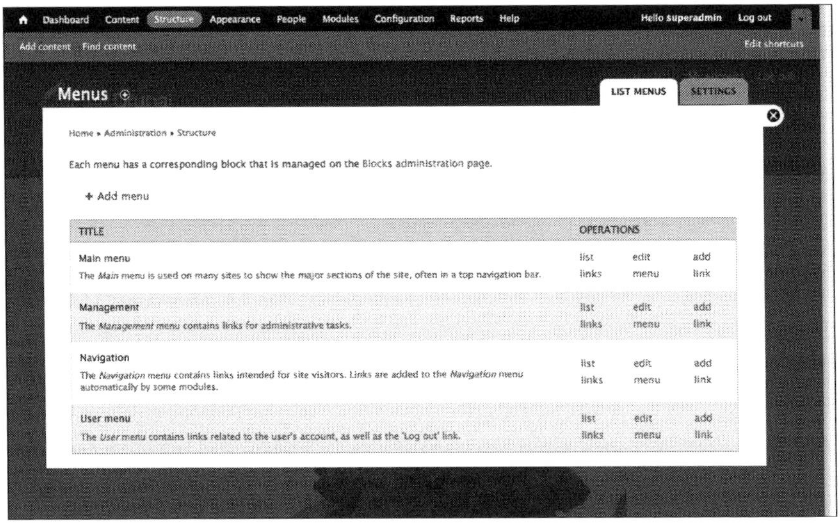

FIGURE 4.1 The menu overview is found at structure, menus.

At the top of the list of menus is a link *add menu* used for adding further menus. The only difference between menus that you create yourself and those provided by modules (or the standard installation) is that your custom menus can be deleted.

LIST MENU LINKS

The page listing menu links allows you to manage the content of the menu in a few different ways (see figure 4.2):

- You may change the menu structure by clicking and dragging the sorting arrows. Sub menu items are created by indenting a menu item.
- You may enable or disable a menu item with the checkbox *enabled*. Disabled items won't be displayed in the menu, and any child items will also be hidden – but the pages they lead to are not affected.
- You may edit each menu item, using the *edit* link. This leads to a page similar to the one used for creating new items – see below.
- Each item managed by Drupal's Menu module also has a *delete* link. Links defined by other modules are managed by their respective module settings, but can still be disabled in the menu link list.

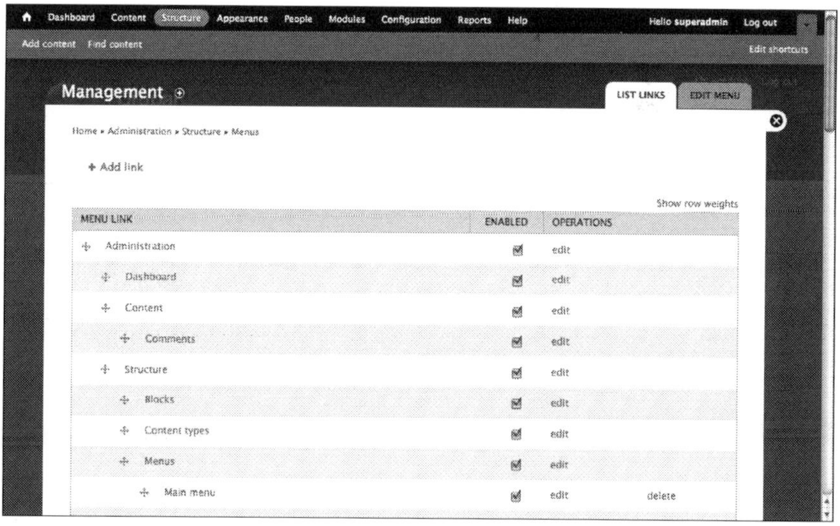

FIGURE 4.2 Each menu has a list of all links included in that menu.

CREATING AND EDITING MENU ITEMS

Right above the list of menu items there is a link *add item*, used to add new links to the currently viewed menu. The form for creating or editing menu items has the following information:

- Menu link title: This is the clickable text that will be displayed to users.
- Path: This is the URL the menu link leads to. When creating menu links it is strongly recommended to use the internal path ('node/1') rather than absolute paths ('http://example.com/node/1'), since internal paths makes it possible to move the site without breaking links. It also makes it possible for Drupal to replace links with any URL aliases.
- Description: This is a tooltip, usually shown when hovering over the menu item.
- Enabled: This corresponds to the enabled setting in the menu item list (see above).
- Show as expanded: If this option is checked, all child items to this menu link will be loaded and displayed, even if the user has navigated to another part of the menu.
- Parent link: This setting dictates which menu link this item should be placed under, if any. This option can be replaced by manual click-and-drag sorting in the menu item list.
- Weight: This setting determines the sorting order for menu items with the same parent – with lower weight numbers floating to the top. This option can be replaced by manual click-and-drag sorting in the menu item list.

> TIP
>
> Menu links don't have to lead to pages on your Drupal site, but can point to any valid URL.

Creating menu links for nodes

A quick and easy alternative when creating menu links is to use the menu options available on node edit pages, under *menu settings*. If the option *provide menu link* is checked, a number of new options become available

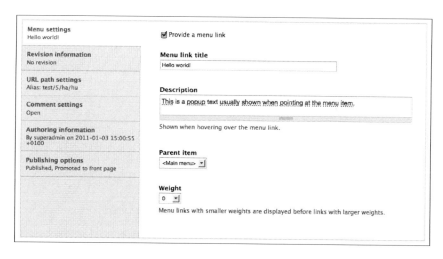

FIGURE 4.3 You can create menu links to nodes right from the node's edit form.

(see figure 4.3) – all settings are analogous with the menu item configurations described in the previous section.

By default, articles and basic pages may only be placed in the *main menu*. There are settings on each node type determining which menus should be available in the node edit form, as well as default settings for the *parent item*.

Try your skills

The tasks described below continues the suite in the previous chapter – with a fictive Boss issuing orders about changes to a standard Drupal installation. The tasks are not full user stories – as used in exercises in part B and C in this book – but rather quick tasks with a clear goal. These exercises are also available at nodeone.se/learn-drupal.

ADDING MENU LINKS

Hi, it's Boss

I've started a Wordpress blog to tell people about the stuff happening at our website. It is found at http://bossblog.wordpress.com/. Could you link to it from the left-hand menu?

Thanks.

//Boss

ADDING MENU ITEMS TO THE SECONDARY LINKS

Hi, it's Boss

You know the about us page we created some time ago? There should be a link to it at the top of the site – where the My account link is. Will you fix this?

Ok thanks.

//Boss

ADDING ARBITRARY INTERNAL LINKS TO MENUS

Hi, it's Intern

I've been thinking – you know how Boss often wants some selected pieces of new to get more attention? If we have a tag Important news, we could use the list for the tag to collect all the stuff Boss thinks is extra important. Then we could also link to this list from the tabs on the site.

Could you do this?

//Intern

CHANGING MENU ITEM SETTINGS

Hi, it's intern

You know, when I post content on the site I almost always create articles but never basic pages. Having to click "add content" and then "articles" seems unnecessary – and it must be the same for you. I suggest that we make the menu items hidden under "add content" in the navigation menu visible all the time. I could do this myself, but I don't want to change any site settings without asking you first. Should I do it? (Or do you want to make the changes?)

//Intern

Other basic Drupal core settings

This chapter collects some miscellaneous administrative settings a Drupal developer should know.

Administration aids

There are a number of shortcuts and nifty tools enabled in a standard Drupal installation, all with the purpose of making site administration easier. They are summarized below.

- The black list at the top on Drupal pages is provided by the *Toolbar* module. It contains links to the top-level items in the menu *management*.
- The administrative overlay – the frame appearing when clicking on administration links – is provided by the *Overlay* module. One of its points is to make it easier to find the page you were at when starting your administration.
- The *Contextual links* module adds a number of links in drop-down menus at various elements on your Drupal site. The menu is accessed by clicking on the gear icon that appears when hovering over elements that have contextual links – such as blocks.
- The *Dashboard* module makes it easier to build a collection of blocks on one single administration page (found under the dashboard link in the toolbar).
- The gray list just below the black toolbar is provided by the *Shortcuts* module, which also provides the plus-marked links *add to default shortcuts*. The latter are used to add links to the former, which is a handy way

to always have your most-visited administration pages one click away. It is possible to create different sets of shortcuts from the toolbar select *configuration, shortcuts*. Users with relevant permissions may select themselves which shortcut sets to use on a separate tab on their user pages. Note that while shortcuts remind us of menus, they are technically separated.

> **TIP**
>
> The modules *Administration menu* and *Admin* are popular complements to Drupal's built-in tools for administrators. They both provide alternative, and in some aspects more user friendly, administration menus.

Text formats

In Drupal, all text that may contain markup is handled by one of the website's *text formats* – rules determining how the text should be processed before being displayed. The *text formats* have three main purposes:

- Security: The text formats make sure that any malicious code or script, entered by malicious users, doesn't have malicious effects on the site or its visitors.
- Sanitation: The inputted text is processed to make sure that any markup is clean and follows common standards. This is one of the reasons for Drupal being naturally search-engine friendly (as well as friendly towards screen-readers).
- Comfort: Text formats may also be used to convert certain expressions to HTML. In Drupal core this is used to automatically create things like line breaks and links from URLs, but could also for be used for allowing the same type of markup as used on Wikipedia (for example).

Each text format consists of one or more *filters*. The formats and most filters can be managed at the toolbar, *configuration, text formats*.

> **TIP**
>
> Even if Drupal processes all formatted text, the original text is never changed – which is an important rule in how to treat user input. Since the original, potentially malicious input, is stored in the database it is as Drupal coder important to always keep in mind that user-provided text always should be sanitized.

Other settings

This last section of the Drupal core basics chapter contains some loosely coupled items you as site administrator or Drupal developer may find useful.

- The page used as your site's home page can be set form the *toolbar, configuration*, site information. The default setting is 'node', which gives a list of teasers of nodes marked with *promote to front page*.
- Drupal depends on a number of scheduled activities being carried out on a regular basis – for example allowing indexing new content for searches. If your server has native *cron*-functions you can turn off Drupal's backup functionality for scheduled activities, found at the toolbar, *configuration, cron*. On the same page you can also trigger cron activities manually, for example to make new content immediately searchable.
- If things starts behaving weirdly while you're building your Drupal site, it is wise to first empty Drupal's cache – processed data that is temporarily stored to speed up the website – and if this doesn't help check error logs for interesting messages. The cache can be cleared from the toolbar, *configuration, performance*. The most interesting log messages are found from the toolbar, *reports, recent log messages*.
- When performing system updates on your site, you should put it in maintenance mode to make sure that site visitors aren't affecting the database while it is being updated. This setting is found from the toolbar, *configuration, maintenance mode*.

Try your skills

The tasks described below continues the suite in the previous chapter – with a fictive Boss issuing orders about changes to a standard Drupal installation. The tasks are not full user stories – as used in exercises in part B and C in this book – but rather quick tasks with a clear goal. These exercises are also available at nodeone.se/learn-drupal.

MODIFYING TEXT FORMATS

Hi, it's Intern

In some of the longer texts on the site I have included sub headers using <h2>, <h3> and <h4> HTML tags. I have so far been using the full HTML text format to make these tags appear, but this seems a bit bad. Could you make it so the filtered HTML text format accepts these sub headings?

Thanks in advance.

//Intern

A BONUS TASK

It's Boss

Today I typed example.com/aboutus in the URL bar to view our about us page, and I got an ugly and boring page not found message. I immediately called our web consultants and asked if the message is something that you can change. They said that it is, technically, but that it has not been included in the training you got from them. They asked if they should update the administration manual or schedule a training session, but I figured it is probably cheaper to let you figure this out yourself. Ask Intern if you like – she actually seems quite capable when it comes to web.

So – could you provide me with a new message for page not found pages? I have faith in you. Thanks.

//Boss

Part B:
Information structure in Drupal

An important factor in Drupal's success as a publishing system is the possibility to quickly and flexibly create information structures. This functionality stems from Drupal's way of handling information fields, combined with the Views module. This part of the book covers the basics of how to leverage Drupal's tools for information structure.

Fields

Articles and basic pages are both node types, but they hold different information – while basic pages only stores header and body, articles may also have images and tags. The difference between them is that the two node types have different *fields*.

In short, fields work like this:

- Node types have a number of fields attached to them, used to store text, images or other data. Which kind of data is being stored is determined by the *field type*.
- When creating or editing a node, you can input data to each field attached to that type of node. How data is inputted is determined by the fields *widget*, and could for example be select lists, text fields or file uploads.
- Each field has settings that determine how the field data should be displayed when viewing the saved node – such as which image size should be used, or if text should be displayed in trimmed or full version. Field data can also be hidden.
- Administrators may add, remove and change settings for fields, thereby customizing the kind of information that could be stored on the website.
- Other parts of Drupal – in particular the Views module – may access and use field data to filter, sort, display and in different ways process content on your site.

The bullets above summarize most cases of how fields are used in Drupal. It may seem a short list, but when you have mastered it you will be able to create powerful web applications in short time.

In a standard Drupal installation, it's not only nodes that can have fields – but also comments, users, and taxonomy terms (see separate chapter). These are collectively called *entities* (together with some non-fieldable parts of Drupal). The fact that there is a point-and-click interface for building information structures for all these parts of a website gives Drupal a unique flexibility that should not be underestimated.

The following section describes how to manage fields for nodes. Field management for comments, users, and taxonomy terms is carried out in an almost identical fashion – some notes about these are summarized in a separate section..

> TIP
>
> The term *fields* can denote several, quite different things in the Drupal-verse. In this book the term *entity fields* is used where there is need to explicitly point out that we're talking about fields that can be added to nodes, users and other entities.

Fields on node types

To get an overview of the fields a node type contains, you visit the toolbar, *structure, content types*, and the link *manage fields* for the node type you wish to inspect. The overview page for fields allow a number of operations (see figure 5.1):

- You may change the order of the fields by clicking and dragging the sorting arrow for each field. This order is reflected on the node edit form and, unless otherwise is set, also on the node view page.
- You may edit the settings for each field by clicking its *edit* link.
- You may change a field's type by clicking the field type name. (This can only be done if nothing has yet been stored in the field, since it would otherwise risk destroying user inputted data.)
- Each field may be deleted – which also deletes any data stored by the field.
- The widget used for data input may be changed. You do this by clicking on the widget name for the relevant field.
- New fields may be added.

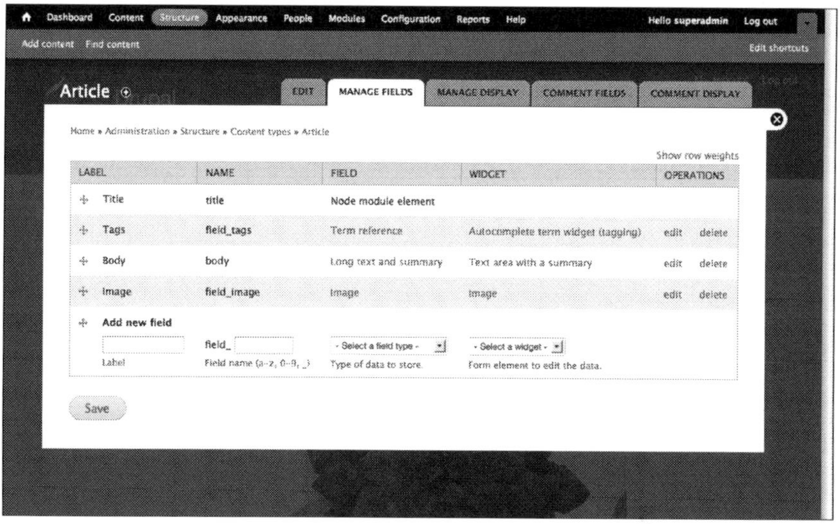

FIGURE 6.1 The node type "Article" has a number of fields, which you can edit and reorder.

- Fields used on other entities may be reused, as an alternative to adding new fields.

Below is a closer description of all of these operations.

Editing fields and widgets

When clicking the *edit* link for an entity field you are brought to a page full of settings for that field, while a click on the widget name opens a corresponding page for the widget. (You can switch between these pages using the tabs on top of the page.)

The settings available for a field depends on its field type, and its widget – usually the help texts explains quite well how the different settings are used. Below are descriptions for the most common settings.

- Required: Users will get an error message if trying to save a node (or other entity) while required fields are empty.

- Help text: Any help text will usually be displayed in small font below the input field. Best practice dictates that every field should have help text, unless there is a good reason otherwise.
- Default value: This sets the default value when creating new nodes/ entities. (The default value will *not* be automatically used if the field is left empty – it just saves the effort of filling in the most common value by hand.)
- Number of values: If there is a need, fields can accept multiple values – you may for example allow users to upload several images to an article. This setting either allows a fixed number of values (normally just one), or *unlimited* – usually providing a button with the text *add another item* below the field, allowing the user to add more input fields when required. If the field uses a *check boxes/radio buttons* widget, multiple-value fields will be displayed as check boxes instead of radio buttons.
- Allowed values (list fields only): In this text area you may enter a list of values the user should be able to select from, one per line. It is possible to separate the data stored in the database and the value presented to the user by writing lines on the form *stored data|displayed data*. Only the data stored in the database has to match the field type – a number list could for example have o|*free of charge* as a possible value, displaying *free of charge* to all users while still storing a number in the database.
- Text processing (text fields only): This option determines if a text input should be able to hold markup, or if it is always plain text. See the section on text formats for more information.

Adding new fields

At the bottom of the field list for a node type is a row used to add new fields. Each field requires a label, a machine name, a field type and finally also a widget that matches the selected field type.

When adding a new field you are automatically redirected to the pages for configuring the field and its widget. (See figure 5.2.)

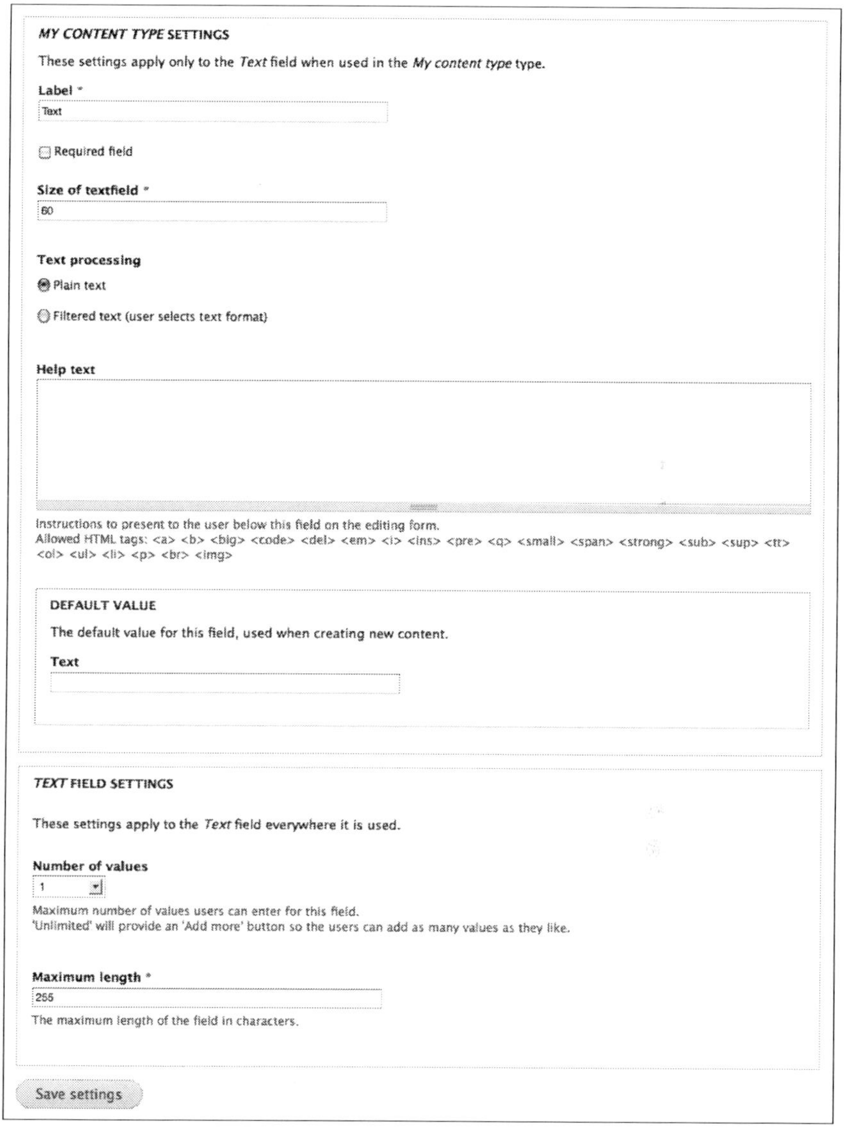

MY CONTENT TYPE SETTINGS

These settings apply only to the *Text* field when used in the *My content type* type.

Label *

Text

☐ Required field

Size of textfield *

60

Text processing

⦿ Plain text

◯ Filtered text (user selects text format)

Help text

Instructions to present to the user below this field on the editing form.
Allowed HTML tags: <a> <b> <big> <code> <del> <em> <i> <ins> <pre> <q> <small> <span> <strong> <sub> <sup> <tt>
<ol> <ul> <li> <p>
 <img>

DEFAULT VALUE

The default value for this field, used when creating new content.

Text

TEXT FIELD SETTINGS

These settings apply to the *Text* field everywhere it is used.

Number of values

1 ▾

Maximum number of values users can enter for this field.
'Unlimited' will provide an 'Add more' button so the users can add as many values as they like.

Maximum length *

255

The maximum length of the field in characters.

Save settings

FIGURE 6.2 Different field types have different settings. The figure shows the settings for textfields.

FIELD TYPES IN A STANDARD DRUPAL INSTALLATION

The field types included in a standard Drupal installation are:

- Boolean: This stores a zero/one value in the database, but could for users be displayed as any text (such as no/yes).
- Decimal: This stores a number with a specified number of decimals. The character used for decimal mark is configurable, and you may optionally add a prefix or suffix to the number – for example '$'.
- File: This stores file data to a node/entity (while the actual file is stored in the file structure and not the database). Settings for this field include accepted file types, folder where the files should be stored, file size limitations, and a few more options. It is possible to store files without making them publicly accessible if you have entered a path to use for private files on the toolbar, *configuration, file system*.
- Float: This stores a float number – the most exact type of number used in Drupal. As with decimals you may add prefix and suffix to the field.
- Image: This stores metadata for an image (while the actual image file is stored in the file structure and not the database). Field settings are similar to those for files, but also include alternate and title text settings, as well as limitations for image sizes.
- Integer: This stores a light-weight integer number. As with decimals you may add prefix and suffix to the field.
- List (integer/float/text): This stores number and text data for pre-defined lists. The field type is useful to create select lists or check boxes.
- Long text: This can store a large amount of text in the database, and is normally only used when you want a text area input.
- Long text and summary: This saves a text along with a summary in the database – the field type used in a standard article. Field settings include the possibility to write a customized summary.
- Term reference: This stores a reference to a taxonomy term – see the taxonomy chapter for details.
- Text: This stores a shorter text in the database, usually inputted via a single-line textfield.

Drupal modules may provide more fields and widgets to your site, making it possible to have fields customized for e-mail addresses, geodata, video, and much more.

TIP

Drupal modules may provide more fields and widgets to your site, making it possible to have fields customized for e-mail addresses, geo-data, video, and much more.

Reusing fields

It is possible to use the same field on more than one entity – an image field can for example be used on both users and a node type. You do this by using the row *add existing field* in the list of fields.

When reusing fields only parts of the configuration may be changed for each node type or entity – such as help texts – while others must be the same for all entities where the field is used – such as number of values to store.

It is recommended to create new fields instead of reusing existing ones, unless you have a clear reason for the opposite. The biggest reasons for this are the increased flexibility you get for field configuration, and that shared fields can make it more difficult to export only selected parts of the configuration on your site. (See the section on exporting configuration in appendix 1 for more information about why configuration export is useful.)

TIP

Reusing fields will normally *not* give you any performance improvements on the site – if anything your site risks becoming slightly slower when the data table for a shared field becomes unnecessarily large.

Comment and user account fields

Just as with node types, you may add and configure fields for comments and user accounts. Field settings for comments are found at their respective node type settings, by clicking the tab *comment fields*. Field settings for users are found at the toolbar, *configuration, account settings* and the tab *manage fields.*

Fields applied to user accounts have additional settings that determine if the field should be displayed on the user registration page. Required user fields are always included on the registration form.

Creating relations with fields

An important part of building information structure is to create relations between nodes, and also between other entities – this fact box *belongs to* this article, this press release *relates to* these products, and so on.

In Drupal these relations are created with *reference fields* or *relation fields* – fields connecting entities on your site.

At the time of writing there are two options available for creating references between entities:

- The *References* module is a port of the most common reference fields in Drupal 6 – node references and user references. The module provides two new field types, pointing to nodes and users, respectively.
- The *Relation* module is new for Drupal 7 and provides a way to relate any kind of entities. It also includes options to have directional or undirectional relations – and the possibility to add fields to a relation.

> **TIP**
>
> At the time of writing the References module is more stable and easy to use than the Relation module, but it is likely that the Relation module will be the de facto standard in Drupal 7. That said, References will most likely be used by many sites migrating from Drupal 6 to Drupal 7, meaning that it will continue to be used and updated. See the chapter about modules in appendix 1 for more information about how to find and evaluate modules.

ELABORATION: THE PROBLEM OF DIRECTIONAL REFERENCES

As a Drupal developer you will find yourself considering which direction a reference should have – should you put a reference field on node type A pointing towards a selected user, or should the field be placed on the user and point towards selected A-type nodes?

Factors influencing these choices are usually, in order:

1 The technical consequences of the choice, and limitations on how easy it will be to store, retrieve and display the data.
2 The workflows on the site, and which solution will be most comfortable for end users.
3 The information structure on the site, and which solution gives the most clean result.

When these factors do not agree, you can often provide tools for improving (primarily) the workflows on the site, but these tools will not be described further in this book.

Determining how references should be directed is an art that requires training, and it is common that unfortunate choices don't have consequences until you have reached half-way through a website project.

> **TIP**
>
> If one direction, but not the other, should lead to a reference field having *one* value instead of many, it is probably the best choice – a fact box relating to exactly one article is usually a better choice than one article relating to any number of fact boxes.

Example implementations of fields

This section contains examples of how the concepts and functionalities in this chapter may be used. You can find more examples in the exercises.

ATTACHMENTS TO ARTICLES

As editor on my news site I want to be able to attach PDF documents to articles. This will allow visitors to view and download the files. This is important since we often have useful extra information in PDFs that we want to offer to our visitors.

The functionality above can be achieved by the following steps:

1 Visit the page for overviewing the fields for the node type article.
2 Add another field of the type *file*. Give it the label attachment and the name *field_article_attachment*.
3 Drag and drop the field to a suitable place in the field list.
4 Save the field list, opening the settings for the new field.
5 Use the default field-wide settings by clicking save *field settings*.
6 Add a help text, explaining that any attached files will be shown along with the article.
7 Change the allowed file extensions to pdf.
8 *Set file directory* to *article/attachments*.
9 Check *enable description field*.
10 Change *number of values to unlimited*. Save!

YEAR OF BIRTH IN THE USER PROFILE

As an administrator on my forum site I would like all members to state their year of birth when registering. This is important since it helps me understand how popular the site is among different user groups.

The functionality above can be achieved by the following steps:

1 Edit the fields for user accounts.
2 Add a new field of the type integer, for example with label *year of birth* and the name *field_user_birthyear*.
3 Saving the field list will open the settings for the new field.
4 As integer fields lack site-global settings you can just hit *save field settings* to continue to the configuration used on user accounts only.
5 Mark the field as *required*, which automatically includes it on the registration form for the site.
6 Write a help text explaining how the information they provide will or will not be used.
7 Set *minimum* to 1900 and *maximum* to 2011 to prevent users from providing nonsense years.

TIP

The *Date* modules provides entity fields for dates and times, which in this case would be a good alternative to using an integer field.

Exercises: Documentation site

These are the first exercises in the *documentation site* suite. They include building the basic information structure for a website used by a community for building software documentation collaboratively. Carrying out these exercises requires using the concepts described in this chapter, as well as concepts covered by part A of this book.

Video recordings of the suggested solutions to these exercises can be found at nodeone.se/learn-drupal.

DOCUMENTATION PAGE

As site member I want to be able to create and edit documentation pages, containing text, screenshot uploads and file attachments. This is important since it allows me to contribute to building the on-line documentation.

FIGURE 6.3 An example of how the finished documentation page may look.

How to demo

1 Log in to the site.
2 Create a new documentation page, containing text, images and file attachments.
3 Verify that text, images and file attachments are displayed when vie-wing the saved documentation page.
4 Log out. As anonymous visitor, verify that the documentation page is not editable.
5 Log in with another account. Verify that the documentation page is editable.

Required preparations

- An empty Drupal site.

Suggested solution

1 Add a new content type *Documentation page*. Provide it with a des-cription of how the content type will be used, such as *Documentation pages are editable by all site members, and contain documentation about a given concept.* (See *node types and node administration* in the nodes chapter.)
2 Click the *save and add fields* button to go to the fields overview page for the node type.
3 Add a new image field to the content type. Give it the label *images*, pro-vide it with a help text, and allow an unlimited number of images to be uploaded into the field. (See *adding new fields* in this chapter.)
4 Add a new file field to the content type. Give it the label *attachments*, provide it with a help text and change the allowed file extensions to *txt pdf doc xls zip tar.gz odt ods docx xlsx*. Enable the description setting, and allow unlimited number of uploads in this field. (See *adding new fields.*)
5 Change the permissions settings on the site, to allow all authenticated users to add and edit documentation pages. (See *permissions and roles* in the users and persmissions chapter.)

Comments

- Since documentation pages probably won't be put in any menus, it could make sense to deselect all menu options in the node type setting.
- There are a lot of settings when adding new fields to content types. In most cases you can just use the default settings, and change whatever you need afterwards.
- It is useful to have conventions when deciding machine names for fields – it makes it easier for yourself and others to find and recognize them. One convention is to start each machine name with the name of the node type it is used on. (Or any other entity.)
- The content of the fields may not be displayed in the best way – but that is actually not a part of this user story. Writing and reading user stories in concise ways will help you focusing on the right tasks.

DOCUMENTATION COLLECTION

As site member I want to be able to create documentation collections, referring to one or several documentation pages. There should be room for entering a description for each collection. This is important since it allows

FIGURE 6.4 An example of how the finished documentation collection may look.

me to organize the on-line documentation in a way that is meaningful to me, as well as take part of documentation structures others find useful.

How to demo

1   Log in to the site.
2   Create a new documentation collection, containing a description and referring to at least two documentation pages.
3   Verify that collection description and links to the documentation pages are displayed when viewing the saved documentation collection.
4   Edit the collection and change the order of documentation page references. Verify that the list order has changed accordingly when viewing the saved collection.
5   Log out and log in with another account. Verify that the documentation collection is not editable.

Required preparations

• A number of documentation pages should be available on the site (see previous exercise).
• The References project should be downloaded and the Node Reference module installed. (Alternatively, a stable release of the Relation module could be used.)

Suggested solution

1   Add a new node type *Documentation collection*. Provide it with a description. Click *save and add fields* to go to the fields overview page. (See *node types and node administration* in the nodes chapter.)
2   Make sure that the *Node reference* module is enabled. Then add a node reference field, for example using the label *documentation pages*. (See *adding new fields* in this chapter.)

3 Allow the node reference field to point to documentation pages only. Mark it as *required*, provide it with a help text, and allow users to enter an unlimited number of references in each field. (See *adding new fields*.)

4 Go to the permissions list for the website, and set permissions to allow authenticated users to create and edit *their own* documentation collections. (See *permissions and roles* in the users and permissions chapter.)

Comments

- The Relation module is more flexible and more powerful than the References module – but is at time of writing not stable enough to document. See the elaboration on using fields for creating references for more information.
- As with documentation pages, it does not really make sense to add collections to menus – so all menus may be deselected in the node type settings.

USER INFORMATION

As site member I want to be able to view details about other site members, such as real name, a user image and in which country they live. It should be possible to enter this information when creating an account on the site. This is important since it makes it easier to get to know the people I'm cooperating with on the website.

How to demo

1 As anonymous visitor, create a new account on the website. Verify that it is possible to enter real name, upload a user image, and enter which country you live in.

2 Verify that your user information is displayed when viewing the new account. (Copy the URL for use in the next step – the unique URL for this user account can be found by going to the user edit page and copying all but the */edit* part of the path.)

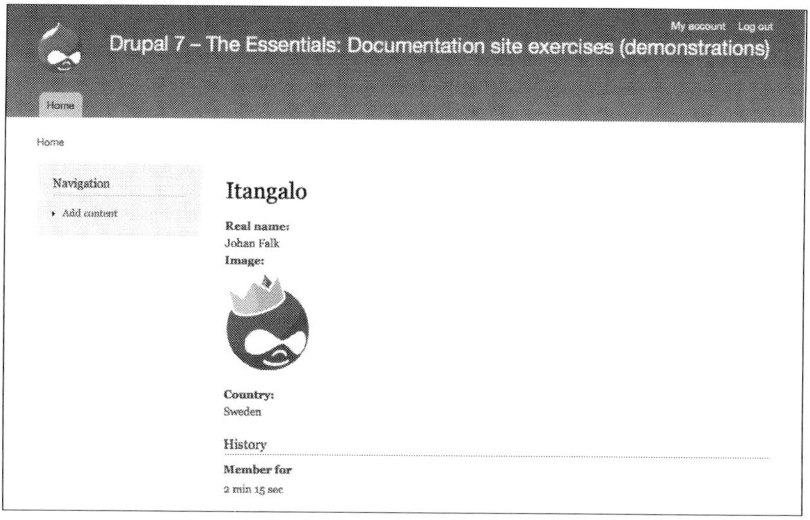

My account Log out
Drupal 7 – The Essentials: Documentation site exercises (demonstrations)

Home

Home

Navigation
• Add content

Itangalo

Real name:
Johan Falk
Image:

Country:
Sweden

History

Member for
2 min 15 sec

FIGURE 6.5 An example of how a user page may look.

3 Log out. As anonymous visitor, verify that you cannot access the page with the user information. (Manually paste the URL into your browser.)

4 Log in as another user. Verify that you can view the user information for the newly created account.

Required preparations

• An empty Drupal site.

Suggested solution

1 Go to the account settings on your site, and change the registration settings to allow people to register without administrator approval. Also turn off the default image used for user accounts. (See *other user account settings* in the users and permissions chapter.)

2 Go to the *manage fields* tab on the account settings page. Add a new text field with the label *real name*. Give it a help text and set it to be

displayed in the user registration form. (See *comment and user account fields* plus *adding new fields*, in this chapter.)

3   Add another field, for user images. Add a help text, and have the field being displayed on the user registration form.

4   Add a last text field, for country. Provide it with a help text – and have it displayed on the user registration form.

5   Change the permission settings to allow all authenticated users to view the profile pages.

Comments

- The default picture field for user accounts cannot be used in this case, since there is no easy way of having it appear in the user registration form.
- Whenever adding fields to user accounts, it is sensible to have help texts letting the end user know if the information will be displayed publicly or not.

Exercises: News site

These are the first exercises in the *news site* suite. They include building the basic information structure for a website used to publish news. Carrying out these exercises requires using the concepts described in this chapter, as well as concepts covered by part A of this book. The exercises can also be found at nodeone.se/learn-drupal.

NEWS ARTICLES

As news writer I want to be able to create news articles, and also to edit my own news articles. News articles contain title, header image, introduction, body, and non-header images. This is important since it allows me to provide site visitors with news.

How to demo

1   Log in to the site as writer.

2   Create a news article with title, header image, introduction, body and at least one non-header image.
3   Verify that all elements are displayed when viewing the article.
4   Verify that you may edit the article.
5   Log out. As anonymous visitor, verify that you can view the article.
6   Log in as another writer. Verify that you can view but not edit the article.

Required preparations

• An empty Drupal site.

FACT BOXES

As news writer I want to be able to add fact boxes to news articles. Fact boxes should contain title and plain text only. An article should be able to have multiple fact boxes, but each fact box should belong to only one article. Fact boxes are important since they allow me to add valuable site information to articles without weighing down the article body with details. *(Note that this user story does not contain any functionality for viewing the fact box with the articles – only to create fact boxes.)*

How to demo

1   Log in to the site as writer.
2   Create a new fact box. Enter title and text. Verify that you must select an article the fact box belongs to in order to be allowed to save.

Required preparations

• At least one news article created on the site (see previous exercise).
• The References project should be downloaded and the Node Reference module installed. (Alternatively, a stable release of the Relation module could be used.)

Taxonomy

Taxonomy is the word by Drupalistas (and biologists) when talking about *categorizing*. The tags used on articles in a standard Drupal installation is an example of how Drupal's taxonomy system may be used.

Categories – such as individual tags on articles – are collected in what is Drupal-speek is called *vocabularies*: A vocabulary *cities* could contain categories like *Miami* or *Mumbai*, while a vocabulary called *news sections* could contain categories like *sports, science* and *politics*. In a standard installation, the article tags are collected in a vocabulary simply called *tags*.

Since a good Drupal developer needs to know Drupal-speek well, you should also know that categories in Drupal technically are referred to as *terms*.

It may take a little while before you use these words without getting confused, but it helps knowing them when reading or talking about Drupal it helps to know the lingo. Here is a quick summary for your phrase book:

- *Taxonomy* is the framework for categorizing – the practice of classifying things.
- A vocabulary is a set of categories, used to separate different kinds of categories. Could for example be *cities*.
- *Terms* are the actual category words, such as *Miami* or *Mumbai*. Each term belongs to exactly one vocabulary.

Using the taxonomy system

As the articles in a standard Drupal installation show, it is possible to use Drupal's taxonomy tools to categorize content – you can add tags (terms) to an article. These terms are usually displayed as links, leading to a list of all nodes marked with the same term. (See figure 7.1.)

These lists – *term lists* – have some similarities to the front page list in a standard Drupal installation: Nodes are displayed as teasers, and the option *sticky at top of lists* make nodes appear on top of the list. Just as with the front page, there is also an RSS feed for each term list. In contrast to the front page, though, each term list has a title – the term name – and if the term has a description (see below) it, too, will be displayed.

Users with access to edit terms will see tabs at the term lists – one to view the list and one for editing the term.

TAXONOMY AND FIELDS

Terms are added to nodes an other entities by virtue of *term reference* fields. The settings for term reference fields include an option to set which vocabulary should be used, and there is also a somewhat unusual widget available – *autocomplete term widget (tagging)*. This widget makes Drupal display suggestions matching what the user types, and it also allows the

FIGURE 7.1 Each taxonomy term has a list page displaying teasers of all nodes marked with the same term. Here is a list of all content marked with the example tag *alpha*.

user to add new terms if the typed text doesn't match any existing term (in the relevant vocabulary).

Creating and managing vocabularies and terms

At the toolbar's option *structure, taxonomy* is a list of all the vocabularies on your website – in a standard Drupal installation only *tags*. (See figure 7.2.) Each vocabulary is presented along with some management links – for editing the vocabulary settings, listing all existing terms, and adding new terms.

FIGURE 7.2 The administration page for taxonomy has links to manage each vocabulary, and create new ones.

The list of taxonomy terms allows you as administrator to reorder the terms – which includes creating tree structures. It is also possible to edit each term (See figure 7.3.) The for for adding or editing terms holds information about the term name, any URL alias for the term, and also a term description. (See figure 7.4.) The term description is actually an entity field, and it is possible to add more fields to terms – see the section below for details. The edit page also allows you to set any parent terms, but this is usually more easy to manage in the drag-and-drop list of terms.

Above the list of vocabularies you will find a link *add vocabulary*, leading to a form used for – you guessed it – adding new vocabularies. (Like in many other cases, the add and edit forms are extremely similar.) Each vocabulary has a name and, optionally, a description. Drupal will automatically suggest a machine name for the vocabulary, based on its plain-text name.

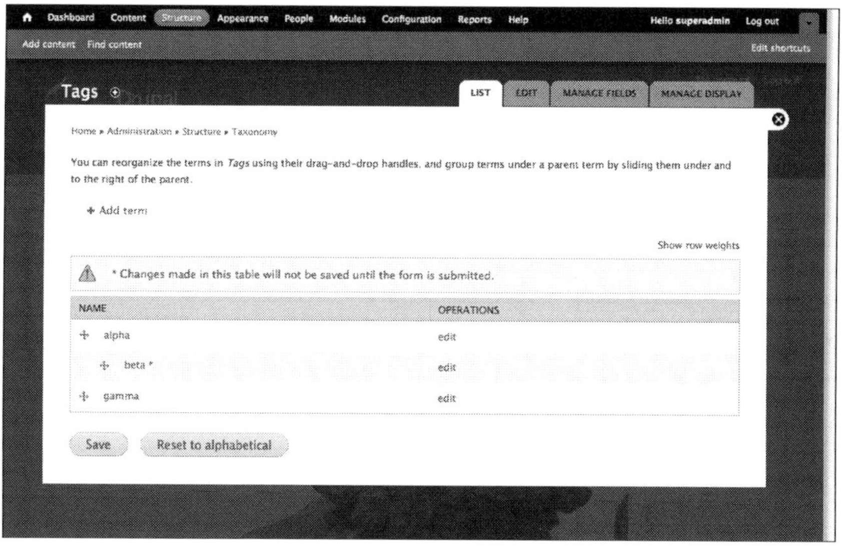

FIGURE 7.3 Each vocabulary has a list of all its terms. Terms can be sorted into a tree structure.

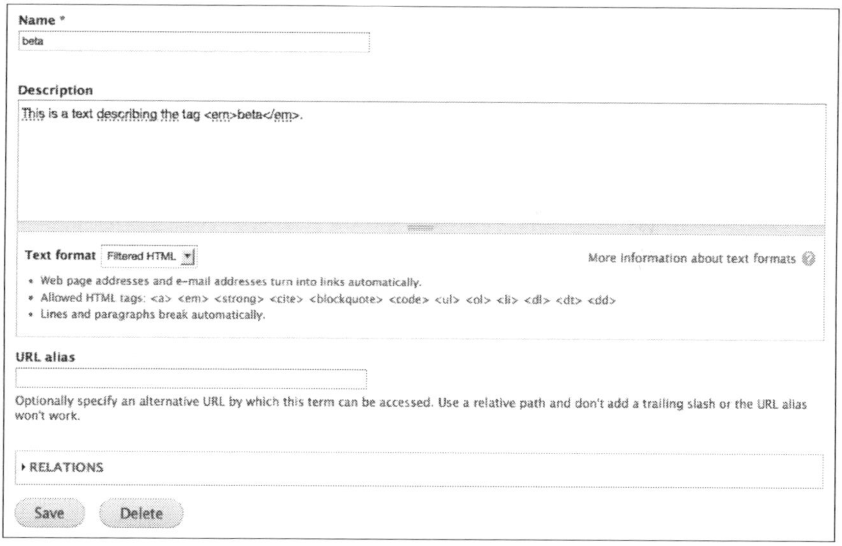

FIGURE 7.4 Each term may be edited. You can change the fields available on terms, for example adding images to terms.

> **TIP**
>
> It is possible to select more than one parent term on the term edit page. This allows for interesting relations between terms, but makes it impossible to use the click-and-drag list for managing the list of terms. If you set more than one parent term, the click-and-drag list is disabled.

FIELDS ON TAXONOMY TERMS

Just as with node types, comments and user accounts, you can add entity fields to taxonomy terms. The fields are set on a per-vocabulary basis, and the field settings are available from the edit page for the vocabulary and the tab *manage fields*.

Elaboration: taxonomy terms, text fields or nodes?

In basically all medium-complex Drupal sites you will face one or two decisions relating to taxonomy:

1 Should a particular field (for example *section*) be a text list field, or should I use taxonomy terms? Both could give me a selection list for sections when creating content.

2 Should a certain type of data (such as *product types*) be a node type, or should they be taxonomy terms? Both are fieldable and may contain whatever information I need.

Deciding these questions usually requires both good knowledge about the website and its data, and experience of managing data with Drupal. Sometimes it has little or no consequence what you choose, but an unfortunate choice may also lead to a lot of extra work later on in the site project.

Here are some tips for approaching these kinds of decisions.

• What is good or bad is, at the end of the day, determined by what works and what doesn't work.

• That taxonomy terms give you automated lists of content is not a reason to choose terms in front of text fields or nodes – the Views module allows you to build similar lists yourself, based on text fields or other data. (See separate chapters for more information about Views.)

- When deciding between text fields and taxonomy terms, ask yourself (or the client!) if the information is a necessary part of the node/entity. If so, text fields are usually the better choice. If you're dealing with meta information, on the other hand, taxonomy terms are usually the best choice.
- When deciding between text fields and taxonomy terms, be aware that taxonomy terms may be edited and even deleted independently of the node/entity – the term information is separated from the node/entity.
- When deciding between node types and taxonomy terms – ask yourself (or the client!) if you need any of the functionality available to nodes only; publish states, revisioning, access control, authors, et cetera.
- When deciding between node types and taxonomy terms – will the data only be used to describe other content on the site? If so, taxonomy terms could be the best choice. If it makes sense to look at the data in itself, nodes are probably better.

Example implementations of taxonomy

This section contains examples of how the concepts and functionalities in this chapter may be used. You can find more examples in the exercises.

USING CATEGORIES IN PARALLEL

As editor on my recipee site I want to be able to categorize recipiees as either startes, main courses, desserts or other. I also want to be able to categorize recipees according to dietary preferences such as free of gluten, free of lactose and vegetarian. This is important since it helps the site visitors find recipees they are interested in.

The functionality above can be achieved by the following steps:
- A new vocabulary with the name *type of corse*, where the terms *starter, main course, dessert* and *other* are added manually.

- A new vocabulary with the name *dietary preferences*, where the terms *free of gluten, free of lactose* and *vegetarian* are added manually.
- The node type for recipees (assumed to exist already) gets a new term reference field, referring to the *type of course* vocabulary. The field is set as required, accepts one single value, and uses the *select list* widget.
- The node type gets another term reference field, referring to the vocabulary dietary preferences. The field is not required, accepts an unlimited number of values, and uses the *check boxes/radio buttons* widget.

FACULTIES AND DEPARTMENTS

As editor on the university information site I want to be able to mark a piece of news as relevant to only selected departments. I also want to mark entire faculties to denote that all departments on that faculty are affected. This is important since it lowers the amount of irrelevant information the university staff has to read.

The functionality above can be achieved by the following steps:
- A new vocabulary with the name administration unit.
- Each faculty at the university is entered as terms in the vocabulary.
- Each department on the university is entered as terms in the vocabulary, and sorted as child terms of their respective faculty.
- The node type for news (assumed to already exist) gets a new term reference field, referring to the *administration unit* vocabulary. The field is set up to allow unlimited number of values, and will probably use the select list widget.

> TIP
>
> Note that both cases described above strictly speaking aren't user stories, for two reasons. One: The new functions are described from the editors point of view, but the functionality should be useful for the site visitors. Two: There is no actual use case described in the cases – only descriptions of how data should be stored. User stories like these should be avoided in real projects, since they border to technical specifications rather than value added to the website. (These kinds of user stories may still be useful as pedagogical examples, though!)

Exercises: Documentation site

These exercises build on previous exercises in the *documentation site* suite. They can be carried out individually, with some preparations, or in sequence with the previous exercises. The exercises require using the concepts described in this and the previous chapter, as well as concepts covered by part A of this book.

Video recordings of the suggested solutions to these exercises can be found at nodeone.se/learn-drupal.

TOPIC TAGS

As site member I want to be able to add freely chosen topics as tags to documentation pages and collections. This is important since it allows me to create another level of structure to the on-line documentation, making it easier to browse and search.

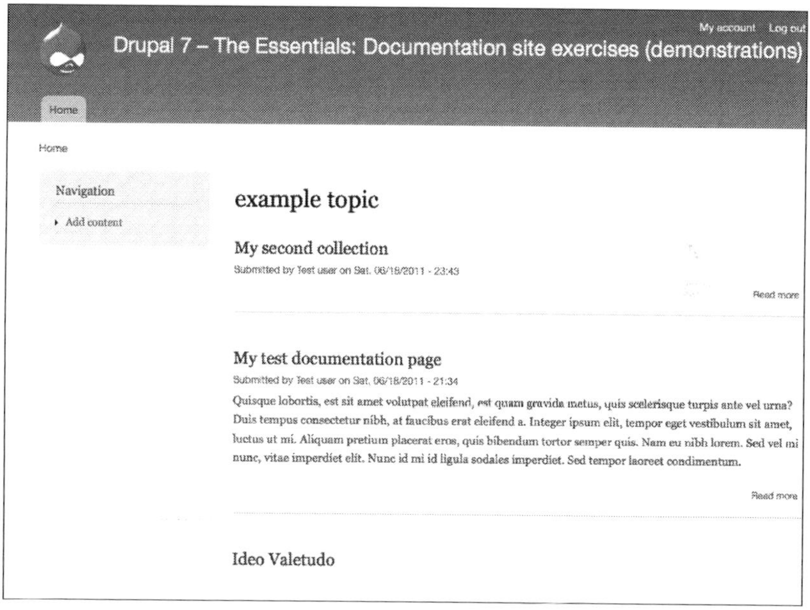

FIGURE 7.5 An example of how topic tags may be utilized on the documentation site.

How to demo

1 Log in to the site.
2 Edit an existing documentation page and add one or several topic tags. Verify that you can add new topics.
3 Add a documentation collection and add topics to it. Make sure you reuse at least one of the topics from the documentation page.
4 Verify that topics appear as links when viewing documentation pages and collections. Also verify that the links lead to lists of all content tagged with the selected topic.

Required preparations

• The site should have documentation pages and collections, as described in the first exercises in this suite.

Suggested solution

1 Go to the taxonomy overview page and add a new vocabulary called *topic*. Give it a description before saving. (See *creating and managing vocabularies and terms* in this chapter.)
2 Go to the field overview for documentation pages and add a new field of the type *term reference*, using the *autocomplete* widget. (See *taxonomy and fields* in this chapter.)
3 Give the field a label *topics*, and let it refer to the *topic* vocabulary. Enter a help text and allow the user to add an unlimited number of terms to the field. (See *adding new fields* in the fields chapter.)
4 Add a similar field to the documentation collection node type.

Comments

• In this user story it would work fine to reuse the taxonomy reference field for documentation pages in collections as well. But if the client in the future would like documentation pages to have exactly one topic, while collections can have several, you would have to break up a shared field into two separate – possibly with a lot of user-entered data being lost. Better is to use two separate fields, though identically configured.

- Whenever using the autocomplete field, it is a good habit to let the help text inform users that *terms are separated by commas* – not spaces.

- It is not completely obvious that we should use taxonomy terms for topics – maybe we should use simple text fields, or perhaps node references and have topics as nodes? But since everything we know about the topics (so far) tells us that it is metadata, taxonomy terms is a good choice. As a bonus, we get the listings wanted in this user story.

Exercises: News site

These exercises build on previous exercises in the *news site* suite. They can be carried out individually, with some preparations, or in sequence with the previous exercises. The exercises require using the concepts described in this and the previous chapter, as well as concepts covered by part A of this book.

SECTIONS AND SUB SECTIONS

As writer I want to categorize my articles according to news sections and sub sections. The main sections should be *world* (sub sections *Asia, Europe, Middle East, Africa, Americas* and *U.S.*) and *science* (sub sections *environment* and *space & cosmos*). This is important since it helps site visitors to find news stories they are interested in.

How to demo

1 Log in to the site as writer.
2 Create a news article. Verify that you have a get a select list of all sections of the site, with sub sections sorted by their main sections.
3 Verify that you cannot save the news article without selecting a section, and that you can only select a single section.

4   In the saved article, verify that the section appears as a link to all articles in that section.

Required preparations

- The site should have a news article content type, as provided by the first exercise in this suite.

SECTION EDITORS

As site builder, I would like to mark user accounts belonging to section editors with the section for which they are editors. This is important since it allows me to re-use this information in upcoming development tasks, connecting section editors with sections. *(Note that this is not a proper user story, since it does not add any value to end users of the site.)*

How to demo

1   Log in to the site as administrator.
2   Edit a user account. Verify that you can select a section for the account – the same sections as in previous exercise – but that you can also leave the section selection emtpy.

Required preparations

- The site should have a section vocabulary set up, as described in the previous exercise.

View modes and field display

You as administrator can add different types of fields to node types, comments, users and taxonomy terms – as the previous chapters have shown. These fields can be used to story just abou any kind of data you need on the site, but it is also important that the data is displayed in the way you want.

Getting all data on your website displayed in a correct and aesthetic way is an art in itself, and far from all tricks are covered by this book. But the first steps are easy – changing the field display settings, and tweaking these settings for different *view modes*.

Field display settings

A good place to start looking at field display settings are nodes. At the page for overviewing your node types (*structure, content types*) are links named *manage display*. They lead to a page where you can configure how the fields for the selected node type should be displayed. (See figure 8.1.)

On that page you will find each entity field in the node type, along with settings for how the field content and field label should be displayed. You may change these settings in the following ways.

- You may change the order of the fields by clicking and dragging their sorting arrows.
- Labels can be set to be displayed above the field, inline with the field content, or not at all.
- The *format* setting dictates how the field content itself should be displayed. Which formats are available depend on the field types and widgets. For example, texts may be displayed in full or trimmed version,

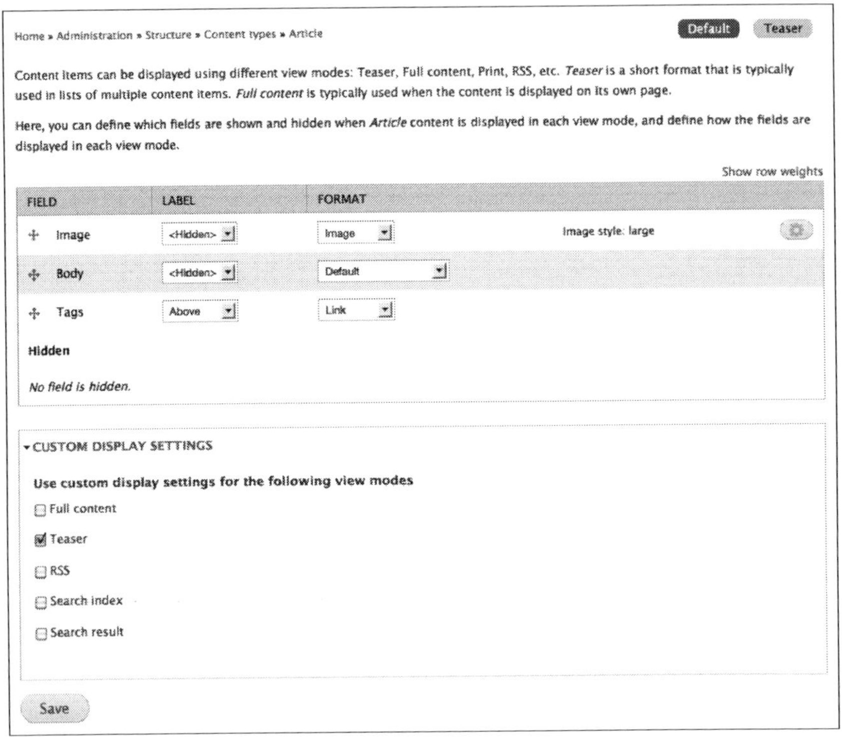

FIGURE 8.1 The field display settings for articles allow you to select which fields should be displayed, and how.

term references could be links or plain text, and files can be displayed with file names or full URLs – to mantion a fiew. Some fields and widgets, such as images, have further settings you can access by a gear button on the field's row on the page.

- All fields may have the *<hidden>* format, meaning that they aren't displayed at all. Hidden fields are moved to the bottom of the list and marked as *disabled*.

View modes

How a node is displayed may depend on the contexts where it is viewed – where the canonical examples are full nodes and teasers. On the page for field display management there are some settings hidden under the label *custom display settings*. The settings consist of a check box list of all view modes available for nodes, marking which view modes should have customized display settings. In a standard Drupal installation only the *teaser* is checked, resulting in two sub tabs on the manage display page – *default* and *teaser*. The sub tabs lead to separate settings for each view mode.

In a standard Drupal installation, the following view modes are available:

- Full content: This is normally used only when visiting the URL for a particular node.
- Teaser: This is used on two list types – the front page and taxonomy term lists.
- RSS: These settings are used when including the node in RSS feeds.
- Search index: This is used when Drupal's Search module indexes content on the site. Fields that are hidden in this view mode will not be searchable.
- Search result: This is used when presenting search results on the website.

While nodes have a number of different view modes, other entities only have one view mode each. They are *full comment* (comments), *user account* (users) and *taxonomy term page* (taxonomy terms).

All entities have their own pages for managing field display. They can always be accessed as a tab from the pages used for managing their field settings.

> **TIP**
>
> The *Display suite* module makes it possible to add more view modes to your entities.

Image styles

Drupal has built-in functionality to automatically scale and resize images. This is managed by *image styles*, which – in classic Drupal style – may be manipulated and extended by administrators. Each style becomes availablen in the field display settings, where you can select which style fits each view mode best.

Home » Administration » Configuration » Media

Image styles commonly provide thumbnail sizes by scaling and cropping images, but can also add various effects before an image is displayed. When an image is displayed with a style, a new file is created and the original image is left unchanged.

+ Add style

STYLE NAME	SETTINGS	OPERATIONS
thumbnail	Default	edit
medium	Default	edit
large	Default	edit

FIGURE 8.2 A standard Drupal installation contains three image styles – pre-defined ways of displaying images.

Image styles are created and edited from the toolbar, *configuration, image styles*. The resulting page contains an overview of all available image styles, links to edit each style, and also a link to create additional styles. (See figure 8.2.)

> **TIP**
>
> Image styles create image derivatives that are stored in the file system – but will never change the original images.

CREATING AND EDITING IMAGE STYLES

The first step in creating a new image style is to provide it with a machine name. (This is one of the few places in Drupal where you have to enter machine names manually.) The name will be used in the path to style's image derivatives, and should only contain lowercase alphanumericals, dashes (-) and underscores (_). A common practice is to name a style by their use case ('sidebar_small') or their actual sizes ('180x180').

Saving the machine name creates an empty image style and redirects you to the page to edit it. (See figure 8.3.) On the resulting page you may add one or several *effects*, used to manipulate the image. A standard Drupal installation provides the following effects:

- Crop: This cuts the image down to selected measurements. You can specify which part of the image should be in focus.
- Desaturate: This converts the image to grey scale.

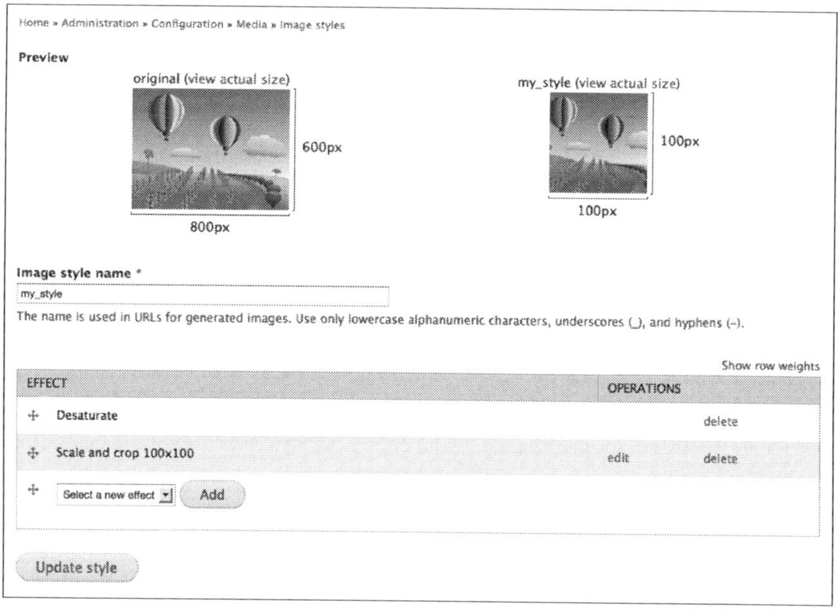

FIGURE 8.3 Image styles consists of a number of effects, used to process the image.

- Resize: This streches or shrinks the image to a size that you define, without any cropping.
- Rotate: This rotates the image an integer number of degrees. You can set which background color should be used on any blank spots revealed by the rotation, and you can optionally have a random rotation, with a specified maximum angle.
- Scale: This scales down the image to fit it all within a specified width and height. (You may set one dimension only to fit the scale to that dimension only.) You may optionally allow the images to be scaled up too, if it is smaller than the given dimensions.
- Scale and crop: This scales the image to cover a given width and height, cropping any parts outside the given frame after scaling.

The most commonly used effects are *scale* and *scale and crop*. You may chain several effects to create combined image effects. Administrators may reorder effects in a style, add more or remove existing effects.

> **TIP**
>
> Image styles defined by modules – such as the ones included in a standard installation – can't be deleted. Furthermore, you must actively override the standard settings to be able to edit their effects. You can revert the styles to their default settings later on, if need be.

> **TIP**
>
> The *ImageCache Actions* module provides a number of new effects for image processing.

Example implementations of view modes and field displays

This section contains examples of how the concepts and functionalities in this chapter may be used. You can find more examples in the exercises.

SEPARATE IMAGES ON THE FRONT PAGE AND NODE VIEW PAGE

As editor on my news site I want to be able have separate images for articles when viewed on the front page compared to the article's own page. This is important since it allows me to create more attractive article teasers.

The functionality above can be achieved by the following steps:
- A new image field *teaser image* for articles.
- The display of the teaser image is hidden on the full node view.
- The display of the original image field is hidden on teaser view.
- The teaser image is set to be displayed in a suitable image style, on teaser view mode only.

KITTEN-STYLE IMAGES

As member of a forum for kitten lovers, I would like uploaded kitten photos to be displayed slightly aslant rather than in the regular, right-angled fashion. This is important since it gives me cuddly feeling that I appreciate.

The functionality above can be achieved by the following steps:

- A new image style, *aslant*, is added.
- The style gets two effects that (1) scales and crops the image to 240 by 240 pixels, and then (2) rotates the image a random number of degrees – maximum 15°.
- A new image field is added to the node type *kitten photos* (assumed to already exist).
- The field display is set to show the image in the aslant style.

Exercises: Documentation site

These exercises build on previous exercises in the *documentation site* suite. They can be carried out individually, with some preparations, or in sequence with the previous exercises. The exercises require using the concepts described in previous chapters in this book, including part A.

Video recordings of the suggested solutions to these exercises can be found at nodeone.se/learn-drupal.

TABLES OF ATTACHMENTS ON COMMENTS

As site member posting a comment on a documentation page, I want to be able to attach files – just as I can when editing the *documentation page*. I want the attached files to be displayed in a table. This is important since file attachments are useful when discussing documentation.

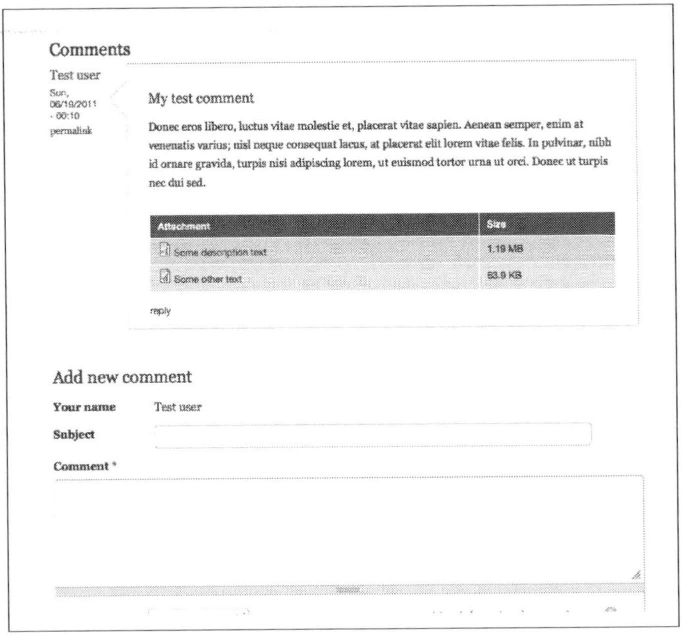

FIGURE 8.4 An example of how the file attachments on comments may look.

How to demo

1   Log in to the site.
2   Post a comment to a documentation page, attaching at least one file.

3   Verify that the accepted file types are the same as when attaching files to documentation pages.
4   Verify that the attached files are displayed in a table.

Required preparations

• The site should have a documentation page content type, as provided by the first exercise in this suite.

Suggested solution

1   Go to the tab *comment fields* for the documentation page node type. (See *comment and user fields* in the fields chapter.)
2   Add the existing field – the attachment field used on documentation page nodes. Set the configuration identical to how it is used in the documentation page node type. (See *reusing fields* in the fields chapter.)
3   Go to the tab *comment display*. Set the format for the attachment field to *table of files* and hide the label. (See *field display settings* in this chapter.)

Comments

• Since the user story explicitly says that files should be managed in the same way on comments as on documentation pages, it may be a good idea to reuse the field rather than create a new one. Still – while creating a new field takes a few more minutes, it may save you many hours of work later on.
• Since the client seems interested in using attachments in the same way in both documentation pages and their comments, it is probably a good idea to display files as tables on the node as well.

RETRO STYLE USER IMAGES

As site member I want user images to be displayed in a retro coarse-grained pixel style. This is important since it reminds me of old video games, providing a positive feeling on the site

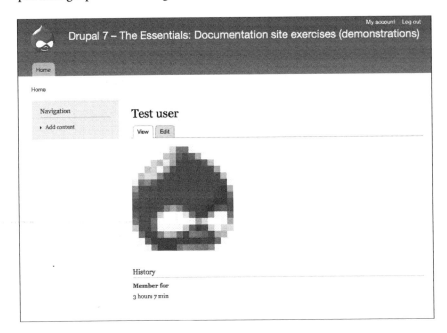

FIGURE 8.5 An example of how retro style user images may look.

How to demo

1 Log in to the site.
2 Edit your user account and upload a user image of normal quality.
3 Verify that the image is displayed in a coarse-grained pixel style on the account page.

Required preparations

- The user accounts should allow image upload, as described in the exercise *user information* in the fields chapter.

Suggested solution

1   Go to the overview page for image styles. Add a new image style *retro*. (See *image styles* in this chapter.)
2   Add an action *scale and crop* to reduce the image size to 16 times 16 pixels. (See *creating and editing image styles* in this chapter.)
3   Add another action *scale*, to increase the image size to 240 pixels squared. Make sure to check the option *upscaling allowed*. (See *creating and editing* image styles.)
4   Go to the *display fields* tab for user account fields. Change the image format to *retro*. (See *field display settings* in this chapter.)

Comments

- When using so heavily distorted images, it makes sense to use the same format for the image preview used when uploading the image. This setting is changed within settings in the field itself.

Exercises: New site

These exercises build on previous exercises in the *news site* suite. They can be carried out individually, with some preparations, or in sequence with the previous exercises. The exercises require using the concepts described in previous chapters in this book, including part A. These exercises can also be found at nodeone.se/learn-drupal.

SECTION BANNER IMAGES

As editor I would like to be able to set section banner images, appearing at the top of each section's news list. This is important since I believe that it helps visitors recognize each section and feel more comfortable reading news on our site. *(Note that this user story would be better phrased in terms of what site visitors want – not site editors. Investigating end user needs and expectations is imperative when developing websites.)*

How to demo

1 Log in to the site as editor.
2 Edit a section list page and add an image to it. Save.
3 Verify that the image appears in a flat and wide style at the top of the section's article list.

Required preparations

- The site should have a section vocabulary, as described in the exercise *sections and sub sections* in the previous chapter.

Views basics

The *Views* module is the most used of all Drupal modules. The flexibility and generality of Views makes it difficult to describe what the module does, but in the simplest use cases it is used to make lists of nodes, users, files or other content on the website. In more complex cases Views could be used for:

- listing titles of content related to an article;
- creating image slideshows;
- displaying a map marking latest news pieces published on the site;
- showing a block with a calendar containing lessons related to the course a visitor is viewing; and
- creating a page with a timeline containing all comments posted during the last 24 hours.

Technically, Views is a tool to *fetch data*, *process data* and *display data* – which is a quite broad field to work in.

Using Views in an efficient way is one of the most important skills a Drupal developer has to learn – indeed, it is often the difference between a beginner and an experienced Drupalist. This chapter covers the basics of Views, but is written more like an inventory of functionality than description of cases of how to use them. It is strongly encouraged that you look closer at a few of the implementation examples and exercises to see how to use Views in real life.

Installing Views

Views is installed like most modules – the module is downloaded, extracted and moved into the *sites/all/modules* folder. (See appendix 1 for more details about how to install modules.) To be able to set up views you will need both the *Views* and the *Views UI* modules (while the latter may be turned off once your views have been built). The Views project also holds the module *Views exporter*, which can be completely replaced by the Features module (described in the chapter about exporting settings, appendix 1).

To enable Views you must also have the *Chaos Tools* module available on your site. (The module is a part of the *Chaos tools suite* project.)

Views overview

The overview page for the Views module is found at the toolbar, *structure*, *views*. It contains a list of all views available on your website (see figure 9.1). With Views comes a number of pre-configured default view that you can be enabled – this is done by clicking the *enable* link available in the drop-down menu on the right side of each view.

In the overview, each view is listed with a short description, any path used by the view, and some more information. If you have not spent a lot of time with Views, this information won't tell you very much – but eventually the list will provide you a quite good summary of many of the functions on a Drupal site.

At the right side of each view, there is a drop-down menu with some links. They are used to enable/disable the view, edit it, clone it, export it and finally also delete it. Note that views provided by modules – such as the default views included in the Views project – cannot be deleted manually.

TIP

Views has excellent support for the *Advanced Help* module, providing help links in different parts of the graphical interface. Views will notify you of this if you do not have Advanced Help installed and enabled – you can turn these messages at the tab *settings* found at the Views overview page, should you grow tired of the reminders.

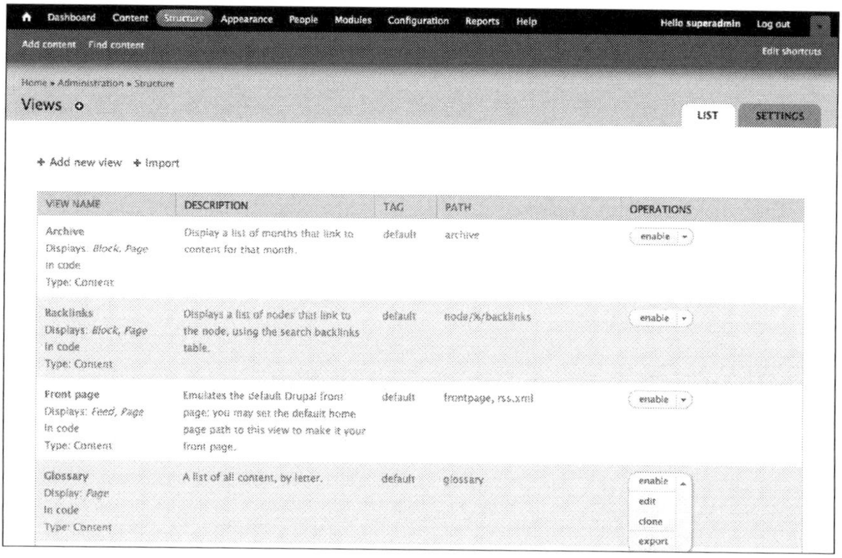

FIGURE 9.1 Views provides a number of pre-configured views you can enable. Any manually created views will also be displayed in this list.

Instead they have the *revert* option, removing any overrides you have made to its original configuration.

Creating new views

According to Ancient Wisdom, the best way of learning the Views module is to start using it. A good way of starting to use the module is to create yourself a new view. This is done at the Views overview page, and the link *add new view*, found just above the list of views. (These kind of links are called *local actions*.)

The link takes you to a page where you can set the most common and important settings for a view (see figure 9.2) without having to interact with the rather scary page containing all the view settings (see figure 9.3).

The quick-wizard for adding a view allows you to create a view through the following steps:

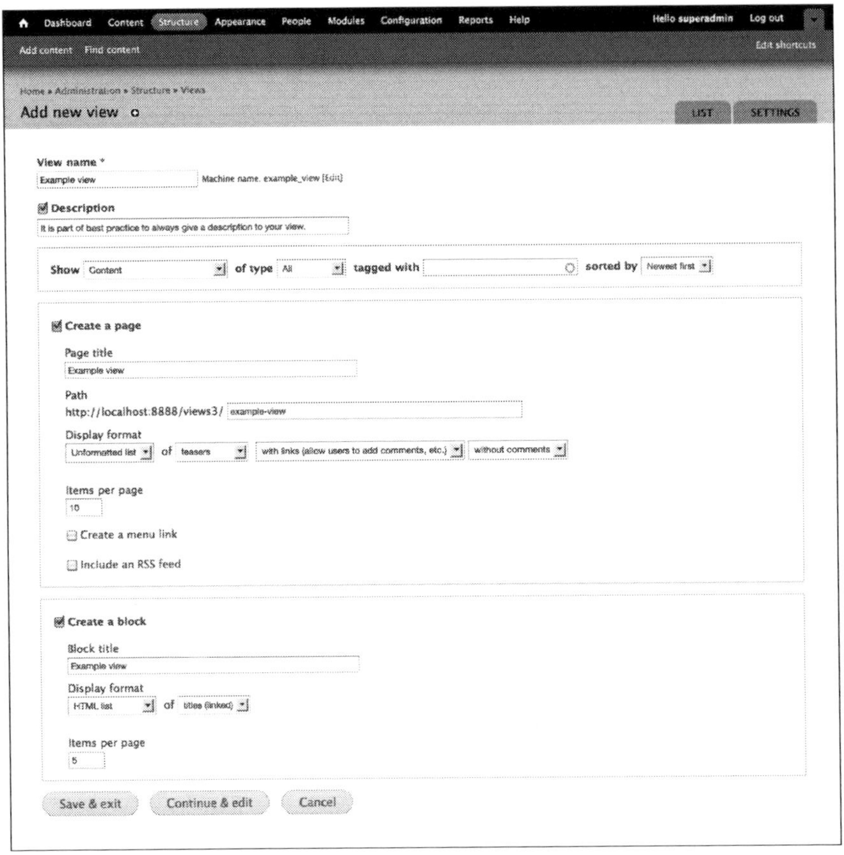

FIGURE 9.2 The quick-wizard for creating a new view is indispensible for anyone wanting to create a view without hazzle – and a good tool even for people enjoying digging around in advanced Views settings.

1   Give your view a *view name* – an administrative name not visible to end users. Based on this, Views will also suggest a *machine name* – which cannot be changed once saved.

2   Check the *description* box to provide your view with a short administrative description, explaining what it does or where it is used. Best practice dictates that each view should have a description.

3   Select what kind of site data should be displayed in the setting starting with *show* – for example useres, files or content (nodes). If you select nodes you may also limit the view to display only certain content types, or nodes marked with selected taxonomy terms. Finally you can also

select how the view should be sorted. Note that the type of data listed – the first choice on this row – cannot be changed once the view is created.

4   The option *create a page* provides you with a page of listed results. If you check this option you will get a few more options, such as which path the page should be available at and if it should have a menu link. You also get to choose how the data should be formatted – default is a teaser list similar to the default front page.

5   The option *create a block* provides you with a block containing the list results. This block can then be placed in a region, just as other blocks on the site. Further options include specifying the formatting of the results, as well as the number of results to display. (Note that you can have results provided as both a page and a block!)

6   The button *save & exit* completes the configuration and redirects you to any page that you have set up for the view. The button *continue & edit* brings you to the full configuration panel for the view – where the real fun starts.

The most common data to list with Views is content (nodes), which explains why this option has more options and settings than other data types. Nodes are, however, far from the only data type with great use cases in Views.

TIP

Views can fetch and process data *outside* your Drupal site, too. Usually this requires specific modules for each web service or databank you want Views to access – check out the modules *Apache Solr Views, SharePoint, YQL Views Query Backend*, and *XML Views* if you want some examples.

The Views main configuration panel

The brave souls choosing the *continue & edit* button at the quick-wizard page will be confronted with Views' main configuration panel (see figure 9.3). The same challenge awaits those who click the *edit* link for any existing view, be it from the Views overview page or the shortcuts available to administrators when looking at views on the website.

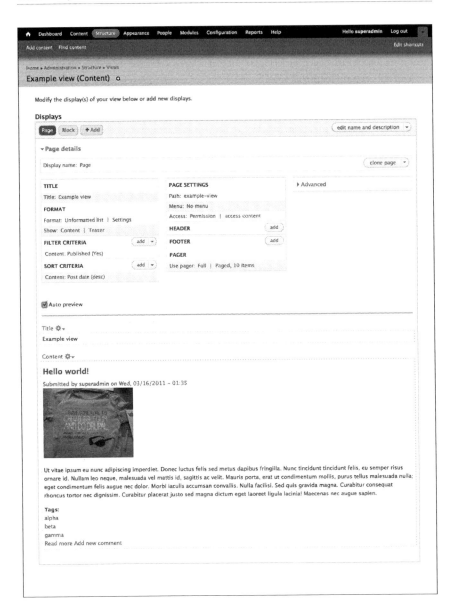

FIGURE 9.3 The Views main panel contains an overview of the view's settings, and links to change them. A lot of information, and a lot of possibilities.

The main configuration page – in this book called the *Views main panel* – contains an overview of the settings in the view, divided into groups to make them more lucid. The efforts of creating and configuring views almost entirely consists of clicking and editing these settings – and to an equally large part, the efforts of learning Views consists of learning what all the settings mean and how they interact.

All the buttons and options in the Views main panel may seem overwhelming, especially the first hundred times you encounter them. It is of little comfort that what you see in the Views main panel is the tip of an iceberg: configuring a view is usually a process of opening new settings by clicking somewhere in the main panel – settings which in turn open further settings (which pretty often result in even further settings). Learning to use Views efficiently takes time and effort. It is without doubt worth it.

Below is a summary of the most important settings, in the order they are usually configured when creating views.

> **TIP**
>
> Views that never have been saved may be lost if leaving the Views main panel. It is a good habit to save your view early – note that the *continue & edit* button doesn't save it for you. A view displaying error messages, such as *Display "Master" uses fields but there are none defined for it or all are excluded,* cannot be saved until the error is addressed.

> **TIP**
>
> The user interface for Views described in this book is a recasted version of an older interface. Much of the online documentation is still adapted for the old interface – don't be confused if you see screenshots displaying a different user interface.

Configuring filters

A good start to configuring views is to set *filters*. A view will, by default, fetch all available objects of the data type the view is based on – a node view will fetch all (accessible) nodes on the website. Filter settings makes it

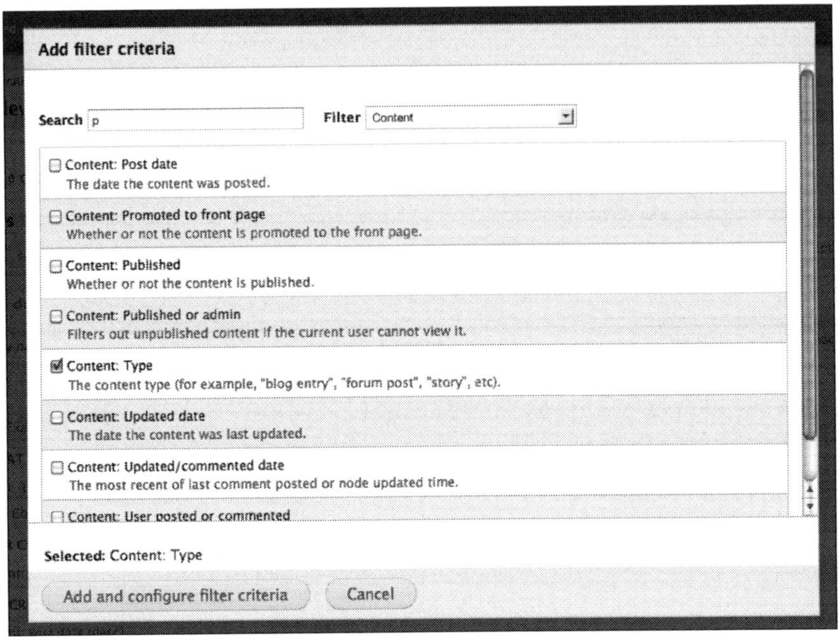

FIGURE 9.4 You can select which filters should be applied to the view by marking them in the a long list of available data fields.

possible to restrict the results to nodes of a certain type, created by a selected user, or those that have been updated the last week.

ADDING AND EDITING FILTERS

You add a new filter to your view by clicking the *add* link at the group *filter criteria* in the main panel. This opens a dialogue containing a list of all the data fields Views can use for filtering. (See figure 9.4.)

The magnitue of the list depends on the data type of the view, and node views has enough data fields to fill a few screens. You will learn a lot by browsing this list and see which options you have for filtering. Once you have become more familiar with the filtering options it is comfortable to use the *search* or *filter* options to quickly find the data fields you want.

New filters are added by marking one or several data fields and clicking the button *add filter and configure criteria*. This opens another dialogue of settings, where you set how you want to restrict the selected data fields –

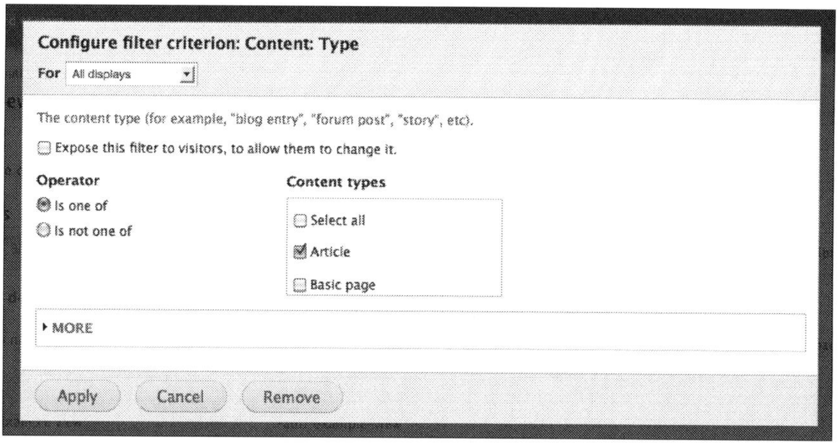

Configure filter criterion: Content: Type

For All displays ▾

The content type (for example, "blog entry", "forum post", "story", etc).

☐ Expose this filter to visitors, to allow them to change it.

Operator
◉ Is one of
○ Is not one of

Content types
☐ Select all
☑ Article
☐ Basic page

▸ MORE

(Apply)   (Cancel)   (Remove)

FIGURE 9.5 Filters are configured individually.

you can for example require that the data field *content: type* should have the value *article* to restrict your node view to articles only. Which options are available depends on the selected data field – you can for example require that a node title contains (but isn't necessarily equal to) a given string, or that a time stamp is later than *-7 days*. (See figure 9.5 and 9.6.)

Hidden under the *more* settings in the filter dialogue is an option to set an *administrative title* to the filter, making it easier to overview your settings. If no administrative title is set, the name of the data field will be used.

The filter settings contain two options that are described in separate sections: The checkbox *expose this filter to visitors, to allow them to change it* is explaind further in in the section about exposed settings. The option *configure [...] for all displays* in the dialogue head makes it possible to have different settings between (for example) pages and blocks for the same view – see the section about displays for details.

When you save your filters, the dialogue is closed. You can change settings for existing filters in three different ways:

- You can change settings for individual filters by clicking their name, thereby re-opening their configuration dialogue. (See figure 9.7.)
- You can create logical AND and OR groups from your filters by clicking the *and/or* option available in the menu at the *add* link for filters. (See figure 9.8.)

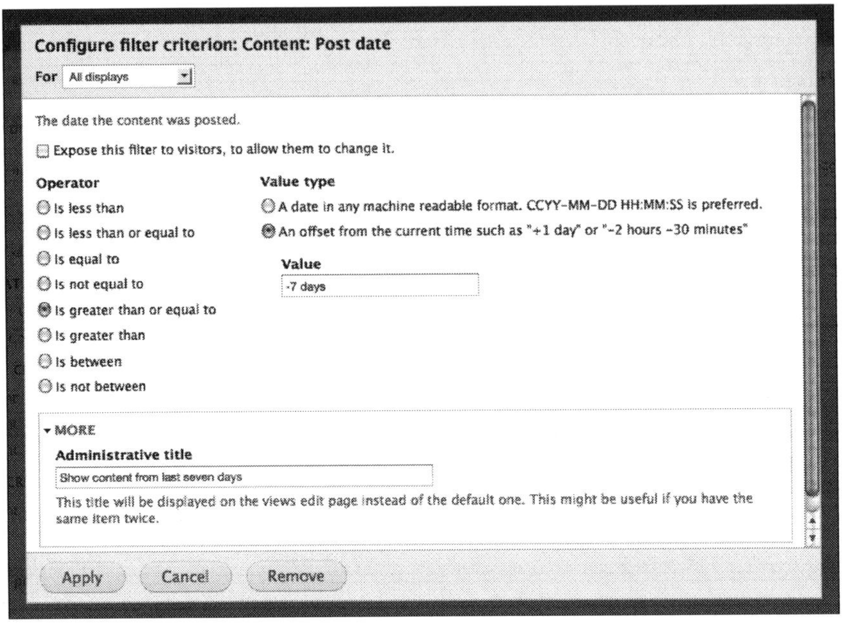

Configure filter criterion: Content: Post date

For [All displays ▾]

The date the content was posted.

☐ Expose this filter to visitors, to allow them to change it.

Operator   **Value type**
○ Is less than   ○ A date in any machine readable format. CCYY-MM-DD HH:MM:SS is preferred.
○ Is less than or equal to   ◉ An offset from the current time such as "+1 day" or "-2 hours -30 minutes"
○ Is equal to   **Value**
○ Is not equal to   [-7 days   ]
◉ Is greater than or equal to
○ Is greater than
○ Is between
○ Is not between

▼ MORE

Administrative title
[Show content from last seven days   ]

This title will be displayed on the views edit page instead of the default one. This might be useful if you have the same item twice.

(Apply)   (Cancel)   (Remove)

FIGURE 9.6 The settings for each filter varies with its data field. It is a good habit to give administrative titles to filters and other Views components that you configure.

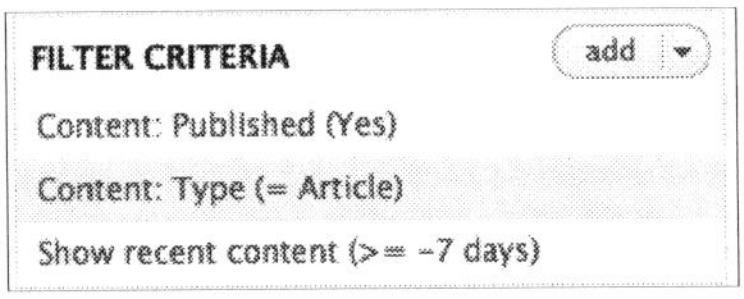

FILTER CRITERIA   (add ▾)

Content: Published (Yes)

Content: Type (= Article)

Show recent content (>= -7 days)

FIGURE 9.7 Each added filter becomes available in the group Filter. A click on the title of a filter opens its configuration dialogue.

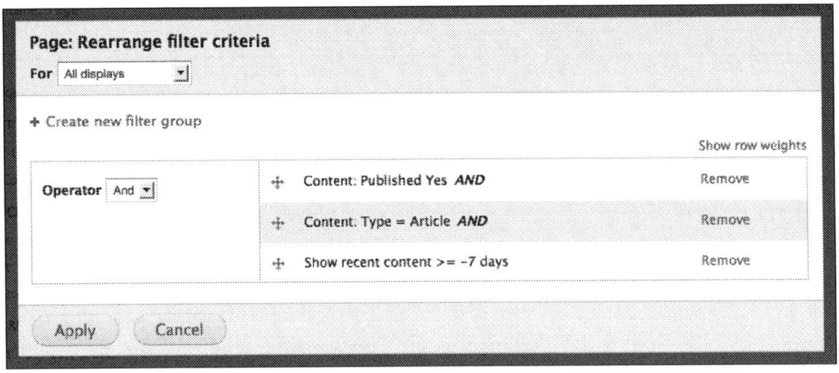

Page: Rearrange filter criteria

For [All displays ▾]

✚ Create new filter group

                                                        Show row weights

Operator [And ▾]   ✛ Content: Published Yes *AND*   Remove

                        ✛ Content: Type = Article *AND*   Remove

                        ✛ Show recent content >= -7 days   Remove

(Apply)   (Cancel)

FIGURE 9.8 You can create logical groups of filters to allow more complex filtering.

- You can delete filters from their respective configuration dialogues, or from options available drop-down menu at the *add* link.

> **TIP**
>
> Views does not automatically exclude unpublished nodes from its results. A filter to exclude unpublished nodes is added by default when a node view is first created, and if you remove this filter you should make sure that only trusted users are able to access the view.

Configuring view fields

As soon as the filters are set – and sometimes even before that – you usually add your *view fields* (labelled *fields* in Views, but here called view fields to separate them from entity fields). View fields are the data fields that the view will display to end users – even if the view has access to all data about (for example) a node, you can choose to only display title, author and the time when the node was updated.

> **TIP**
>
> Depending on settings in the Views quick-wizard, your view will either display entire nodes or single fields. To be able to configure view fields you must have the *row style* (in the *format* group) set to *fields*. See the section about row style for more information.

ADDING VIEW FIELDS

New view fields are added in the same way as filters – a click on the *add* button in the *field* group will open a dialogue, allowing you to choose from all available view fields. (See figure 9.9.) By checking one or several data fields and clicking *add and configure fields* a new dialogue opens, where you provide further settings for each view field. (See figure 9.10.)

The settings for view fields are more extensive than those for filters, and may vary considerably between different types of view fields. The settings usually include the following:

- Formatter: This setting is available for entity fields, to determine how they should be rendered in the view. You can either choose the default formatting (accordning to the display settings for the entity field), or any of the other formatting options provided by the field and its widget.
- Link this field to the original piece of content: This option creates a link to the node this view field belongs to. (You may combine this setting with the *output this field as a link* option, to manipulate the link properties – see the *rewriting view fields* section.)
- Create a label: This provides the view field with a label, usually displayed right before the view field's value.
- Exclude from display: This make the view read and process the view field, but won't display it publicly with the other view fields. This may be useful in more complex manipulation of the view output – see the *rewriting view fields* section.

Add fields

Search [   ]   Filter [Content   ▼]

☐ Content: Add comment link
Display the standard add comment link used on regular nodes, which will only display if the viewing user has access to add a comment.

☑ Content: Comment count
The number of comments a node has.

☐ Content: Comment status
Whether comments are enabled or disabled on the node.

☐ Content: Delete link
Provide a simple link to delete the content.

☐ Content: Edit link
Provide a simple link to edit the content.

☐ Content: Has new content
Show a marker if the content is new or updated.

☐ Content: Last comment author
The name of the author of the last posted comment.

Selected: Content: Comment count

(Add and configure fields)   (Cancel)

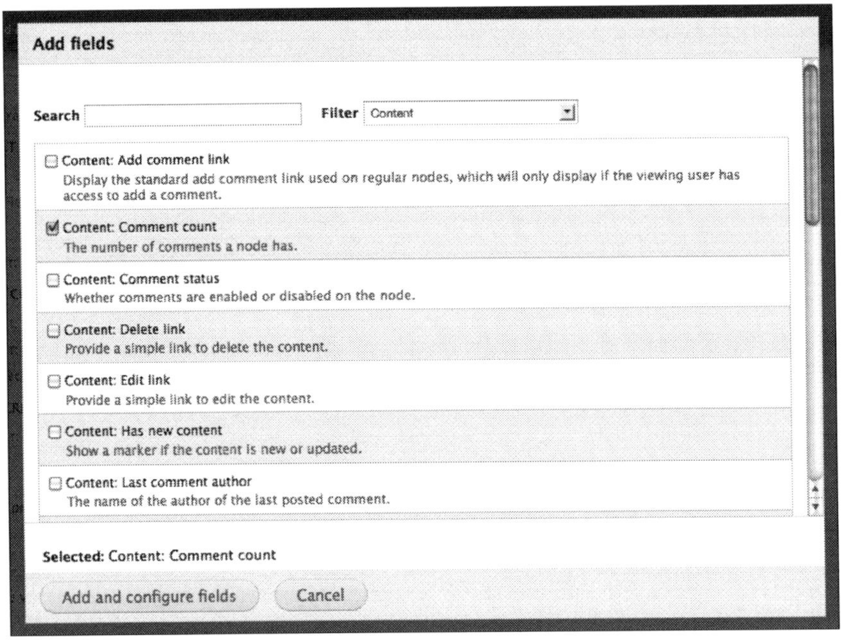

FIGURE 9.9 You add new view fields in the same way as filters – by checking one or several of the choices in a long list of data fields.

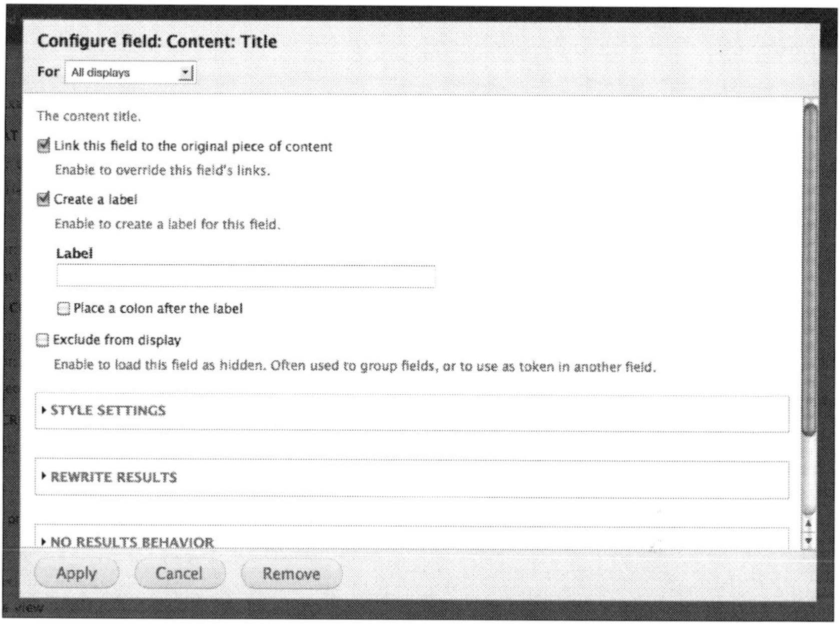

FIGURE 9.10 Each view field is configured separately. More options are hidden inside the collapsed fieldsets.

- Style settings: These settings allow you to change the markup for the view field, which can make it much easier to style the view field with CSS.
- Rewriting: These options allows you to change the content of the view field before further processing, including options to turn the view field into a link. See the *rewriting view fields* section for details.
- No results behavior: With these settings you may affect how the view should interpret and react on empty view fields – for example by completely hiding the field (including any label).
- Multiple field settings: View fields with multiple values can be displayed on a single row – these settings allow you to control how this should be done.
- More/administrative title: The administrative title will be used in the Views interface to represent the view field. Setting a customized title is especially useful if you use the same view field multiple times in a view, to tell the fields apart.

EDITING VIEW FIELDS

You handle and edit existing view fields much in the same way as you do with filters:

- The configuration for each view field may be changed by clicking its title, thereby opening its configuration dialogue.
- The order of the view fields may be changed by clicking the *sort* option in the drop-down menu accessed at the *add* button.
- View fields can be deleted from their configuration dialogues or by a link in the drop-down *add* menu.

Configuring sorting

The settings for controlling how view results are sorted follow the same patterns as filters and view fields – you add new sorting criteria by clicking the add link in the *sort criteria* group, selecting one or more data fields to use for sorting, and in the following dialogue also select whether the sorting should be ascending or descending.

It is worth mentioning that more than one data field may be used for sorting. If so, any additional sorting criteria will be used only as tie breakers for previous fields. (See figure 9.11.)

Sorting settings may be exposed to site visitors – see separate section for details.

FIGURE 9.11 By clicking the *rearrange* button you may change the order of the sort criteria.

A few more basic Views settings

You can make a View considerably more useful with the help of the following settings:

- Title: A click on this setting opens a dialogue where you can enter a text to use as title for the view.
- Header/footer: You can add elements above and below the view, for example to insert help texts. It is also possible to add views as headers and footers.
- No results behavior (in the *advanced* settings): This setting controls what should be displayed if the view doesn't yield any results. An interesting alternative is to load another view, but you can also display a text telling the visitor just how sorry you are that no results could be found.

PAGER

You may limit how many results should be fetched by a view, and you can separate the results on different pages. You access these setting at the *pager* option.

The setting has four main options:
- Display a specified number of items: This limits the number of results in the view, and have them all displayed on the same page.
- Display all items: As advertised, this displays all the results at once.
- Paged output, full pager: This makes the view fetch all results, and by default divide them to show 10 results per page – with a pager allowing the visitor to go forward and backward in the result. You may change the number of results per page, and you can also put a maximum number of pages to display. Furthermore, you can expose the pager settings, to have the user change these settings – see separate section for details.
- Paged output, mini pager: This option is similar to the one above, but has a more compact pager (without overview of page numbers).

All the alternatives above include the *offset* setting, making the view skip a number of results at the top of the list. If a pager is used you can also set a *pager ID* – if more than one pager is on the same web page, all pagers with the same ID will be affected by the same forward/backward links. This is usually, but not always, an unpleasant effect.

Modules that you install may change or extend the pager options.

> **TIP**
>
> Settings that include sub settings are in the main panel separated by a vertical bar, for example *Use pager: Full | Paged, 10 items.* When changing the main settings you are automatically forwarded to the sub settings, but the next time you want to change the sub settings you have to click the sub setting title.

ACCESS SETTINGS

In the middle column in the main configuration panel is a small but important setting with the name *access*. It can be used to limit the access to the view in three different ways:

- None: This means no access restriction – anyone may see and use the view.
- Permission: This allows all users with a selected permission (such as *administer content*) to use the view.
- Role: This allows all users with at least one of the selected roles to use the view.

Node views have the access setting to the permission *view published content* by default. Views showing unpublished content should have additional access restrictions.

Displays

Before a view can be shown on a Drupal site it must have one or more *displays*. Displays determine how a view may be called from Drupal – without any display a view is only an abstract database query without the possibility to be executed or rendered on the site (unless you write custom PHP code to embed it).

A default Views installation has four types of displays available for you to use:

- Page: This makes the view available as a web page on the site, with its own URL and optionally also a menu link.
- Block: This creates a block of the view, which can be used on the site as any other block.
- Feed: This creates an RSS feed at a given URL, and is optionally attached to other displays in the same view.
- Attachment: This display time will be attached and displayed before or after other displays in the same view, much like using the header/footer setting and embedding a view.

CREATING AND DELETING DISPLAYS

You can create both a page and a block display in the Views quick-wizard, but it is also possible to add and delete displays at the Views main configuration panel.

All the configured displayes are listed as buttons at the top of the main panel. (See figure 9.12.) A click on each button changes the main panel to shown the settings relevant for the selected display. To the right of the display buttons there is another button, used to add new displays to the view.

Just below the display-switching buttons are settings used to change

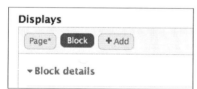

FIGURE 9.12 At the top of the Views main configuration panel are tools to switch between, and add more, displays.

TIP

At the time of writing it is not possible to change the order of displays, but this is expected to be available soon. Changing order of displays useful when access to the view is restricted – as the first a visitor is allowed to access will be used – or if you have several attachment displays and you want to control the order in which they attach their content.

141

name and description of the display – particularly useful to keep track of several displays of the same kind – and also options for cloning or deleting the display.

DISPLAY SPECIFIC SETTINGS

Most displays add a new group of settings to the mid column in the main configuration panel. Page displays, for example, add the options to set path and menu items – while block displays allow you to set an administration name for the block.

Apart from these settings, each display has three specific settings hidden in the *advanced* section:

- Machine name: This is the display's unique name within this view. It is usually not displayed for visitors (except as CSS classes).
- Comment: This setting allow you to add comments about how the view is configured, which is highly useful if it contains unexpected settings that other developers might overlook.
- Display status: This setting allow you to disable the display, making it unavailable without deleting it.

> TIP
>
> Some display specific settings are required, and will yield error messages if missing. Make sure to set all required options to be able to save your view.

OVERRIDDEN CONFIGURATION

Often you will want to have several views that display all but the same information – a page with the ten most recent news, and a block with the three most recent. In these cases you will find it very useful to have several displays in one view and use *overridden settings* to vary each display individually.

When editing settings you will (when possible) get a select list in the settings dialogue header allowing you to select if you want to save the settings for *all displays (except overridden)* or *for this display (override)* – the exact wording varies depending on the type of display you are editing. (See figure 9.13.)

The latter option is used to apply your settings to the active display only, to make it different from the view's default (*master*) configuration.

By overriding settings, one single view may be reused to many different purposes, and a lot of work can be saved.

There are a few more details worth knowing about overriding view configuration:

- Display specific settings cannot, and does not have to, be overridden.
- You may return overridden settings to the default ones by editing the setting and selecting that the configuration should no longer apply to this display only.
- Overridden settings are displayed with a broken link in the Views main panel. (See figure 9.14.)
- All groups of settings with add buttons are overridden as one unit – you cannot, for example, have a single filter configuration overridden and the other filters in default.

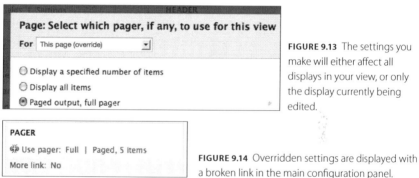

FIGURE 9.13 The settings you make will either affect all displays in your view, or only the display currently being edited.

FIGURE 9.14 Overridden settings are displayed with a broken link in the main configuration panel.

ELABORATION: HOW FAR SHOULD I OVERRIDE?

When working with views you are often faced with the question of what should be the default settings of the view, and what should be the overridden ones. One approach to this is to make the most common settings to default. Another approach is to always keep all the settings in the the most used display in default mode.

A related question is when you should start creating new views, rather than creating yet another display where half of the settings are overridden.

One approach to this is to collect all displays managing the same kind of functionality in the same view. Another, perhaps more common, is to move separate displays into new views when too many settings need to be overridden. There may also be technical limitations forcing your decision – feed displays, for example, can only be attached to displays in the same view.

View formats

How view results are displayed to end users are ultimately determined by the view *format* – a layer of Views formatting, processing and wrapping the data when a view displayed is called to be embedded by Drupal.

A standard Views installation has five view formats (see figure 9.15):

- Grid: This provides a grid with a configurable number of columns, with one view result per grid square. Grid settings include among other things if the results should be ordered horizontally or vertically. It is worth knowing that the grid format uses a HTML table, which some would like to avoid to style presentation.
- HTML list: This provides a ordered or unordered HTML list.
- Jump menu: This creates a shortcut menu, linking to a URL provided by a selected view field. Format settings include whether the current path should be the default option in the jump menu.

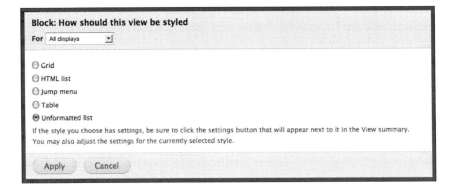

FIGURE 9.15 The view format can change the view presentation completely – for example into maps, tables, calendards or jump menus.

- Table: This provides a table of the view data. Settings include, among other things, making the table headers click-sortable and also the option to display several view fields in the same columns.
- Unformatted: This provides a list of the results without any special markup.
- Unformatted: Detta matar ut träffarna utan särskild formatering.

Each view format can have a number of extra settings. (See figure 9.16.) There are many module providing additional view formats.

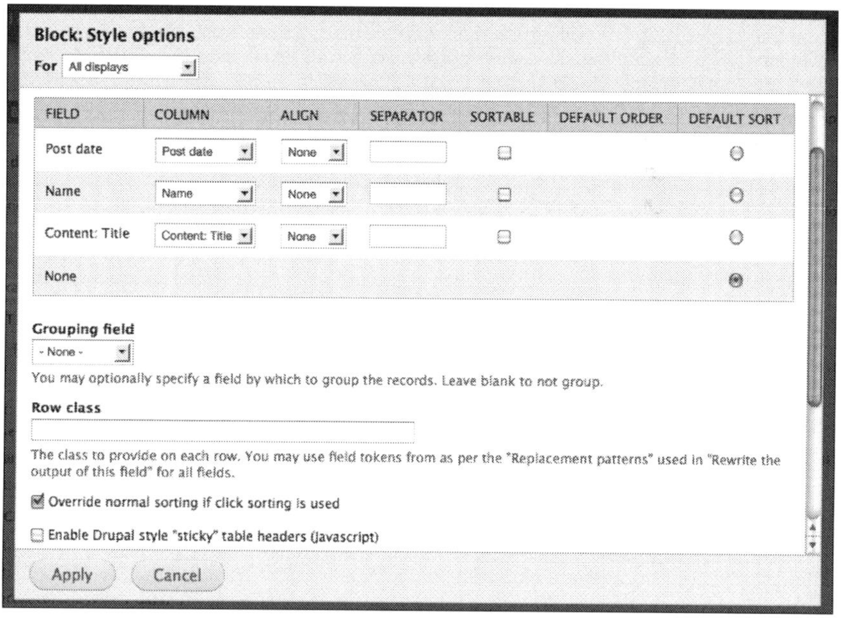

FIGURE 9.16 Each view format may have a number of format-specific settings. These are the settings for the table format, including click-sortable columns.

ROW STYLE

Just below the view format settings is a setting for *row style*. The most common option is *fields*, allowing you as administrator to select which view fields should be included in the view – as described above. Oftentimes, this is the only option available – which usually leads to the row style setting being hidden. But for node views there is one additional row style available – *content*. (See figure 9.18.) The content row style displays each resulting node in one of the view modes available on the website, such as teaser or full node. In some cases, such as the display for RSS feeds, the row style *must* be set to content.

If the row style is *fields*, sub settings are available – including the option *inline fields*. This can be used to output several view fields in the same row, with a configurable separator. There is also a setting for automatically hiding empty fields. (See figure 9.17.)

FIGURE 9.17 You can configure fields to be displayed on the same row.

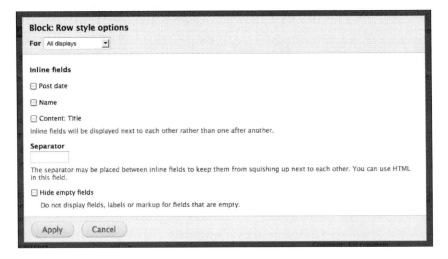

FIGURE 9.18 Node views can either be outputted field by field, or as entire nodes.

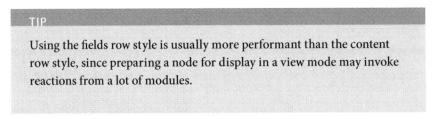

Using the fields row style is usually more performant than the content row style, since preparing a node for display in a view mode may invoke reactions from a lot of modules.

The Views preview

At the bottom of the Views main configuration panel is a preview of the view content, offering great feedback for assuring that your settings work as intended. It is also possible to use the preview to change most of the settings in a view – clicking any of the gear links will display menus to change a lot (but not all) of the view's configuration. (See figure 9.19.)

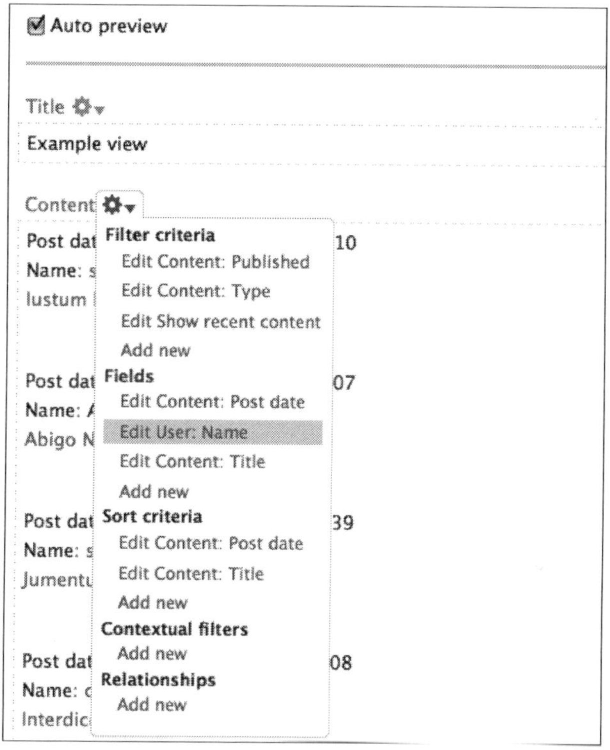

☑ Auto preview

Title ⚙▾

Example view

Content ⚙▾

Post dat	**Filter criteria**	10
Name: s	Edit Content: Published	
Iustum	Edit Content: Type	
	Edit Show recent content	
	Add new	
Post dat	**Fields**	07
Name: A	Edit Content: Post date	
Abigo N	Edit User: Name	
	Edit Content: Title	
	Add new	
Post dat	**Sort criteria**	39
Name: s	Edit Content: Post date	
Jumentu	Edit Content: Title	
	Add new	
	Contextual filters	
Post dat	Add new	08
Name: c	**Relationships**	
Interdic	Add new	

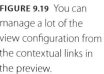

FIGURE 9.19 You can manage a lot of the view configuration from the contextual links in the preview.

If you prefer to configure your view from its preview, you can collapse the main panel by clicking the header *page details* just below the display buttons. (The actual link name depends on the current display.)

Example implementation of basic Views configuration

This section contains examples of how the concepts and functionalities in this chapter may be used. You can find more examples in the exercises.

A BLOCK WITH A RANDOM IMAGE

As visitor on a photo site I want a random photo uploaded the recent week to be displayed in the sidebar. This is important since it helps me find photos I otherwise would have missed.

The functionality above can be achieved by the following steps:
- A node type for photos, containing images (such as the article node type).
- A new node view, with the name *random image*. In the quick-wizard, the *block* is checked (while page is left unchecked), and the block is set to display one result only.
- In the main configuration panel, a filter *fields: field_image – fid* is added to filter out nodes where the relevant image field is empty.
- Another filter *content: post date* is added, configured to only display nodes posted the most recent week.
- A new view field *fields: field_image* is added, displaying the content of the relevant image field in a style that fits the websites sidebar. The view field for node title, automatically added by the quick-wizard, is removed.
- The *use pager* is inspected, to assure that only one result is displayed, without any pager.
- A new sort criteria *global: random* replaces the one added by default, to allow selecting a random image.
- The view is saved, and the site's block settings are updated to display the new block in a suitable region.

PAGE, BLOCK AND RSS FEED WITH THE LATEST ARTICLES

As visitor at a news site I want to always be able to see the three most recent headlines. Along with the headlines I want a link to a page displaying more news, and there should also be an RSS feed for the news. This is important since it makes it easier for me to follow the recent news.

148

The functionality above can be achieved by the following steps:

- A new new, with the name *recent articles*. The quick-wizard is set to list nodes of the type articles, sorted with newest on top.
- In the quick-wizard, the option for creating a block is also checked, the option for adding an RSS feed to the page display is checked, and both displays are set to display an appropriate number of results.
- In the main configuration panel, the block display's setting *more link* overridden and enabled.
- The view is saved and, from the block administration page, the view is placed in a suitable region.

Exercises: Documentation site

These exercises build on previous exercises in the *Documentation site* suite. They can be carried out individually, with some preparations, or in sequence with the previous exercises. The exercises require using the concepts described in previous chapters in this book, including part A.

Video recordings of the suggested solutions to these exercises can be found at nodeone.se/learn-drupal.

RECENTLY UPDATED DOCUMENTATION PAGES

As site member I want a list of documentation pages that were updated recently. This is important since it helps me keep track of updates in the documentation on the site.

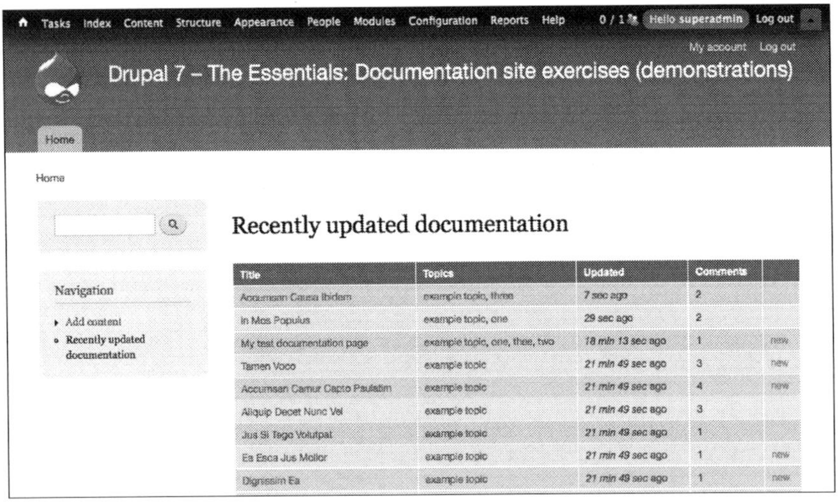

FIGURE 9.20 An example of how the list of recently updated documentation pages may look.

How to demo

1   Log in to the site.
2   Verify that there is a clearly visible link on the site with the text *Recently updated documentation.*

3   Verify that the link leads to a page with a table of (at most) 25 documentation pages, containing information about page title, topic, update time, number of comments and a text marking any pages that were changed since they were last viewed.

4   Verify that the list gets a pager if there are more than 25 documentation pages available.

5   Edit a documentation page and re-save it. Verify that it appears at the top of the list, as most recently updated.

Required preparations

- The site should have a documentation page content type, as provided by the first exercise in this suite.

Suggested solution

1   Go to the views overview page and add a new view. (See *views overview* in this chapter.)

2   In the quick-wizard, give the view a name and a description explaining what it does – such as *recently updated documentation pages* and *a table of most recently updated documentation pages on the site*. (See *creating new views* in this chapter.)

3   In the quick-wizard, also select that you want to display *content* of type *documentation page*. Check that you want a *page*, and that it should display a table of fields, 25 results at a time, using a pager. Also check the option for creating a menu item, adding it to the navigation menu with the link text *recently updated documentation*. (See *creating new views*.)

4   Click *continue & edit* to enter Views' main configuration panel.

5   Add a new view field *content: all taxonomy terms*, and at the *more* settings, limit the terms to the *topic* vocabulary only. (See *configuring view fields* in this chapter.)

6   Add a new view field *content: updated date*, and set the format to *time ago with "ago" appended*. (See *configuring view fields*.)

7   Add view fields *content: comment count*, and *the content: has new content*. (See *configuring view fields*.)

8 Edit the title field added by Views by default. Add a label *title*, to provide the related table column with a header. (See *configuring view fields*.)

9 Remove any existing sort criteria and add a new, *content: updated date*, with sort order *descending*. (See *configuring sorting* in this chapter.)

10 Save the view.

Comments

- Adding customized administrative titles to the view configuration may help you and other developers in the future.
- Don't forget to save your view often.
- An alternative to adding a menu link to the navigation menu would be to add it to the primary links – having it appear as a large tab. However, the long link text makes it unsuitable in a tab.
- In the quick-wizard there's an option for adding an RSS feed to the view. It is not a feature mentioned in the user story, but since the list will change often it could make sense to add a feed even without a request to do so.

Exercises: News site

These exercises build on previous exercises in the news site suite. They can be carried out individually, with some preparations, or in sequence with the previous exercises. The exercises require using the concepts described in previous chapters in this book, including part A.

SECTION EDITOR OVERVIEW

As site visitor I would like to have a list of all news section editors on the site, along with their e-mail addresses and a link to the section news list. This is important since it makes easier for me to trust news when I can contact the people responsible for publishing the news.

How to demo

1 As anonymous user, verify that you can find a link *section editors* on the site.

2 Verify that the link leads to a page listing all users responsible for a news section, along with name, e-mail address and a link to the section news list.

3 Log in as administrator. Edit a user account and either add or remove the user's section. Verify that the list of section editors is reflects the changes.

Required preparations

- The site should have a sections vocabulary, as provided by the *sections and sub sections* exercise in the taxonomy chapter.

Comments

- Public listing of e-mail addresses should only be made with the consent of the e-mail owners.

Advanced Views configuration

There are many ways of describing what Drupal is. One of the better ones is: *Drupal is a tool for making easy things difficult, and difficult things easy.*

This statement is particularly true for Views – while it may thirty minutes or sometimes several hours to create a simple list, just a handful extra clicks may transform the list into an image slideshow, a sortable table or a customized search page.

The difficult part is of course to know where these handful clicks should be made. This chapter presents some of the more complex and powerful functions in Views.

Grouping view fields

The sub settings for view formats contains an option *grouping field*. (See figure 10.1.) This allows you to select a view field used to group all results before they are sorted – all results with the same value in the view field will be grouped together, using the view field as header for the group. (See figure 10.2 for an example of where an image tells more than fourty words.)

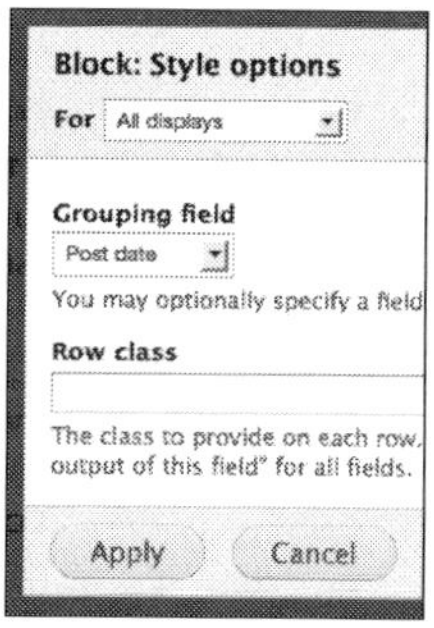

FIGURE 10.1 You can choose to group your view results according to (at most) one view field.

FIGURE 10.2 Grouped lists get sub headers, based on the selected view field.

Grouping of view fields may for example be useful for displaying all comments on your site, grouped by the day they were written.

> **TIP**
>
> If you don't want that a view field used for grouping should appear inside the actual list, you can use the *exclude from display* setting in the view field configuration.

Rewriting view fields

You sometimes find yourself in situations where view fields contain data that you want to show in the view, but it doesn't quite fit your needs. You got the author name, but you would like it to say *written by James Joyce* rather than just *James Joyce*. In these situations you will find great use of the option *rewrite the output of this field* and also *output this field as a link*, both revealed when clicking the *rewrite results* option when configuring view fields. (See figure 10.3.) The options allow you to take control over the text (or otherwise) shown in the view field, and also any link that Views creates from the view field.

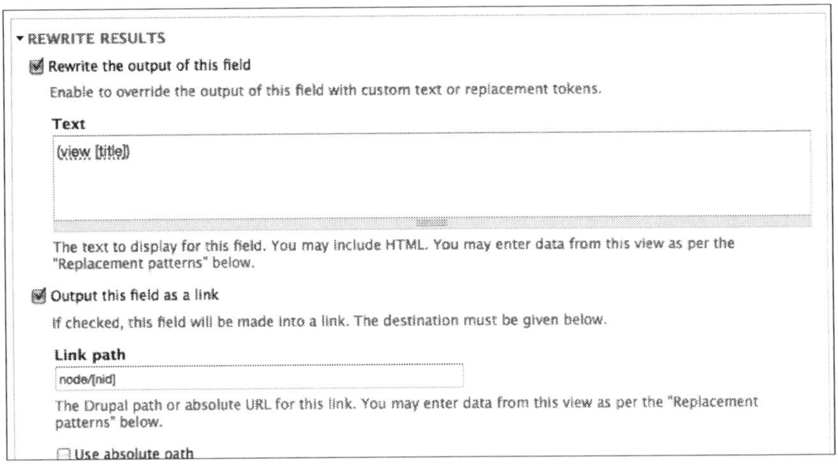

FIGURE 10.3 You can rewrite text and links in view fields, and even include data from other view fields in the rewriting.

An important feature is that you may use all view field *so far loaded by Views* as variables when rewriting your field – meaning that you could, for example, include a user ID when building a link, or a node title when setting a link tooltip. The rewrite settings in the view field configuration contains a list of available variables.

> **TIP**
>
> The options to output a field as a link only works for affecting links created by views (such as the *link this field to the original piece of content* setting) – not if the view field itself contains the link (such as image fields rendered as links to a node).

Exposed settings

Views can *expose* a number of settings to end users, allowing them to change the settings when using or viewing the view. The settings that can be exposed are filters, sorting and pagers. The settings can, for example, be used to build comment list only displaying comments written by an entered user, a node

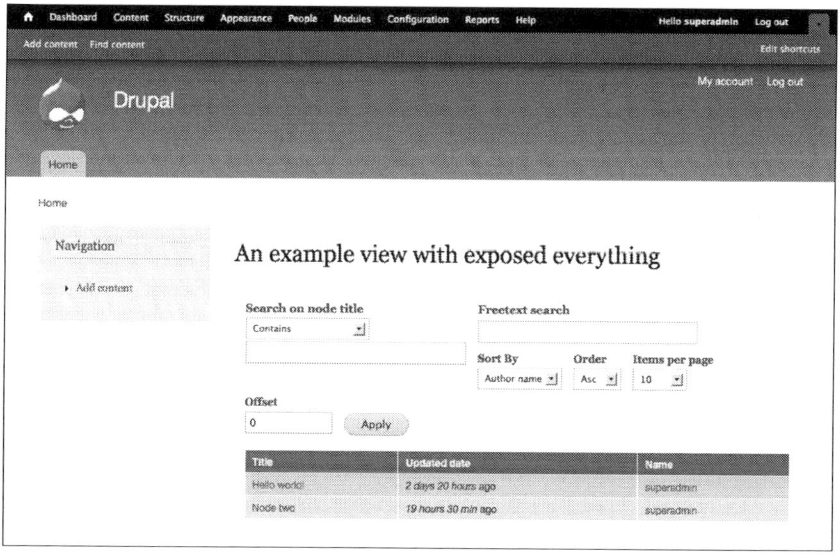

FIGURE 10.4 An example view with a lot of exposed settings – filters, sorting and pager.

list where users may search for words in the node title, lists where users select how many results should be displayed on each page, or switching sorting between most recent or most popular content. (See figure 10.4.)

Filters are exposed by checking the option *expose this filter to visitors, to allow them to change it*, visible in the filter configuration dialogue. Sort criteria and pagers have similar options.

SETTINGS FOR EXPOSED FILTERS

When exposing a filter, a number of new settings become availabe. (See figure 10.5.) The most important ones are:

- Label: This text will be shown at the input box for the exposed filter, promting users to enter something.
- Expose operator: This option allows you to expose the operator for the filter – not only filtering value.
- Remember: This setting allows storing the parameter values for the exposed settings in the user's session cookie for the site, instead of passing them in the URL.

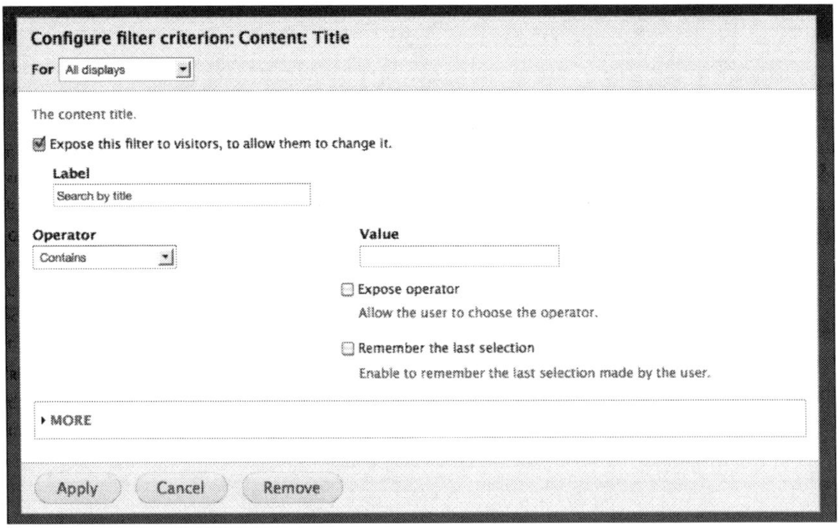

FIGURE 10.5 Exposed filters have a number of new settings, such as which label should be used for the exposed filter.

158

> **TIP**
>
> With the *Search* module enabled (which is the case in a standard Drupal installation), a filter option *search: search terms* is available. It can be used as an exposed filter to get the same search hits as Drupal's built-in search. Using Views to build search pages drastically increases the possibilities to customize search filtering and display.

If a filter value is entered into the filter configuration, it will be used as default value in the exposed filter (unless other settings says otherwise).

SETTINGS FOR EXPOSED SORT CRITERIA AND PAGERS

When sort criteria are exposed, you get the option to set which text should represent the sorting – the data field *user: name* could for example have the label *author* or *user*. End users can, when using the view, choose which of the exposed sort criteria to use and also switch between ascending and descending sorting.

The exposed settings for pagers include how many results should be displayed per page, and optionally also offset. You may include or exclude the option to display all results on one page.

EXPOSED SETTINGS IN BLOCKS, AND FURTHER SETTINGS

The Views main configuration panel contain two further settings for exposed settings, under the *advanced* section. They allow the following options:

- Exposed form in block: This option moves the exposed settings from the view header to a completely separate block. Placing exposed search filters in a block on your site may serve as a customized search box. The block must, as other blocks, be placed in a region to be visible.
- Exposed form style: This allows you to set whether end users are required to set exposed filter values, or if all fields may be empty. Sub settings allow you to set a number of the strings displayed to the end users, such as the button to execute the settings. (See figure 10.6.)

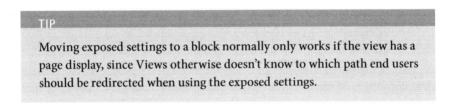

FIGURE 10.6 You can customize the text strings displayed together with exposed settings.

> **TIP**
>
> Moving exposed settings to a block normally only works if the view has a page display, since Views otherwise doesn't know to which path end users should be redirected when using the exposed settings.

Contextual filters

Views is a highly flexible module to start with, but the *contextual filters* increase the use cases for the module at least by a factor of ten. Contextual filters in many ways work as regular filters, but there is one important difference – instead of setting a filter value manual, the value is fetched from variables in one way or another sent programmatically to the view. A regular filter could give you all nodes written by a specified user. A contextual filter for node author would be able to, for example, display all nodes written by the currently viewed user, or the same user who wrote the currently viewed node. The concept is that contextual filters prepare a view for filtering in one way or another, but the filter value is not yet determined. When the view is eventually called, it is also provided with data used to complete the contextual filters.

The canonical example of how contextual filter values are provided to views is by the view path – if a view has the path *example.com/my-view*, the URL *example.com/my-view/story/22* will call the view along with two values for contextual filters (in this case *story* and 22). But there are more ways of providing contextual filter values – see the chapter about Page manager and Panels in part C for examples.

The difference between standard filters and contextual filters may seem trivial, but in practice it is huge. Contextual filters allow you to reuse views in many different situations, and they also allow Views to interact with other parts of the website. It is not uncalled-for to write a whole book about how to use contextual filters in Views.

> **TIP**
>
> Until recently the contextual filters were called *arguments* in Views, and there is likely a lot of documentation, tutorials and Views-compatible modules still using that term. If you see the term *argument*, it should be interpreted either as contextual filter, or the value provided to a contextual filter.

CONFIGURING CONTEXTUAL FILTERS

Contextual filters are added and managed at the *advanced* section in Views main configuration panel. They generally follow the same patterns as filters, but have a number of settings that normal filters lack. (See figure 10.7.) Take a deep breath:

- When the filter value is *not* in the URL: This setting determines the view behavior, should the view be called without any value for the contextual filter – a more or less essential setting when using contextual filters in block displays. See separate section for more information.
- Override title: This setting is used to alter the view's title, if there is a contextual filter value present. You may use variables on the form %1, %2, and so on, to include the first, or second filter values in the title (and so on). If there is any title element associated with the filter value – such as a node title for node IDs or user names for user IDs – the title element will be used. A typical use case is the title *articles written by %1*.

- Override breadcrumb: This somewhat peculiar setting allows you to set the breadcrumb to use when a filter value is present – or default to using the view title. The breadcrumb will lead to the view *without* this contextual filter value (and the view must have a valid response to this – see separate section).
- Specify validation criteria: Since you cannot limit what users may input as contextual filter values in the path, there may be reasons to verify that the filter value corresponds to what you expect. This seting allows you to validate the filter value in a number of ways, and also determine the view behaviour if the validation fails. A typical example is to only allow filter values that are node IDs for selected node types.
- More/allow multiple values: This setting allows for several values for the contextual filter. Values separated by commas are by Views interpreted as AND conditions, while values separated by plus signs are interpreted as OR conditions. A typical example is allowing several taxonomy term IDs, to display all content marked with any of the terms.
- More/exclude: This setting inverts the filtering – the rows matching the filter criteria will be excluded rather than included. A typical example is applying this to a node ID filter to exclude the node currently viewed from a list of similar content.
- Reduce duplicates: When filtering on several criteria, Views may end up repeating some of the results (should they fulfill more than one condition). This option reduces any duplicates – but also makes the database query heavier. A typical example is reducing duplicates occurring when filtering on multiple taxonomy terms.

It is worth pointing out that contextual filters lack some of the settings available for normal filters:
- There is no functionality for grouping contextual filters in OR or AND groups.
- There are no options for selecting which operator should be used with contextual filters (save the *exclude* option). All defaults to *is equal to*.

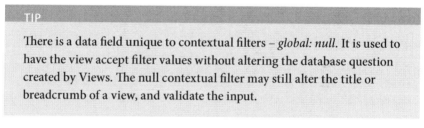

FIGURE 10.7 The settings available for contextual filters vary between different data fields. This is the settings for content: nid.

> **TIP**
>
> There is a data field unique to contextual filters – *global: null*. It is used to have the view accept filter values without altering the database question created by Views. The null contextual filter may still alter the title or breadcrumb of a view, and validate the input.

MANAGING MISSING FILTER VALUES

It often happens – even deliberately – that views with contextual filters are called without the data to set the contextual filter values. This is in particular true for block displays, which without any paths don't have a natural way of receiving contextual filter values.

You can configure each contextual filter to set how the view should react if the filter value is missing. (See figure 10.8.) The options are:

- Display all results for the specified field: This will ignore the contextual filter all together – no further filtering is done.
- Provide default value: This is used to fetch/create an artificial filter value, should a real one be missing. (See below.)
- Show "Page not found": This hides the view.
- Display a summary: This alters the view, having it display a list of all filter values that would lead to results in the view – linked to the view with each contextual filter value present. The list may be configured in a number of ways, for example to display the number of results for each filter value, or displaying a jump menu rather than an HTML list.
- Display content of "No results found": This gives the same result as when the view has no results to display.

The functions for creating or fetching default values for contextual filters are used rather frequently – especially for block displays – and there are a numbers of options available for how to do this. These options may vary between different data fields, but the most common ones are:

- Fixed value: This gives a static value, provided by you as administrator when the view is built.
- Content ID from URL: This is used to fetch a node ID from the current path, assuming it contains a node ID.
- PHP code: This allows a manually entered PHP script, with access to local data, to build a default filter value. Having PHP code in configuration is bad for a number of reasons (such as security and performance), but may be useful during prototyping.
- Taxonomy Term ID from URL: This is used to fetch a term ID from the current path. You may optionally fetch term IDs from a currently viewed node, and also limit the terms to selected vocabularies.
- User ID from URL: This is used to fetch a user ID from the current path and, optionally, the user ID for the author of the currently viewed node.
- User ID from logged in user: This fetches the user ID from the acting user.
- For contextual filters for date and time fields there are some settings available to fetch current date and time, or time values from a currently viewed node.

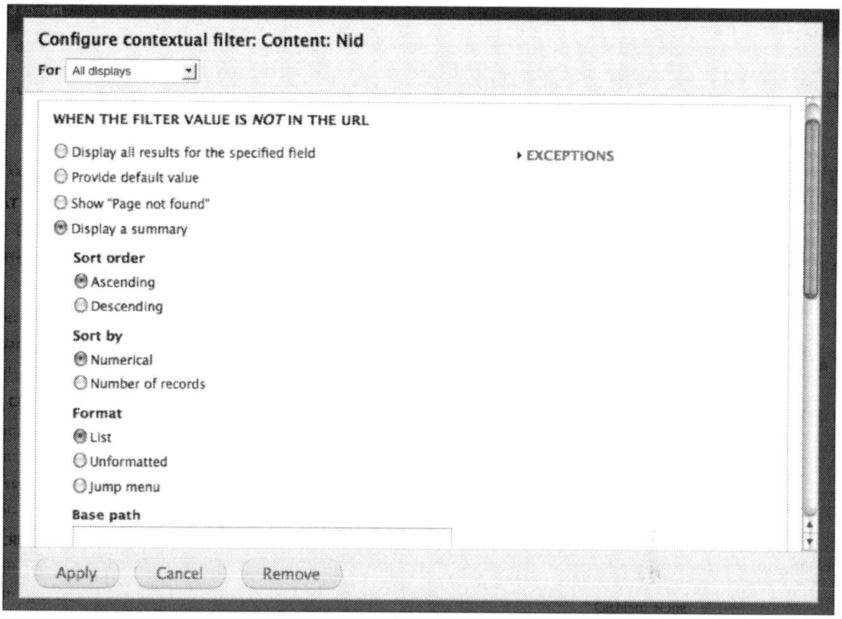

FIGURE 10.8 A view may react in a number of different ways, should a value for a contextual filter be missing. Possible reactions include displaying a summary of possible filter values, or having the view generate a value by itself.

CONTEXTUAL FILTERS AND PATHS

The natural way for a view to get values for contextual filters is by the view path. The easiest way of doing this is by appending filter values to the path, separated by slashes – but it is also possible to have contextual filter values *within* a path. This is accomplished by, when configuring the path for a view, using a parcent sign where the view should expect a contextual filter value (for cxample *user/%/comments*).

Having contextual filter values inside paths is particularly useful when creating menu tabs – see next section.

Creating menu tabs

Page displays have settings for creating menu items, found in the group *page settings*. The options *no menu entry* and *normal menu entry* are rather self-explanatory, but there are to more options that require some explanation.

MENU TAB

The first of the more obscure options is *menu tab*. (See figure 10.9.) Menu items of this kind will be visible as tabs on a given path – here called the tab's *main page* – rather than being displayed as normal menu items. Two requirements must be met to use menu tabs:

- The path to the menu tab must be the same as the tab's main page, but one step deeper. If you want a tab to show up on *example.com/main-page*, the path to the menu tab could for example be *example.com/main-page/my-tab*.
- There must be at least two (accessible) tabs on the main page. If there is only one tab present, it will be hidden by Drupal to avoid displaying tabs unnecessarily.

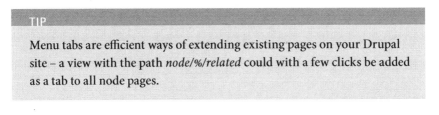

FIGURE 10.9 The menu option menu tab makes it easy to add new tabs to the pages on your website.

> **TIP**
>
> Menu tabs are efficient ways of extending existing pages on your Drupal site – a view with the path *node/%/related* could with a few clicks be added as a tab to all node pages.

> **TIP**
>
> It is likely that another option for menu links will become availble soon – *local action*. Menu items of this kind are similar to menu tabs in how they are set up, but are displayed as links at the top of pages – in the same fashion as the *add new view* link on the Views overview page.

DEFAULT MENU TAB

The second somewhat mysterious option is *default menu tab*. Creating default menu tabs is similar to creating regular menu tabs, but you are at the same time creating the main page for the tab. (This should only be used if there is not already a main page available.)

If the path to a page display is *example.com/my-view/default-tab*, a default menu tab will make the view accessible from both *example.com/my-view/ default-tab* (the tab page) and *example.com/my-view* (the main page).

When configuring a default menu tab, you are also propted to set which kind of menu item the main page should use.

Relationships

The last group of Views settings presented in this book is *relationships*. Relationships are used to allow Views to bring in data that is, in one way or another, associated with the data already available in the view. A comment view could, for example, use the relationship *comment: content* to tap into data about the node for each comment, and a term view could use the relationship *taxonomy: parent term* to tap into data from the parent term of each listed term.

> **TIP**
>
> People comfortable with writing SQL queries will recognize the relationships as *joins*.

ADDING RELATIONSHIPS

You add, edit and delete relationships in the same fashion as filter, view fields and sort criteria – using the *add* button and its related menu. (See figure 10.10 and 10.11.) The settings for relationships should be interpreted in this way:

- Identifier: This is the name that will be used for the relationship within the Views administration interface.
- Require this relationship: Checking this option will make the view exclude items where this relationships cannot be fulfilled. For the relationship *taxonomy: parent term*, for example, it would mean that terms without parent terms would be excluded.

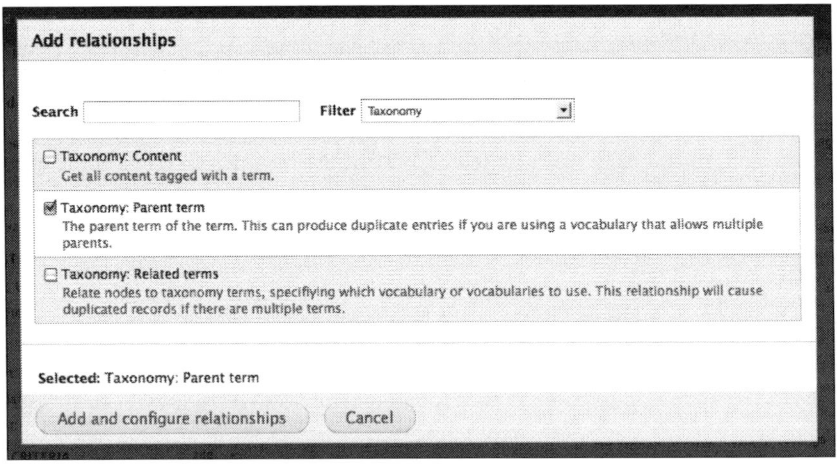

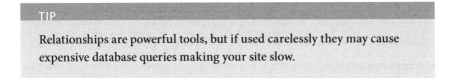

FIGURE 10.10 The number of available relationships in a view is often much fewer than the filters or view fields.

> **TIP**
>
> Relationships are powerful tools, but if used carelessly they may cause expensive database queries making your site slow.

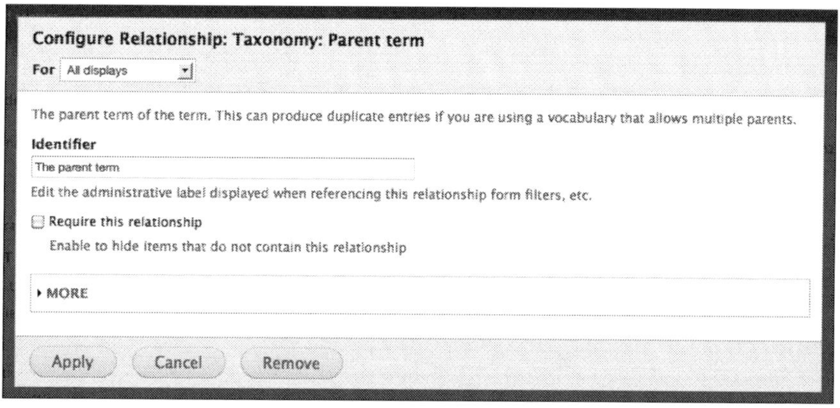

Configure Relationship: Taxonomy: Parent term

For [All displays ▾]

The parent term of the term. This can produce duplicate entries if you are using a vocabulary that allows multiple parents.

Identifier

[The parent term]

Edit the administrative label displayed when referencing this relationship form filters, etc.

☐ Require this relationship

Enable to hide items that do not contain this relationship

▸ MORE

(Apply)   (Cancel)   (Remove)

FIGURE 10.11 Each relation gets a label, used internally in the view configuration.

UTILIZING RELATIONSHIPS IN CONFIGURATION

A view with relationships will, for each result in the view, not only have data for the base object of the view – but also for the objects described by the relationships. When editing configuration for data fields there is (where applicable) an option *relationships* in the fieldset *more*. This setting can be used to select which object should be used for this data field. (See figure 10.12.) This means that in a comment view utilizing the comment: content relationship, you can choose to filter on node type, and if also including the relationship *comment: user* you could sort the results by the name of the user writing the comment.

▾ MORE

Relationship

[The parent term ▾]

Administrative title

[   ]

This title will be displayed on the views edit page instead of the same item twice.

FIGURE 10.12 Data fields can be tied to the base object in the view, or to any of the objects provided by relationships.

169

> **TIP**
>
> When creating a view you select the *base table* for the view – comments, users, nodes, etc – thereby deciding what will be the view's *base objects*. Some functionality in Views always act on the base object, ignoring all relationships. An example of this is the *distinct* option, hidden under *query settings*.

> **TIP**
>
> At the time of writing, it is possible to use the *References* module to provide relationships in Views – node and user references created with References become available as Views-style relationships. Similar functionality is in this very moment developed for the *Relation* module, and while still not completed, the Relation module is expected to become the new standard for configuring relationships between Drupal entities. See the section about using fields to create relations for a few comments about these modules.

Elaboration: Other Views settings

This is the longest chapter in the entire book, and it was proceeded by another whole chapter about Views. Despite this, there are some more aspects of Views that a well-trained Drupal developer should know.

- There are some new functionality in Views allowing grouping directly in the database query generated by Views. The settings are enabled by the option *use grouping* in the *advanced* section. Once enabled, a number of data fields may be used for grouping operations. The functionality is at the time of writing not fully developed, and it is not clear how they will work – but they will for example make it possible to sort nodes by their number of comments, or taxonomy terms by how many nodes are marked with each term.
- At the toolbar, *structure, views* is a *settings* tab revealing a number of global Views settings. The two sub tabs basic and advanced contain some options that are useful if you want to probe how different views

affect your site's performance, or if you discover that the string *<Any>* can't be translated with Drupal's normal translation tools.

That's it.

Example implementations of advanced Views configuration

This section contains examples of how the concepts and functionalities in this chapter may be used. You can find more examples in the exercises.

LIST ARTICLES, GROUPED BY MONTH

As visitor on a blog site I want a list of old blog posts grouped by month, such as February 2011, January 2011, December 2010, and so on. This is important since it helps me find old blog posts I want to read again.

The functionality above can be achieved by the following steps:
- A new node view with the name *blog archive*.
- The quick-wizard is configured to only display blog post nodes, sorted with newest on top, and a page with the path *blog/archive* is created.
- In the main configuration panel, a number of view fields interesting to end users are added (such as *content: title* and *fields: body*).
- A new view field *content: post date* is added, gets marked with *exclude from display*, has no label, and is outputted in the custom format "F Y" (which is the PHP date expression yielding "August 2011", assuming that is the present year and month).
- The style settings are changed to group the view on the excluded date field.
- The view's header is set to *Blog archive*.
- A menu link is added for the page display, to be placed in a suitable menu.

TABS WITH THE EDITOR'S OWN POSTS

As editor on the site for my association I would like each editor's user page to have a tab listing all nodes created by this editor. The list should be accessible only on user pages for editors, and only by editors. This is important since it makes it easier to find your own content.

The functionality above can be achieved by the following steps:

- A new role *editor*.
- A new view with the name *Editor's list*, listing nodes without any particular limitation. The quick-wizard is set to create a page display.
- The access settings for the view is changed, allowing access for editors only.
- The filter for displaying only published content is removed.
- A number of view fields are added, depending on the information editors want to access (for example *content: title, content: post date, content: comment count,* and *content: new comments*).
- The view format is changed to a table, for example, and all columns are made sortable – for example with the default sorting providing the newest content on top.
- The path to the page display is set to *user/%/list*.
- The page display gets a menu item of the type menu tab and the title posts.
- A new contextual filter is added: *user: uid*.
- The contextual filter settings for title is set to *content created by %1*.
- The validation of the contextual filter value is configured to only allow user IDs belonging to editors.

Exercises: Documentation site

These exercises build on previous exercises in the *Documentation site* suite. They can be carried out individually, with some preparations, or in sequence with the previous exercises. The exercises require using the concepts described part A and B in this book.

Video recordings of the suggested solutions to these exercises can be found at nodeone.se/learn-drupal.

CUSTOMIZED SEARCH PAGE

As site visitor I want to be able to search documentation pages based on when they were updated, topics, title, and free text search. I also want to be able to sort the results by relevance, updated time or number of comments. This is important because it helps me find the documentation I am looking for.

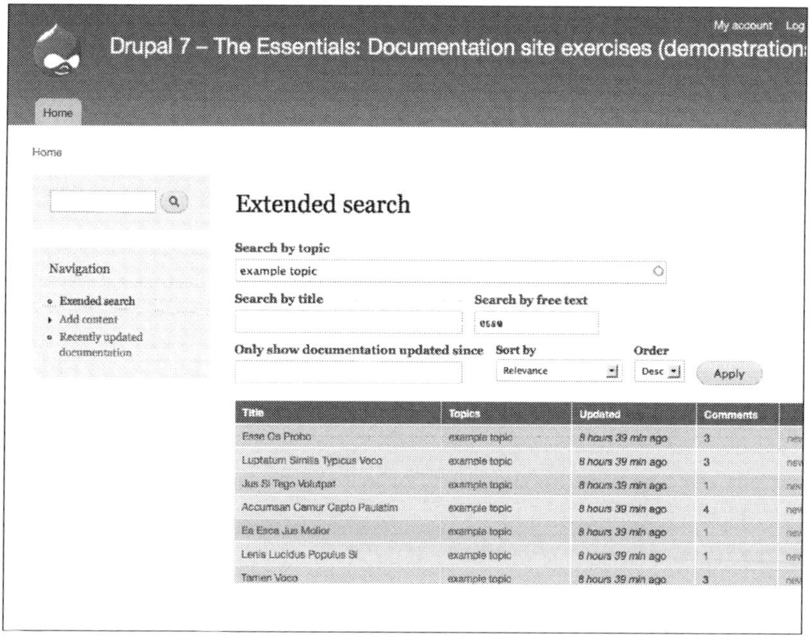

FIGURE 10.13 An example of how the customized search page may look.

How to demo

1   As anonymous visitor, verify that you can find a link *extended search* on the website.
2   At the resulting page, verify that there are search fields for topic, title and free text, as well as a way to show only pages that have been updated since a given date. There should also be controls to change sort order between search relevance, updated time and number of comments.
3   Verify that each of these search criteria work individually.
4   Verify that the sort criteria *search relevance* work, by searching for a word appearing both in titles and bodies on the website – documentation pages with the search phrase in the title should appear first.
5   Verify that the other sort criteria work.
6   Verify that the search results have links leading to the relevant documentation page.

Required preparations

- The site should have a documentation content type, as provided by the first exercise in this suite, as well as topic tags as provided by the exercise in the taxonomy chapter.

Suggested solution

1   Add a new view. Give it the name *extended search*, and have it list content of type *documentation page*. (See *creating new views* in the Views basics chapter.)
2   In the quick-wizard, also add a *page* display, showing 25 results with a pager, in a table of fields. Finally also add a menu link in the navigation menu. (See *creating new views*.)
3   In the main configuration panel, add view fields that seem reasonable to display with search results – see the *recently updated documentation pages* exercise in the previous chapter for suggestions. Make sure to include page title, linked to the documentation page. (See *adding view fields* in the previous chapter.)

4 Add three new filters, and mark all three as exposed – *content: has taxonomy terms* (limit to *topic* vocabulary), *content: title* (operator *contains*), and *search: search terms*. Provide them all with labels that makes it clear to end users that they are search fields. (See *settings for exposed filters* in this chapter.)

5 Add yet another filter, *content: updated date* and set the operator to *greater than or equal to*, in order to display pages updated at the given date or later. (See *settings for exposed filters*.)

6 Remove the existing sort criteria. Add three new criteria, all exposed – *search: score, content: updated date,* and *content: comment count*. Set the default sorting to *descending* in each case, and change their labels to make it clear to end users what each sorting represent. (See *settings for exposed sort criteria and pagers* in this chapter.)

Comments

- If you have done the exercise *recently updated documentation pages* in the previous chapter, the search page could be implemented as an additional page display rather than a completely separate view.
- If you have just recently created content, you may need to run cron before it appears in the search. (See *other settings* in the *other basic Drupal core settings* chapter.)
- The exposed filter for topics could use the *reduce duplicate* setting, preventing content from appearing more than once – which could be the case if you search for two topics and a documentation page has both these. Another option would be to enable the *distinct* setting – which would provide the same effect for the view as a whole. This is found under the *query settings* in the *advanced* section.
- The user story doesn't say that the results should be presented in a table. Usually, search pages result is something similar to a teaser list – which could be implemented in this case too. However, when doing advanced search it also makes sense to present a lot of information condensed into a table.

- Users who are not logged in have no use of the column marking if content has been updated since last viewed – Drupal doesn't keep track of anonymous visitors' page views in the same way as logged in users.
- All the search forms and sorting settings make the extended search page appear quite messy. In a real project, this would most likely lead to a new user story with the objective of making it easier to overview all the options.

LIST USER'S CONTENT ON A USER PAGE TAB

As site member, I would like to have a list of all the content I've written available as a tab on my user page. I would like similar tabs on other users' pages. This is important since it helps me keep track of my own contributions as well as following what other members write.

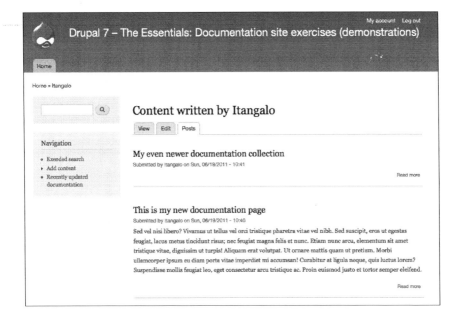

FIGURE 10.14 An example of how content lists may look at a user page tab.

How to demo

1 Log in to the site.
2 Create a documentation page.
3 Visit the user account page and click on the tab "Posts". Verify that the documentation page is listed.
4 Create a documentation collection.
5 Verify that the documentation collection is listed, too, and (since it is newer) is listed above the documentation page.

Required preparations

• The site should have the documentation page and collection content types, as provided by the first exercise in this suite.

Suggested solution

1 Add a new view with the name *content by user*. Have it display content of all types, sorted with newest on top. Create a page with the path *user/%/posts*, with a list of 10 teasers per page, and no menu link. (See *create new views* in the previous chapter.)
2 In the main configuration panel, add a menu item of the type menu tab and give it the link text *posts*. (See *creating menu tabs* in this chapter.)
3 If the contextual filter *user: uid* is not already selectable, add a new relationship *content: author*. (See *adding relationships* in this chapter.)
4 Add a new contextual filter *user: uid*. Use the title override option to set the title to *content written by %1*. Use the validation options to verify that the contextual filter value is a user ID. (See *configuring contextual filters* in this chapter.)

Comments

• You may or may not have to add the relationship in step 3 in the suggested solution – it depends on how the Views module is changed the

177

next few weeks. (Normally, content authors are automatically available in a view of nodes, but this may change.)

- Whenever you have a view using contextual filters, you should have the view returning *page not found* if contextual filter value is missing – unless you have reasons to do otherwise. This prevents the view from being used in unexpected contexts.

- The user story doesn't say how the content should be displayed. A teaser list is easy to make and usually pleasant to look at – changing it to a table, for example, can be made in a future user story if the client would like to change the appearance of the list.

TABLE WITH A COLLECTION'S DOCUMENTATION PAGES

As site visitor viewing a documentation collection, I want to see a table summarizing the documentation pages within the collection. The table should have documentation page title, first 200 characters or so, and comment count. This is important since it makes it easier for me to find documentation I am interested in.

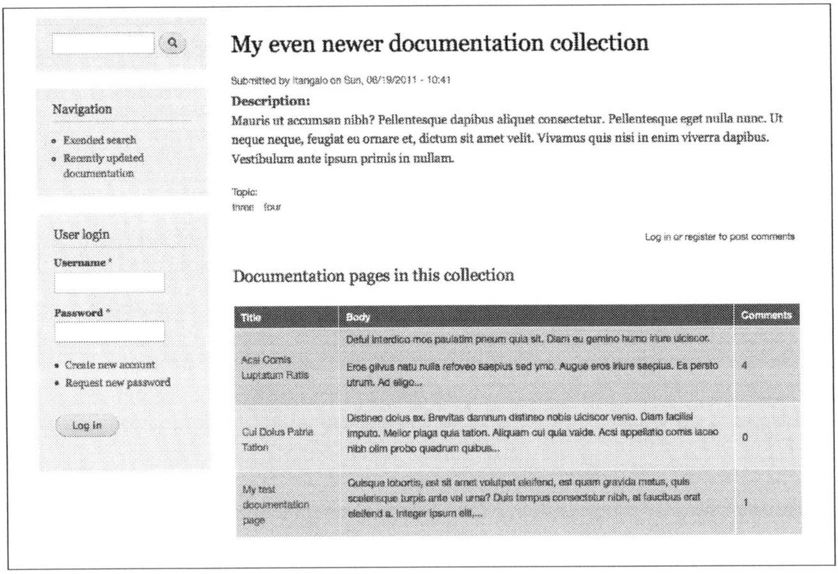

FIGURE 10.15 An example of how a collection table may look.

How to demo

1 Log in to the site and create a documentation collection, if necessary.
2 View a documentation collection. Verify that its related documentation pages are listed in a table at the bottom of the page, with name,
the first 200 characters (or so) of the body, and comment count. Also
verify that the title links to the full documentation page.

Required preparations

• The site should have the documentation page and collection content
types, as provided by the first exercise in this suite.

Suggested solution

1 Add a new view with the name *documentation pages in a collection*,
and have it list content of type *documentation collection*. Create a block
displaying a table, and set the title to *documentation pages in this collection*. (See *creating new views* in the previous chapter.)
2 Add a contextual filter *content: nid*. If no filter value is present, build a
default value with *content ID from URL*. Use validation to assure that
only collection node IDs are accepted. (See *managing missing filter
values* and *configuring contextual filters* in this chapter.)
3 Add a relationship, using the node reference field on the documentation collections. Make sure to use *all* delta, to collect all related documentation pages. (See *adding relationships* in this chapter.)
4 Add the documentation page fields you want to display, using the relationship to the documentation page. Make sure to also update the title
field, provided by default, to use the relationship. (See *utilizing relationships in configuration* in this chapter.)
5 For the documentation page body, either use the *trimmed* formatter
or use the *trim this field to a maximum length* in the *rewrite results*
settings, to limit the body to 200 characters. (See *rewriting view fields*
in this chapter.)
6 Give the view block an administrative title. (See *display specific settings*
in the previous chapter.)

7   In the block administration page, place the new view block at the bottom of the content region. (See *regions and blocks* in the blocks chapter.)

8   Change the field display settings for documentation collections, to hide the default output of the documentation page references. (See *field display settings* in the view modes and field display chapter.)

Comments

- It is logically correct, but not entirely intuitive that you restrict the objects listed in the view to documentation collections – while what's being displayed is documentation *pages*. It might help thinking of relationships as providing new fields on the object you are listing – the collection gets new fields like *collection:page:title* and *collection:page:body*.

- Make sure that you add the fields used on the *documentation page* rather than the documentation collection – and of course to select the right relationship in the field configuration.

- The default order of the relationships will be their *deltas* – their sorting order in the documentation collection. You could, however, sort by documentation page title or any other available data if you want to override this.

- The view's limit on item to display relates to the *base* objects loaded by the view – meaning that even if you restrict the number of collections to one, all related pages will show. This is in parallel to how Views would handle a multiple-value field – if the view is configured to display each value as a separate row, each row won't count as a new result in the database query created by Views.

- At the block administration page, it makes sense to set block visibility to only show at documentation collection pages. The view wouldn't display anything at other pages, but setting the block visibility would prevent Views from ever being called – saving some performance for your site.

LIST USER'S COMMENTS ON A USER PAGE TAB

As site member, I would like to view my own comments on a tab on my user page. I would also like to be able to list comments written by other users on their user pages. This is important since it helps me find my own

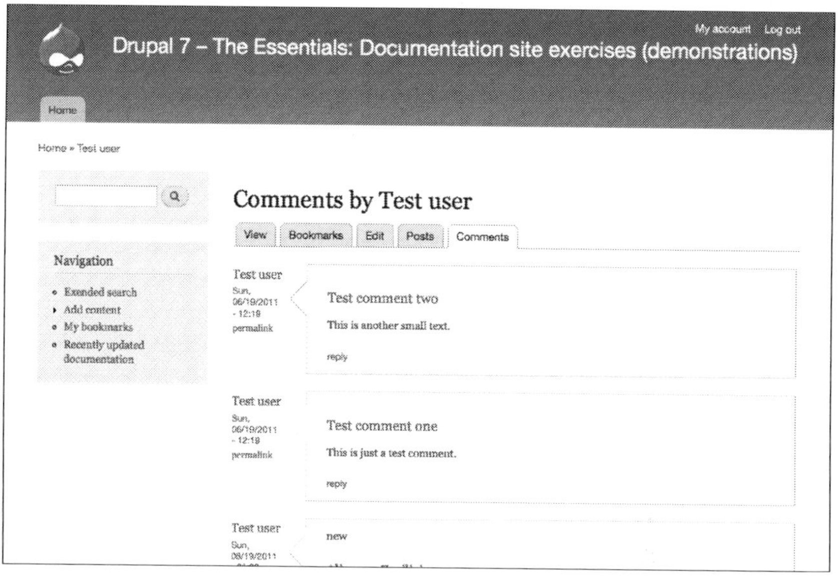

FIGURE 10.16 An example of a comment list at a user page.

comments, follow what other people comment, and also get an overview of a user's contributions.

How to demo

1 Log in to the site.
2 Write two comments.
3 Visit the user account page and click on the tab *Comments*. Verify that the created comments are listed, with newest on top.
4 Log out. As anonymous visitor, visit the same user page. Verify that the comments tab is visible and lists the two comments.

Required preparations

- The site should have the documentation page and collection content types, as provided by the first exercise in this suite.

Suggested solution

1   Create a new view, displaying comments, newest on top. Create a page with the path *user/%/comments*, displaying full comments (not fields). (See *creating new views* in the previous chapter.)

2   Add a new contextual filter, *comment: uid*. Set the title override to *comments by %1*, and also validate that the provided filter value is a valid user ID. (See *configuring contextual filters* in this chapter.)

3   Set the menu settings to a menu tab with the link text *comments*. (See *creating menu tabs* in this chapter.)

Comments

• It makes sense to limit the comment list to display comments only for nodes the user is allowed to view. This can be done using the *content: accessible* filter – however this feature is at the time of writing not fully functional.

• In future versions of Views, it is possible that you will need the relationship *comment: author* to add the contextual filter on user ID.

• The user story does not define how the comment list should be displayed. Defaulting to standard comment view mode is a quick solution, that can be changed in a future user story if the client would like a different list.

Exercises: News site

These exercises build on previous exercises in the *news site* suite. They can be carried out individually, with some preparations, or in sequence with the previous exercises. The exercises require using the concepts described part A and B in this book.

DISPLAY FACT BOXES

As site visitor reading a news article, I would like to have any fact boxes belonging to the article displayed in the sidebar. This is important since it provides me with valuable information without cluttering the main text of the article.

How to demo

1 Log in to the site as writer.
2 Create a fact box, relating to a selected article. (Create an article first, if necessary.)
3 View the article. Verify that the fact box is displayed in the sidebar.
4 View another article. Verify that the fact box is not present in the sidebar.
5 Add another fact box, relating to the same article. Verify that both fact boxes are displayed when viewing the article, with the newest fact box on top.

Required preparations

• The site should have a news article and fact box content types, as provided by the first exercises in this suite.

Comments

• The *DraggableViews* module, combined with some wits and Drupal skills, could be used to allow drag-and-drop reordering of the fact boxes for each article.
• More articles in the same section
• As site visitor viewing an article, I would like to have more articles in the same section listed at the bottom of the page. This is important since it helps me find more articles I'm interested in reading.

How to demo

1 Log in to the site as writer.
2 Create five news articles, all in the section *world*.
3 Log out. As anonymous visitor, go to one of the newly created articles.
4 Verify that the four other articles, but not the currently viewed one, is displayed below the viewed article. Verify that the newest is on top.

Required preparations

- The site should have a news article content type, as provided by the first exercise in this suite, as well as the sections provided by the exercise in the taxonomy chapter.

RECENT COMMENTS, GROUPED BY SECTION

As site visitor I would like to have a list of recent comments displayed on the front page. The comments should be grouped by the (sub) section of the articles they belong to. This is important since it helps me find hot news in the sections I am most interested in.

How to demo

1. Post a comment to an article in the world section. (Create an article first, if necessary.)
2. Verify that the world section appears as the first section in the comment list on the front page, with the new comment listed on top.
3. Post a comment to an article in the Europe section. (Create an article first, if necessary.)
4. Verify that Europe is now the first section in the comment list on the front page – followed by any other comments in the Europe section – and that the world section is second (having the second newest comment).
5. Verify that each item in the comment list contains the name of the related article, linking to the article page.

Required preparations

- The site should have a news article content type, as provided by the first exercise in this suite.

Part C:
Other essential modules

In this part of the book you will have a few essential Drupal modules presented quite briefly, along with their most important functionalities. The purpose of the following chapters is to emphasize a few Drupal modules that are important to learn, rather than presenting all details about how to use them. To balance the somewhat scarce documentation of the modules, there are a number of practical examples intermixed, showing how and when different settings may be useful.

The suggested solutions to the exercises in this part are not as detailed as in part B – instead the comments are a bit richer. The purpose of the exercises in part C is not to give step-by-step instruction in how to create certain functions, but to give an understanding of what you can accomplish with the modules and pointers as to how to do it.

The concepts presented in this part requires that you are very comfortable with the concepts in part A and B – which may very well take several months even if you use Drupal every day.

Flag

The Flag module allows you as administrator to create simple flags, that end users may use to flag nodes, users and comments on your Drupal site. Flag could, for example, be used for:

- allowing end users flag comments as spam;
- allowing editors flagging which nodes should be listed on the front page or in the sidebar; and
- allowing logged-in users flag other users as friends, to follow what they post to the website.

Flags are usually displayed as clickable links at nodes, comments or users. The Flag module integrates well with the *Views* and *Rules* modules.

When installing the Flag module, you get an example flag – *bookmark* – which logged-in users may use used to make their own lists of articles on your site. (See figure 11.1 and 11.2.)

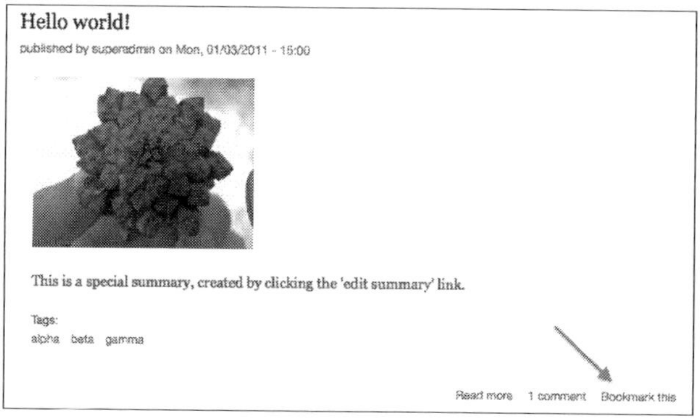

FIGURE 11.1 Note the link *bookmark* at the bottom-right corner – a default flag provided by the Flag module.

189

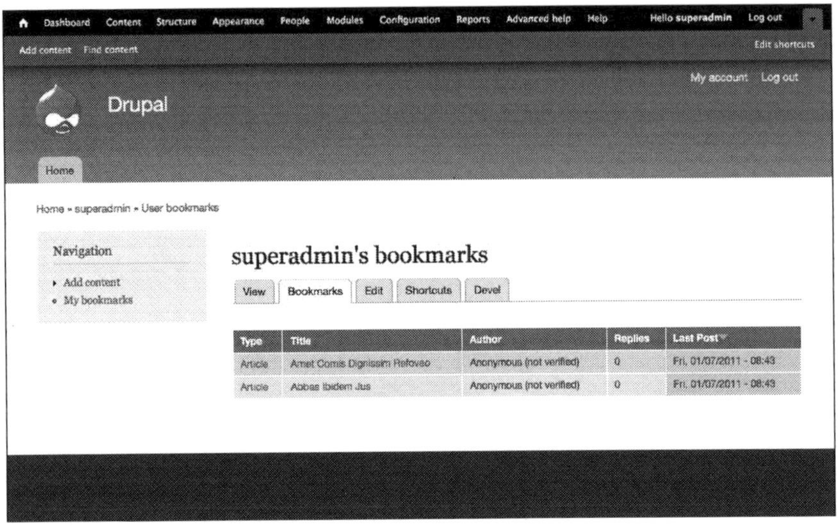

FIGURE 11.2 Bookmarked articles are included in a list of bookmarks, unique to each user.

Installation

Flag is installed in the way as most other modules – the module is downloaded from drupal.org, unarchived, and put in the the *sites/all/modules* folder, and finally also enabled in the modules list. The Flag project also includes the module *Flag actions*, which can be completely replaced by the *Rules* module (see the next chapter).

As previously mentioned, the Flag module provides an example configuration for a flag – the *bookmark* flag, along with two separate views displaying flagged nodes.

Configuring flags

The Flag overview page is found at the toolbar, *structure, flags*. The page lists all flags available on your website, along with links for editing, deleting and exporting each flag. Just above the list is a link *add new flag*. It takes you to a page where basic data for the new flag is set (see image 11.3), after which you are directed to the form used for both adding new and editing existing flags.

There are two basic settings for flags:
- Flag name: This is the machine name for the flag. It must be unique on the site, and may only contain lower-case letter, numbers and underscores.
- Flag type: This determines which kind of entity the flag applies to – nodes, comments or users. (There is currently no version of Flag that works with general entities.)

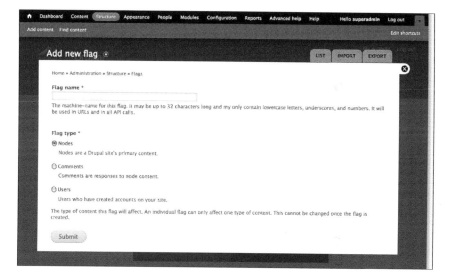

FIGURE 11.3 The first step in creating a new flag is to give it a machine name and determining which type of entity the flag applies to.

Other settings for flags are (see figure 11.4):
- Title: This is the administrative name for the flag.
- Global flag: This setting determines whether all users should share the same flagging (*global*) or if each user should be able to do their own flagging (*per-user*).
- Flag/unflag link text: These are the texts displayed to end users, at the link for adding or removing the flag. You may use *tokens* for including

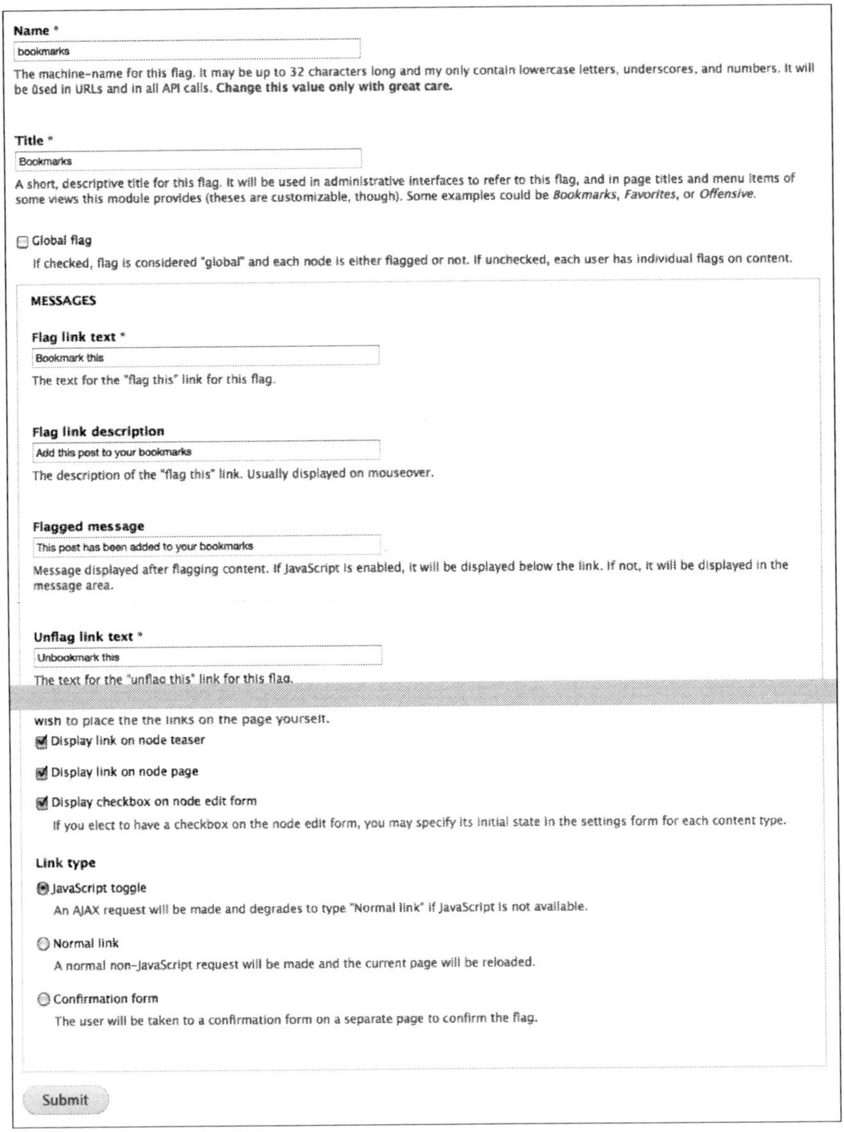

Name *

bookmarks

The machine-name for this flag. It may be up to 32 characters long and my only contain lowercase letters, underscores, and numbers. It will be used in URLs and in all API calls. **Change this value only with great care.**

Title *

Bookmarks

A short, descriptive title for this flag. It will be used in administrative interfaces to refer to this flag, and in page titles and menu items of some views this module provides (theses are customizable, though). Some examples could be *Bookmarks, Favorites,* or *Offensive.*

☐ Global flag

If checked, flag is considered "global" and each node is either flagged or not. If unchecked, each user has individual flags on content.

MESSAGES

Flag link text *

Bookmark this

The text for the "flag this" link for this flag.

Flag link description

Add this post to your bookmarks

The description of the "flag this" link. Usually displayed on mouseover.

Flagged message

This post has been added to your bookmarks

Message displayed after flagging content. If JavaScript is enabled, it will be displayed below the link. If not, it will be displayed in the message area.

Unflag link text *

Unbookmark this

The text for the "unflag this" link for this flag.

wish to place the the links on the page yourself.

☑ Display link on node teaser

☑ Display link on node page

☑ Display checkbox on node edit form

If you elect to have a checkbox on the node edit form, you may specify its initial state in the settings form for each content type.

Link type

◉ JavaScript toggle

An AJAX request will be made and degrades to type "Normal link" if JavaScript is not available.

○ Normal link

A normal non-JavaScript request will be made and the current page will be reloaded.

○ Confirmation form

The user will be taken to a confirmation form on a separate page to confirm the flag.

Submit

FIGURE 11.4 The page for creating or editing flags have a number of settings – most of them self-explanatory.

dynamic text strings. (Installing the *Token* module will give you a list of all available replacement patterns.)

- Flag/unflag link description: These texts are normally displayed as a tooltip popups, when hovering over the flagging or unflagging link. You may use tokens in the texts.

- Flagged/unflagged message: These texts are used as confirmation messages when flaggings have been added or removed. You may use tokens in the texts.

- Roles that may use this flag: This determines which users may set or remove the flag. If you install the *Session API* module, anonymous users may use the flags as well.

- Unflag not allowed text: This is the text displayed to users not permitted to remove a set flag. (If a user isn't allowed to even set the flag, it won't be displayed at all.)

- Flag access by content authorship: This option makes it possible to restrict flagging access to your own content only, or only content written by others. Content flags may also be restricted based on who wrote the node related to the comment.

- Flaggable content (only node and comment flags): This option restricts on which node types the flag should be available.

- Display options: These settings determine in which view modes the flag should be displayed, and vary depending on the type of flag you have. Node flags may be displayed in full node view, teasers, and also as a checkbox in the node edit form.

- Link type: Flags are either displayed as JavaScript links that don't require new page loads, normal links, or links to a confirmation page. (In the latter case you may also set a text displayed when the user is asked to confirm the flagging.)

HOW CAN THIS BE USED?

A flag for flagging comments as spam could be a non-global flag with the message *Report spam*, which all users may set but not remove. A flag for promoting content to the sidebar could be a global flag with the message *promote [node:title] to the sidebar,* and may be set or removed by editors.

Combining Flag and Views

Much of the power in the Flag module stems from its integration with Views. (Indeed, the Flag module was originally written as a Views plugin example!) To use Flag data in Views, you must utilize the flag relationships provided by the Flag module. (See figure 11.5 and 10.6.) There are four types of relationships available:

- Flags: Node/comment/user flag: This provides data about each flagging on a node, comment or user – including the flagging user and when the flag was set. The relationship may also be used to limit the view to objects flagged by the current user.
- Flags: Node/comment/user flag counter: This provides data about how many flaggings a node/comment/user has.
- Flags: User's flagged content: This relationship can be used to limit the view results to users who have used a flag.
- Flags: User: This provides the full user object for the user who has set a flag. To use this relationship you must already have a flag object provided in your view by another relationship.

When adding Flag relationships, you must specify which flag the relation should connect to. Most relationships also have the option *include only flagged content* – which is another way of phrasing *require this relationship* (used by other relationships).

DATA FIELDS FROM FLAGS

With flag objects available in your view, there are a number of new data fields that you may use (see figure 10.7):

- Flags: Flag counter: The total number of flaggings for this view result item.
- Flags: Flagged time: The time a flag was set.
- Flags: Flag link (view fields only): A link used for setting/removing a flag.
- Flags: Flagged (filters only): A value telling if a flag is set or not.

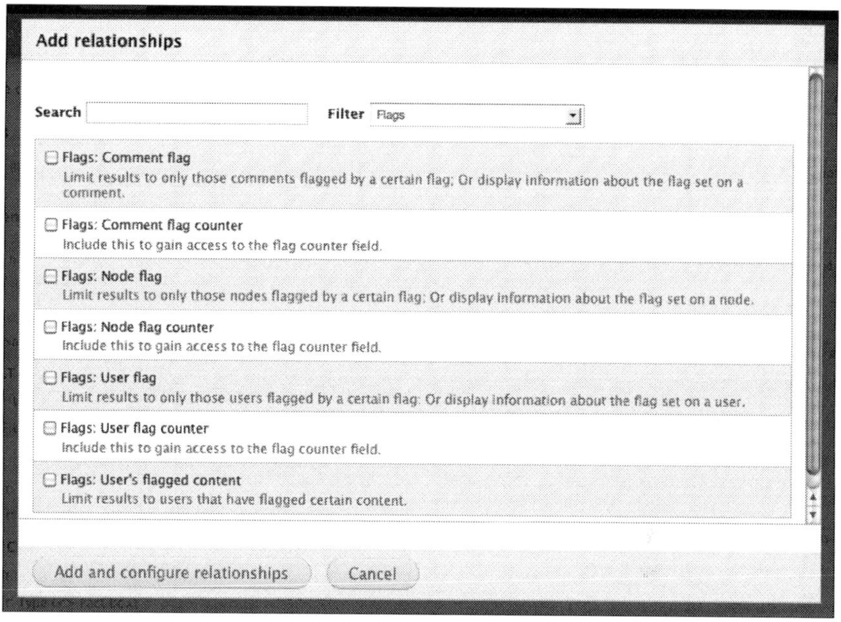

FIGURE 11.5 The Flag module offers a number of new relationships in Views, providing flagging data.

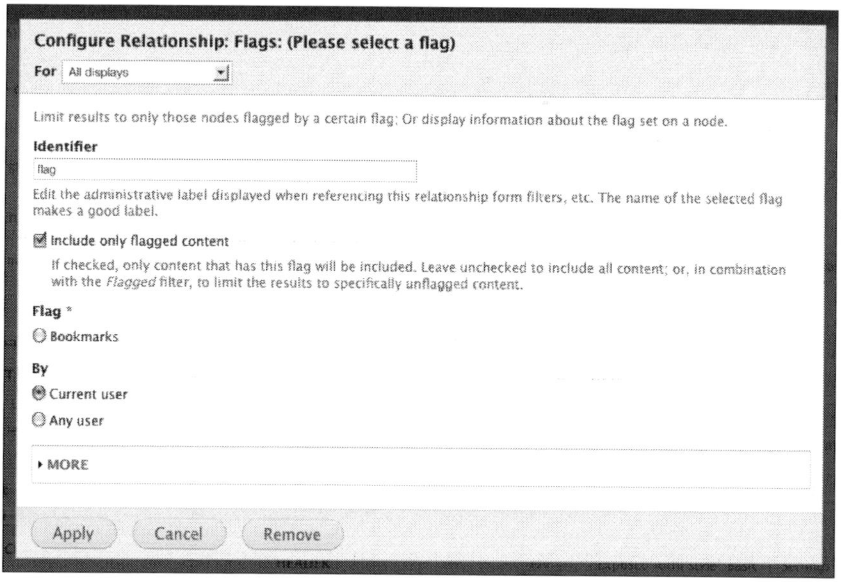

FIGURE 11.6 Each relationship you add will, as usual, have its own settings.

- Flags: Content ID (contextual filters only): The ID for the flagged view result item.

The relationship *flags: user* provides a normal user object to the view, which can be used as alternative to any other user object available in the view.

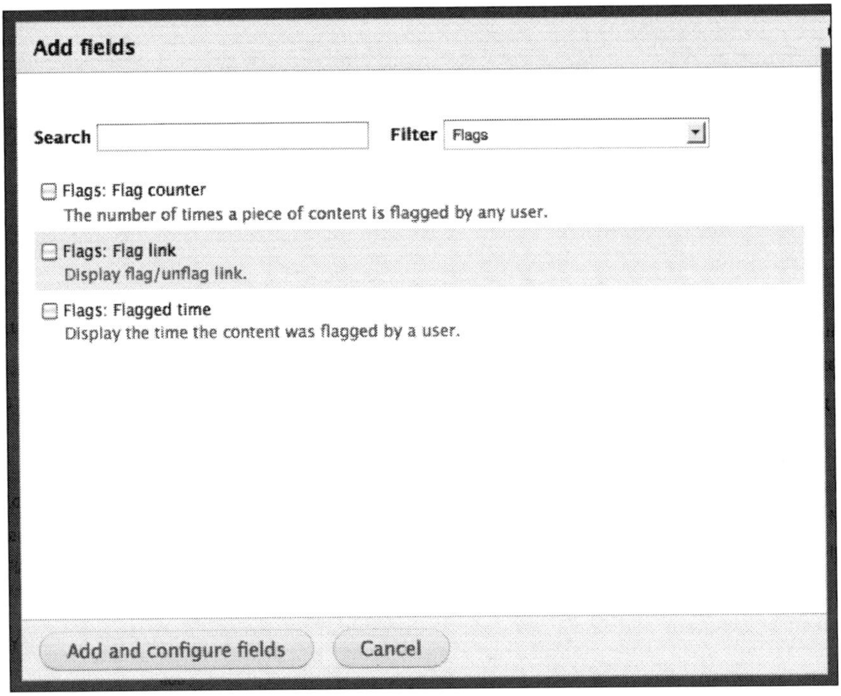

Add fields

Search [   ]   **Filter** [Flags   ▾]

☐ Flags: Flag counter
   The number of times a piece of content is flagged by any user.

☐ Flags: Flag link
   Display flag/unflag link.

☐ Flags: Flagged time
   Display the time the content was flagged by a user.

(Add and configure fields)   (Cancel)

FIGURE 11.7 Each Flag relationship may provide a number of new data fields in the view.

HOW CAN THIS BE USED?

A view of spam flagged comments may built by using the relationship *flag counter* and only include comments flagged with the relevant flag. A view of bookmarked nodes may use the relationship *node flag* and the view field *flag link* to allow users to remove the bookmark flag.

TIP

At the time of writing, the integration of Flag and Rules is still in development.

Exercises: Documentation site

These exercises build on previous exercises in the *Documentation site* suite. They can be carried out individually, with some preparations, or in sequence with the previous exercises. The exercises require using the concepts described part A and B in this book, as well as concepts from the Flag chapter.

Video recordings of the suggested solutions to these exercises can be found at nodeone.se/learn-drupal.

FLAG FRIENDS

As site member, I would like to be able to flag other users as friends. I also want a tab on my user page with a list of links to all my friends' user pages. This is important since it helps me staying up to date with contributions from people I like.

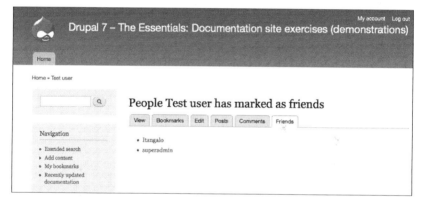

FIGURE 11.8 An example of a friend list.

How to demo

1 Log in to the site.
2 Flag two users as friends. (Create the users first, if necessary.)
3 Go to your user page and click the "Friends" tab. Verify that the flagged users are listed, in alphabetical order, linking to the respective user page.

Required preparations

- A standard Drupal site.

Suggested solution

1 Add a new user flag. Give it the machine name *friend_flag* and the title *friend flag*. Add descriptive flag/unflag texts, descriptions and confirmation message. (See *configuring flags* in this chapter.)

2 Allow all authenticated users to use the flag, but not to flag themselves. (See *configuring flags*.)

3 Add a new view. Give it the name *friends to a user*, and have it list users. Create a page with the path *user/%/friends* and display an unlimited number of items in an HTML list. (See *creating new views* in the Views basics chapter.)

4 Sort the view by user name and add a menu tab with the text *friends*. (See *configuring sorting* in the Views basic chapter and *creating menu tabs* in the advanced Views configuration chapter.)

5 Add a new relationship *flags: user flag* to join flag information to your view. Restrict the list to only flagged users, but users flagged by *any* user (not only the current user). (See *combining Flag and Views* in this chapter.)

6 Add a new relationship *flags: user* to join information about the flagging user to your view. (See *combining Flag and Views*.)

7 Add a contextual filter *user: uid* and make use of the relationship to the flagging user – to require that the flagging user has the user ID specified by the contextual filter value. (See *combining Flag and Views* in this chapter, plus *configuring contextual filters* and *utilizing relationships in configuration* in the advanced Views configuration chapter.)

Comments

- This could be implemented as a tab found on each user page, or merely a tab where you see your own friends. The latter would be difficult to do with Views and Flag only, but quite easy in combination with Page manager.

- If a user hasn't flagged any friends, it makes sense to have a short text displayed in the view – see *a few more basic Views settings* for information about how to do this.
- If you want more challenges, you can also create a list of all users who have flagged the viewed user as friend.

FAVORITE DOCUMENTATION PAGES

As site member, I would like to mark documentation pages as favorites. A list of marked pages should appear as a tab on my user page, and the five most recently added should also appear as a block in the sidebar. This is important since it helps me access content I find useful.

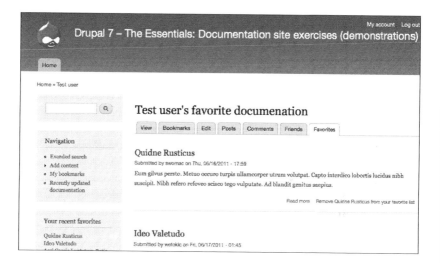

FIGURE 11.9 An example of how the favorite list may look.

How to demo

1   Log in to the site.
2   Flag at least six documentation pages as favorites. (Create the pages first, if necessary.)
3   Verify that the five most recently added are visible in a sidebar block, linking to the respective documentation pages.

4   Verify that the block links to a page listing all six documentation pages, with links to the respective pages. Verify that this page appears as a tab at the acting user's profile page.

Required preparations

- The site should have a documentation page content type, as provided by the first exercise in this suite.

Suggested solution

1   Add a new node flag. Give it the name *favorite* and the title *favorite documentation*. (See *configuring flags* in this chapter.)

2   Give the flag descriptive flag/unflag link texts, descriptions and confirmation messages. Allow all authenticated users to use the flag, and allow flags to be put on documentation pages only. (See *configuring flags*.)

3   Add a new view. Give it the name *favorites*, and have it list content without any specified sort criteria. Create a page with the path *user/%/favorites*, displaying 10 teasers at a time, with a pager. Also create a block, showing five linked titles without any pager. (See *creating new views* in the Views basics chapter.)

4   In View's main configuration panel, add a new relationship *flags: node flag* to get information about all the flags on the listed nodes. Use the favorite flag, and include only flagged content – but include content flagged by *all* users. (See *combining Flag and Views* in this chapter.)

5   Add another relationship, *flags: user*, to get information about the user setting each flag. (See *combining Flag and Views*.)

6   Add a contextual filter *user: uid*, restricting the view to list only content where the *flagging user* has the user ID provided by the contextual filter value. If the filter value is missing – which will be the case for the block – provide default value from *user ID from logged in user*. Also validate that the filter argument is a user ID. (See *configuring contextual filters* in the advanced Views configuration chapter.)

7 Add a sort criteria *flags: flagged time*, for sorting the list with newest flaggings on top. (See *data fields from flags* in this chapter.)

8 In the block display, override the contextual filter settings. Set the title to *your recent favorites*. Also override the *more link* option (in the middle column), setting it to *yes*. (See *overridden configuration* in the Views basics chapter.)

9 Give the block the block name *active user's favorites*. Save the view. In the blocks administration page, place the new block in one of the sidebars.

Comments

• As with the previous exercise, this could be implemented as a tab found at each user page, or only on your own user page – the latter task being drastically simplified using Page manager (and an access rule to compare acting user with the user for whom to list favorites).

• When building the block display, it is possible to use the flag relation option to include content flagged by current user only. However, this would make it difficult to use the *more* link – since the page display expects a contextual filter value. A better, but somewhat more heavy approach (for Views), is to use the same contextual filter settings but allow the block to fetch a default value for the filter.

LIST ALL CONTENT CREATED BY FRIENDS

As site member, I would like a list of all the content created by users I have flagged as friends. I would like this list available as a tab on my user page. This is important since it helps me keep up with contributions from people I like.

How to demo

1 Log in to the site as a user (Alpha). Create at least one piece of content.

2 Log in to the site as another user (Beta). Create at least one piece of content.

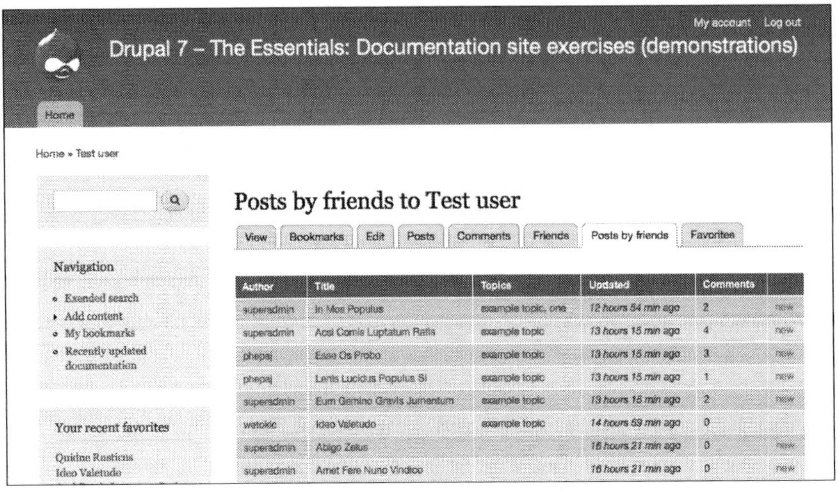

FIGURE 11.10 An example of how the friend feed may look.

3 Log in to the site as a third user (Gamma). Create a piece of content . Flag Alpha and Beta as friends.

4 Go to Gamma's user page. Click on the tab *Friends' posts.*

5 Verify that the content created by Alpha and Beta, but not Gamma, is listed.

Required preparations

- The site should have a documentation page content type, as provided by the first exercise in this suite.
- The site should have the friend flag, as described in a previous exercise in this chapter.

Suggested solution

1 Create a new node view. Give it the name *posts by friends to a given user* and have it list content with newest on top. Create a page with the path *user/%/posts-by-friends,* listing 10 teasers and using a pager. (See *creating new views* in the Views basics chapter.)

2 In Views' main configuration panel, add (if necessary) a relationship *content: author* to access the user object for the documentation author. Then add a new relationship *flags: user flag* to get all the friend flags set on the content author. Finally, add another relationship *flags: user* to join the user setting the friend flag. (See *combining Flag and Views* in this chapter as well as *adding relationships* in the advanced Views configuration chapter.)

3 Add a contextual filter *user: uid*, using the relationship to the flagging user – this will restrict the results to only those where the flagging user matches the provided contextual filter value. (See *configuring contextual filters* and *utilizing relationship in configuration* in the advanced Views configuration chapter.)

4 Add a menu tab item with the text *posts by friends*.

Comments

- This, as the previous two exercises, is a case where it becomes easier to create a tab at *all* user pages to display friend's posts, rather than at your own user page only. (And just as in previous examples, it would be quite easy to solve both these cases if we were using Page manager.)

- Creating a view with three relationships is not something you should do unless you know that you have to. Relationships can result in heavy database queries, resulting in poor performance on your site. If the queries are necessary, though, Views is probably a good way of building them – since you (for example) get optimized queries and caching functionality built-in.

Exercises: News site

These exercises build on previous exercises in the *news site* suite. They can be carried out individually, with some preparations, or in sequence with the previous exercises. The exercises require using the concepts described part A and B in this book, as well as concepts from the Flag chapter.

LIST SPAM-FLAGGED COMMENTS

As editor, I would like site visitors to be able to mark comments as spam. I would also like a list of all comments marked as spam. This is important since it helps me keeping abusive content off the site.

How to demo

1   As anonymous visitor, flag at least two comments as spam. Verify that you cannot remove the spam flag.
2   In another browser, also as anonymous visitor, flag one of the spam flagged comments as spam. Verify that the spam flag was not already set.
3   Log in to the site as editor. Go to admin/content/comment. Verify that there is a tab "Spam" visible.
4   Verify that the list contains all the spam flagged comments, newest comment on top, along with number of flaggings and links for viewing, editing and deleting the comment.

Required preparations

• The site should have a news article content type, as provided by the first exercise in this suite.
• The Session API module must be downloaded and installed.

Comments

• A useful feature would probably be to add an exposed filter, allowing editors to show only comments with (say) three spam flags.
• Including the entire comment body in the list would probably save the editor a lot of time, but also make the list difficult to overview. One solution for this is to have the body comment as tooltip for the link to the comment.
• The *Views Bulk Operations* module can be used to allow editors to select a number of comments and (for example) unpublish or delete all at once.

APPROVE SPAM-FLAGGED COMMENTS

As site editor, I would like mark spam-flagged as approved, removing them from the list of spam-flagged comments. This is important since it prevents me from checking the same potential spam more than once.

How to demo

1   As anonymous visitor, flag a number of comments as spam.
2   Log in to the site as editor and go to admin/content/comment/spam.
3   Verify that each potential spam comment has a link *approve.*
4   Verify that approved comments are removed from the list when reloading the page.

Required preparations

• The site should have a news article content type, as provided by the first exercise in this suite.
• The site should have the spam flag from the previous exercise.

Basic Rules configuration

The *Rules* module is used to configure automized actions on your website – such as sending out e-mails, updating nodes or displaying messages to users. The actions could either be triggered by selected events on your site, or called by other tools and modules. One of the powers with Rules is the flexible ways of evaluating conditions before any actions are executed.

You could for example use Rules for:
- assigning all new users a selected role;
- unpublish all comments flagged as spam by at least three users;
- setting entity field values based on complex conditions;
- allow users to subscribe to comments on selected content;
- send e-mail reminders to users who have not logged in for three weeks; or
- schedule publishing, unpublishing and deletion of content.

When you become skilled in Rules configuration, you will be able to use Rules to replace quite a few small modules – both contributed to drupal.org and custom-written. This chapter only covers basic configuration of Rules.

> **TIP**
>
> Combined with the *RESTful Web Services* module, Rules can be used to connect triggers and actions across different Drupal sites. These functions are still under development and are not discussed further in this book.

Installing Rules

Rules follows the standard procedures for installation. The Rules project include three modules:

- Rules: This is the basic engine used for executing and evaluating rules configuration. It has no graphical interface of its own.
- Rules Scheduler: This module is used to schedule actions on your website. Rules Scheduler is described in a separate chapter.
- Rules UI: This module provides a user interface to Rules. You will need it while configuring Rules settings, but it may in general be disabled once a website is live.

To enable Rules you must also have the *Entity API* and *Entity tokens* available (both being parts of the *Entity API* project).

Configuring reaction rules

The administration pages for Rules are found at the toolbar, *configuration, Rules*. The landing page is used to manage *reaction rules*, a good starting point when learning how Rules may be used. (See figure 12.1.)

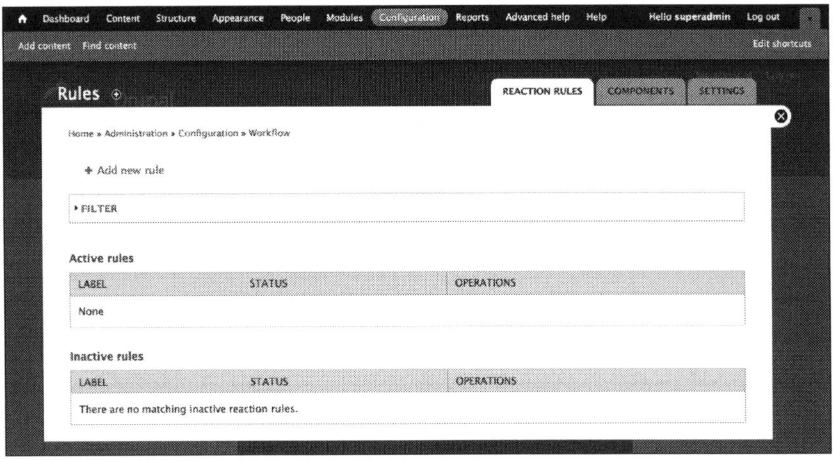

FIGURE 12.1 The landing page for Rules lists all reaction rules on your site – none to start with.

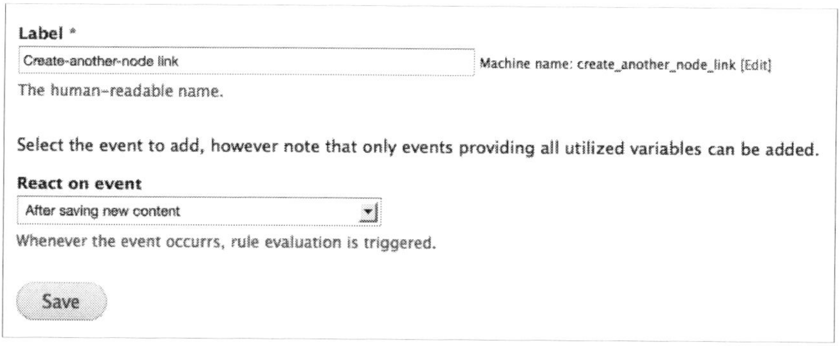

Label *

Create-another-node link

Machine name: create_another_node_link [Edit]

The human-readable name.

Select the event to add, however note that only events providing all utilized variables can be added.

React on event

After saving new content

Whenever the event occurrs, rule evaluation is triggered.

Save

FIGURE 12.2 You create a new reaction rule by entering a name and selecting a triggering event.

The overview page shows a list of all reaction rules on your site – in total zero in a default installation. There is also a link *add new rule*, leading to a form for basic data about the new reaction rule (see figure 12.2):

- Label: This is the administrative title for the reaction rule. A machine name will be suggested based on this name.
- React on event: This select list contains a number of events on your site – select the one you want your reaction rule to trigger on.

The resulting page contains an overview of the configuration for the reaction rule. (See figure 12.3.) The page is divided into *events* triggering the reaction rule, *conditions* that must be met for it to do anything, and the *actions* that will be performed. There are also a number of settings for the reaction rule as a whole collected in the *settings* fieldset.

MANAGING TRIGGERING EVENTS

Maninging events – or *triggering events* – is a pretty straight-forward process. The link *add event* is used to add more triggering events to a reaction rule, and the *delete* link presented at each event removes the corresponding event.

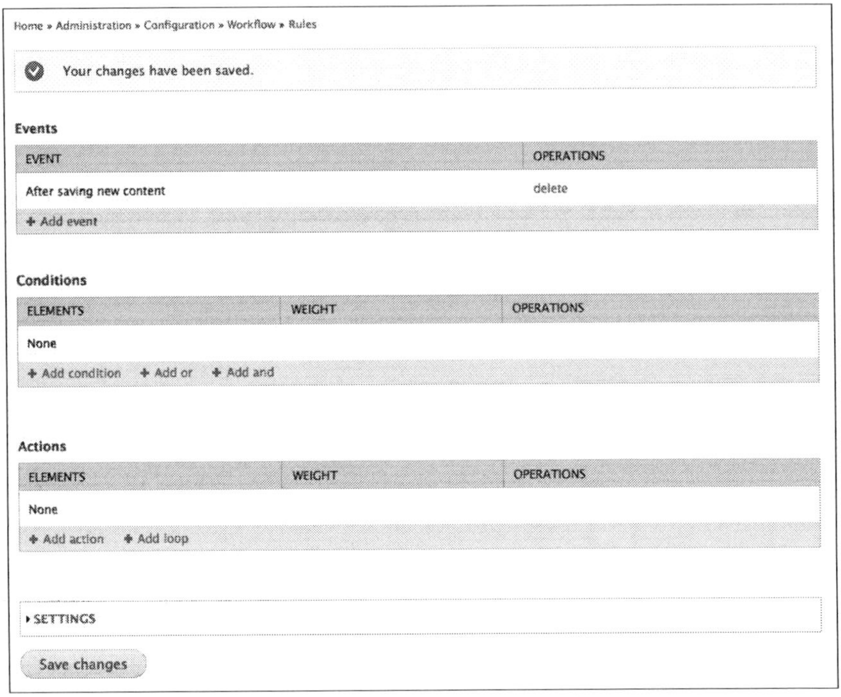

Home » Administration » Configuration » Workflow » Rules

✓ Your changes have been saved.

Events

EVENT	OPERATIONS
After saving new content	delete
✦ Add event	

Conditions

ELEMENTS	WEIGHT	OPERATIONS
None		
✦ Add condition ✦ Add or ✦ Add and		

Actions

ELEMENTS	WEIGHT	OPERATIONS
None		
✦ Add action ✦ Add loop		

▸ SETTINGS

Save changes

FIGURE 12.3 Each reaction rule contains triggering events, conditions and actions. You may add multiple triggering events for the same reaction rule.

HOW CAN THIS BE USED?

A triggering rule used for scheduled deletions of nodes may have use for two separate events – new nodes being created and existing nodes being updated.

Managing conditions

Often you want to condition actions on your website – on a site where comments normally are queued for moderation it may be a good idea to publish the comment immediately *if written by an editor*.

You add new conditions with the *add condition* link, bringing you to a select list of all available condition types, and eventually a configuration page for the added condition. (See figure 12.4.)

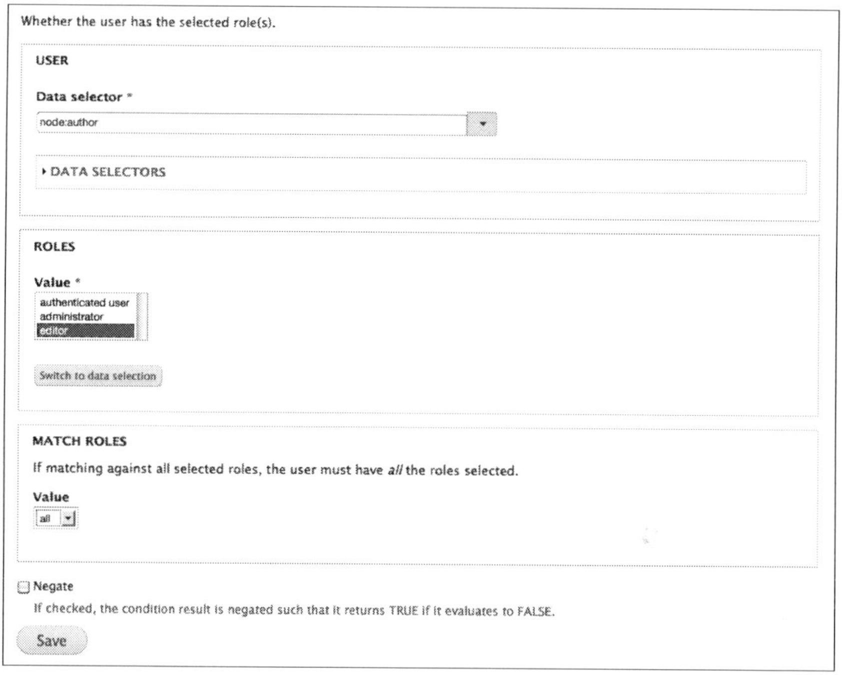

Whether the user has the selected role(s).

USER

Data selector *

node:author

▸ DATA SELECTORS

ROLES

Value *

authenticated user
administrator
editor

Switch to data selection

MATCH ROLES

If matching against all selected roles, the user must have *all* the roles selected.

Value

all

☐ Negate
If checked, the condition result is negated such that it returns TRUE if it evaluates to FALSE.

Save

FIGURE 12.4 The settings for each condition vary depending on the data managed by the condition. Here is a condition used for evaluting a user's roles.

Each condition has a checkbox for negating its result – making the reaction rule to have effect if the conditions are false rather than true. You may configure quite complex logics by adding AND and OR groups to your conditions – this is done by using the corresponding links and then dragging and dropping your conditions to rearrange them within the groups. If you're a really sophisticated Drupal developer you may also try adding logical groups within other logical groups.

HOW CAN THIS BE USED?

A rule redirecting users to their profile pages may kick into action only if the profile is lacking data for some selected entity fields. A rule placing articles in an approval workflow may be skipped if the writer has the administrator role.

211

> **TIP**
>
> Rules automatically creates labels for conditions and actions, based on their settings. At the time of writing it is not possible to set these labels manually, but this option is expected to be available soon.

MANAGING ACTIONS

The *add action* link is used to provide new actions for your reaction rule. (See figure 12.5.) It leads to a list of all actions that may be carried out in the current context – see the section about loading and managing objects for more information about how to make more actions accessible.

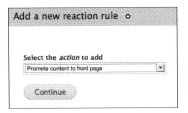

FIGURE 12.5 You may add actions that affect any available nodes, other objects, or the website as a whole.

When choosing an action, a form appears to configure the action – sometimes the settings even consist of several steps of forms.

The settings included in the configuration forms depend on which actions is being configured, and varies so widely that it is unreasonable to try to document them in a book. One of the most important ones is *set data value*, which luckily also serves as a good example of how a typical action is configured. The action is, in essence, used to set just about any piece of data available to Rules – entity fields, node authors, publish state, and much more.

Selecting adding this action to your rule, you first get to select what data you want to set. This is done using *data selection* – something between an autocomplete textfield and a select list, used to browse through the data available to Rules. (See the next section for details.) Once your data is selected, you are prompted to select what information you want to store. This could be done using data selection, for example to set the acting user as a new node author – or by entering a data value manually, for example to set an article body. If entering data manually, you can still use variables available to Rules, by using replacement patterns as listed in a help box below the input field.

A reaction rule may contain multiple actions, and there are also options available for using *loops* to iterate actions – see separate section for details.

REPLACEMENT PATTERNS AND DATA SELECTION

To allow more flexibility when managing dynamic variables, Rules has two different user interfaces for what is often called *tokens* or *replacement patterns*:

- Direct input mode: This is used for text input, and allows you as administrator to isert normal tokens into the text. Next to the text field you will find a list of available tokens, based on the objects currently available in the reaction rule.
- Data selection: The *data selection* input is a kind of auto-completing text field, where you are guided through the variables available to the reaction rule. (See figure 12.6.) When objects relate to each other – which is common – the resulting chain of token parts can tell you how they are related. The token *node:author:mail*, for example, tells you that the resulting variable contains the e-mail address of the user who has written the node handled by the reaction rule.

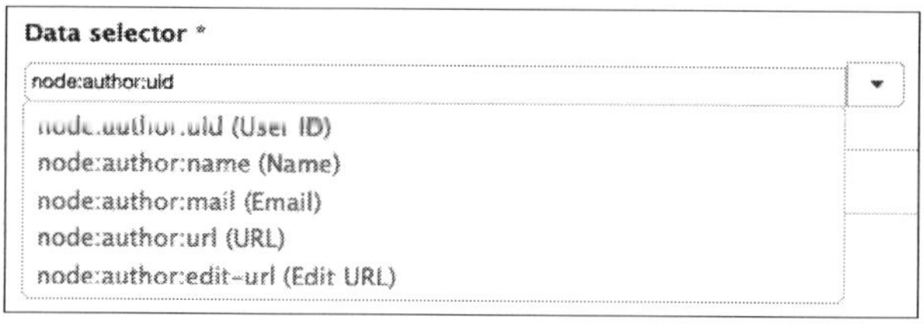

Data selector *

node:author:uid	▼

node:author:uid (User ID)
node:author:name (Name)
node:author:mail (Email)
node:author:url (URL)
node:author:edit-url (Edit URL)

FIGURE 12.6 The data selection input mode guides you through the available tokens.

213

> **TIP**
>
> If the *PHP filter* module (in Drupal core) is enabled, you may use PHP code in all fields normally accepting tokens. Using PHP code in configuration is discouraged.

ACTIONS IN LOOPS

Next to the link for adding actions is a link with the title *add loop*. Loops may be used when an available variable has multiple values, to carry out one or more actions *for each value* in the variable. This could, for example, be used to send e-mail messages to all users listed in a user reference field. (For this to work, the multiple-value variables must be exposed in a way that Rules can interpret, which at the time or writing is not the case for user reference fields.)

Actions are added inside loops using the *add action* link at each loop, and works just as other actions – with the exception that there is a token *list item* available, representing the currently active item in the list being looped. (See figure 12.7.)

It is possible to add loops within loops.

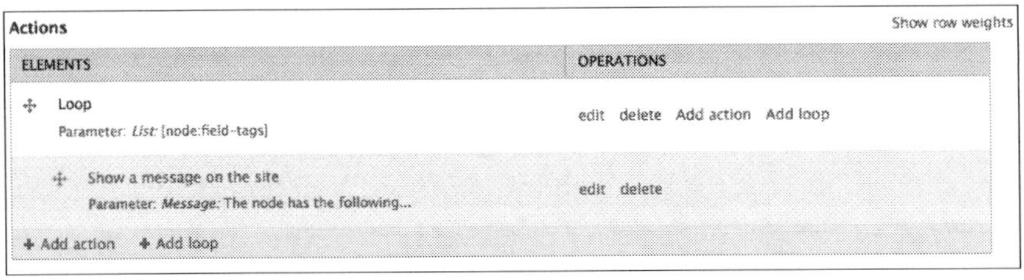
Actions
Show row weights
ELEMENTS
OPERATIONS
Loop
Parameter: List: [node:field-tags]
edit delete Add action Add loop
Show a message on the site
Parameter: Message: The node has the following...
edit delete
+ Add action
+ Add loop

FIGURE 12.7 You can use multiple-value variables to create loops of actions – where actions are executed once for each value.

> **HOW CAN THIS BE USED?**
>
> A loop based on a multiple-value user reference field may be used to send e-mail notifications to each referenced user. A loop based on a multiple-value node reference field may be used to update the node author for all referenced nodes.

OTHER REACTION RULE SETTINGS

The *settings* fieldset, at the bottom of the page when viewing a reaction rule, contains some general settings for the reaction rule (see figure 12.8):

- Label: This allows you to change name (and also machine name) for a reaction rule.
- Provide variables: When several reaction rules are executed in sequence, there is sometimes reason to send along any loaded objects for further processing by other rules. This setting allows you to select which objects should be passed on.
- Active: If this option is deselected, the reaction rule will not have any effect on the site.
- Weight: This setting allows you to change in which order reaction rules are executed – lower weights will be processed earlier.

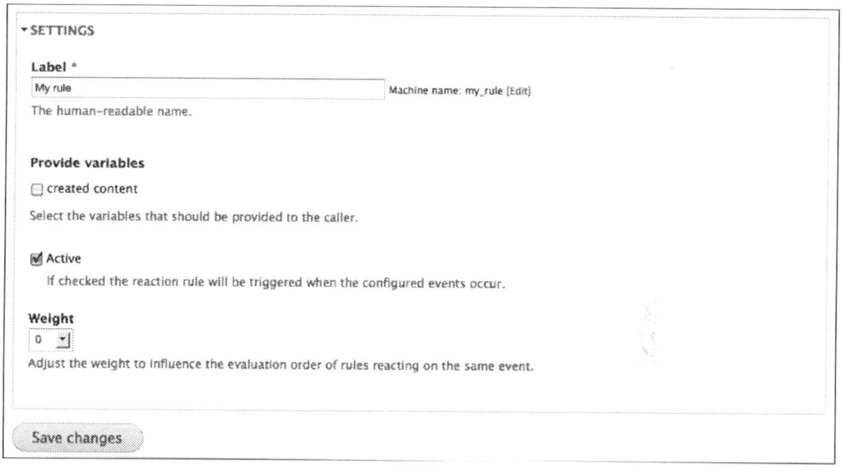

FIGURE 12.8 The *settings* fieldset contains some more settings, for example allowing you to change the name of the reaction rule.

LOADING AND MANAGING OBJECTS

When a reaction rule is triggered, it is handed a number of object that the rule may use to evaluate conditions and carry out actions. The event *before*

215

saving content, for example, provide four objects: the saved node, the node as it was before it was changed, the node author and the acting user.

There are actions loading new objects, and making them available to any subsequent actions. You cannot, however, load new objects and use them for conditions – if you need that kind of logics you should build a *rule set* (see separate section) or let a previously executed rule pass on the relevant object..

> **TIP**
>
> Saving an object is a potentially heavy operation for your website, which is why Rules has built-in functionality for delaying any saving until all actions have been executed. If you need to save an object before the rule is finished – for example to provide a new node with an ID – you can use the action available to save entities.

Rules components

When configuring Rules for doing chores on your website, it doesn't take very long before you feel that you want to use certain sets of conditions or actions over and over again. In those times you wish it was possible to save and reuse configuration – which it also turns out to be!

Reusing Rules configuration is done by creating *components*. All your website's Rules components – and a link to create new ones – are found at a separate tab in the Rules overview. (See figure 12.9.) In a default installation you can create five different types of Rules components:

- Condition set (OR): This is a group of one or several conditions, where only one must be fulfilled for the group to be evaluated TRUE.
- Condition set (AND): This is a group of one or several conditions, where *all* must be fulfilled for the group to be evaluated TRUE.
- Action set: This is a group of actions.
- Rule: This creates a rule without any triggering event – which instead must be called explicitly from other parts of Rules or the website in general.

- Rule set: This creates a group of rules, executed in sequence. See separate section for details about when this is particularly useful. Rule sets don't have any triggering events.

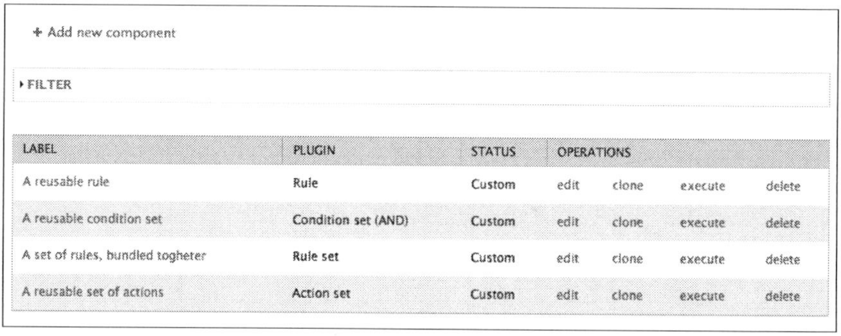

LABEL	PLUGIN	STATUS	OPERATIONS			
A reusable rule	Rule	Custom	edit	clone	execute	delete
A reusable condition set	Condition set (AND)	Custom	edit	clone	execute	delete
A set of rules, bundled togheter	Rule set	Custom	edit	clone	execute	delete
A reusable set of actions	Action set	Custom	edit	clone	execute	delete

+ Add new component

▸ FILTER

FIGURE 12.9 You can create isolated Rules components, for use and reuse on other parts of your site.

Every type of component is created and managed in way similar to their respective parts in reaction rules – with one important difference. Each component has settings for which objects/variables must be included when the component is called. (See figure 12.10.) These objects are selected when calling the component, and are then available for the component to work with.

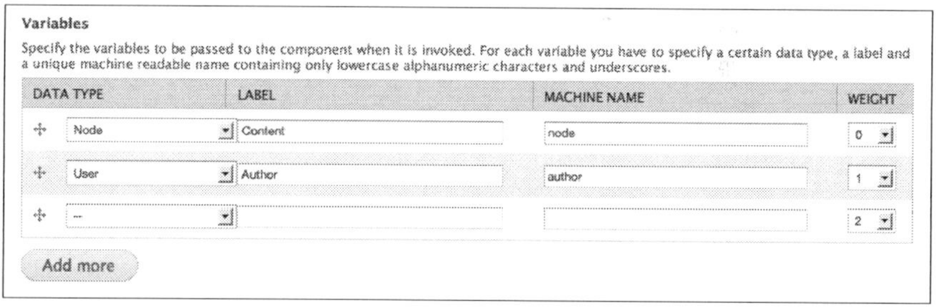

Variables

Specify the variables to be passed to the component when it is invoked. For each variable you have to specify a certain data type, a label and a unique machine readable name containing only lowercase alphanumeric characters and underscores.

DATA TYPE	LABEL	MACHINE NAME	WEIGHT
✛ Node	Content	node	0
✛ User	Author	author	1
✛ --			2

(Add more)

FIGURE 12.10 When creating components, you set which types of objects the component should work with. In order to call the component from other parts of Rules, you must have matching objects available.

> **TIP**
>
> Components are not only useful for reusing configuration, but also for exporting Rules cofiguration efficiently. See the section on configuration export in appendix 1 for details about why configuration export is a virtue.

> **TIP**
>
> The *Views Bulk Operations* module can be used to apply rule components to nodes and other entities. This allows for creating highly customized actions, which site administrators may use to (for example) mark selected articles as reviewed, publish them, and send a message to the author.

Rule sets

Rule sets are, essentially, nothing but a number of stacked rules. This may be useful to group rules together and keep your sanity even when your site have fifty rules – but the possibility to let one rule send along loaded objects to subsequent rules make rule sets particularly useful. An example explains why:

Imagine that you want to create an action that redirects a user to her last post on the site when she logs in – but only if that post is a forum post. You could pretty easily use the action *Load the first node in a Views list* (found in *Rules Bonus Pack*) to load the most recent node by the logged in user – but once loaded you are passed the stage in the rule where conditions are executed.

If using a rule set, you can use one rule for loading the user's most recent node, and a subsequent rule for running conditions against that node – redirecting to the node page if appropriate. Easy as pie!

Scheduling actions with Rules Scheduler

Sometimes you don't want Rules to carry out the actions when a triggering event occurs, but at some later point in time. At a site with events, for example, may find it useful to send reminders 24 hours before an event occurs. It is theoretically possible to use the triggering event *cron mainte-*

nance tasks are performed, combined with slightly insane conditions, but leveraging the powers of the *Rules Scheduler* module will save you a lot of time as well as keeping you from pulling out your hair.

Rules Scheduler (included in the Rules project) allows you to schedule actions at selected points in time. It is used like this:

- A number of actions, rules or rule sets are prepared as rule components.
- A reaction rule (or some other part of Drupal capable of using Rules actions) is configured to *schedule* the selected rule component.
- The scheduling involves setting an ID for the scheduled task, a time when it should be performed, and also selecting any objects that should be sent as variables to the component.
- Once the configured time has been reached, your site will load the scheduled task and execute it.

Some more details are presented below.

> **TIP**
>
> The scheduled tasks are actually not executed right at the scheduled time, but at the nearest following cron run. Depending on your server setup it may take a few minutes or at most perhaps an hour between the scheduled time and the actual execution.

SCHEDULING TASKS

Scheduling tasks with Rules Scheduler is done by adding the action *schedule component evaluation*, availabe as other actions in the Rules interface. (See figure 12.11.) At the resulting page you choose a component of the type *action, rule* or *rule set*. (See figure 12.12.) For a component to be selectable, you must have objects matching all the variables that the component require – if your component is an action set requiring a node, you can't call it unless you have a node object available in your rule.

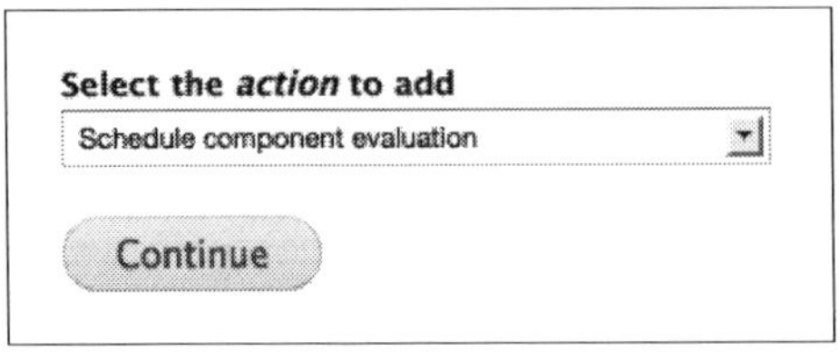

Select the *action* to add

Schedule component evaluation

Continue

FIGURE 12.11 Rules Scheduler allows you to schedule tasks using the action schedule component evalutation.

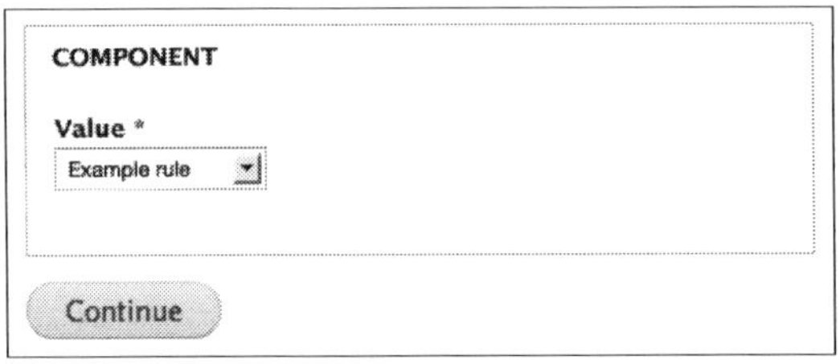

COMPONENT

Value *

Example rule

Continue

FIGURE 12.12 Only components that are action sets, rules or rule sets can be scheduled.

EVALUATION TIME FOR SCHEDULED TASKS

The final configuration page for scheduled tasks allows you to set the time for the component evaluation. (See figure 12.13.) There are three different ways of entering time:

- Static times, such as *2011-08-21 09:00:00.*
- Times specified by entering tokens or using data selection, for example for fetching a time value from an entity field.
- Times specified by *offsets*. The offsets may be combined with tokens or static times (such as *[comment:node:created] +2 days*). There are many ways of specifying offsets – for example will +1 *Monday* give you the nearest following monday.

> TIP
>
> Rules Scheduler expects times in GMT – meaning without any compensation for time zones.

ID FOR SCHEDULED TASKS

Each tasks being schedules must have a unique ID – if a new task with the same ID is scheduled, any previous task with the same ID will be replaced. It is common to use tokens and short texts in combination to build IDs, suchs as *delete node [node:nid]*. (See figure 11.13.)

On the same page used for setting the time and ID for the scheduled task, you can also decide which objects should be sent as variables to the rule component being scheduled.

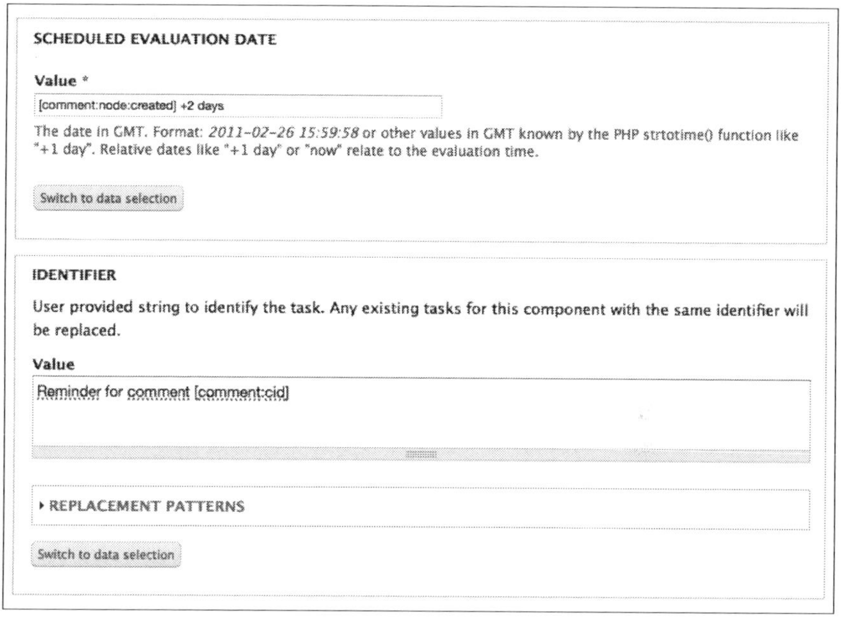

SCHEDULED EVALUATION DATE

Value *

[comment:node:created] +2 days

The date in GMT. Format: *2011-02-26 15:59:58* or other values in GMT known by the PHP strtotime() function like "+1 day". Relative dates like "+1 day" or "now" relate to the evaluation time.

Switch to data selection

IDENTIFIER

User provided string to identify the task. Any existing tasks for this component with the same identifier will be replaced.

Value

Reminder for comment [comment:cid]

▸ REPLACEMENT PATTERNS

Switch to data selection

FIGURE 12.13 The time and ID for the scheduled task is set on the final configuration page.

MORE INFORMATION ABOUT SCHEDULED TASKS

You as administrator can get an overview of all scheduled tasks on your site by visiting the *schedule* tab found from the toolbar, *configuration, rules*. The same page also allows manually deleting scheduled tasks. Inspecting and deleting scheduled tasks is useful while building a website, but is normally not used once the site is live.

It may, however, be necessary to automatically delete scheduled tasks. If you have a rule scheduling deletion of an article, for example, you would probably like the option to cancel the deletion too. Rules can delete a scheduled task with the action *delete scheduled task*, provided by Rules Scheduler. Task deletion is based on the ID of the scheduled task.

> **TIP**
>
> Scheduled tasks are available as a base table in Views, making it possible to create customized site administration pages displaying upcoming tasks.

Bug tracking in Rules

Even with plenty of Rules experience, you will probably find yourself scratching your head trying to understand why your configuration doesn't yield the result you expect. The *settings* tab at the Rules administration pages has an option called *debug rules evaluation*. It makes each step in Rules evaluation being logged and printed to the screen. (See figure 12.14.) Tracking the Rules evaluation you will have a much easier time finding your bugs. Strange as it sounds, you will most likely find that it was you, and not Rules, that introduced the bug.

Rules evaluation log

- 0 ms Reacting on event *Content is viewed.*
- 9.776 ms Evaluating rule *My rule.*
- 10.378 ms The condition *node_is_of_type* evaluated to *TRUE*
- 10.389 ms AND evaluated to TRUE.
- 10.553 ms Looping over the list items of *node:field-tags*
- 19.685 ms Evaluating the action *drupal_message.*
- 20.846 ms Evaluating the action *drupal_message.*
- 21.008 ms Finished reacting on event *Content is viewed.*

FIGURE 12.14 The bug tracking included with Rules will save you a lot of time.

> **TIP**
>
> The Rules debug information also shows a time stamp for each step in the evaluation – information that may help you spot unexpected heavy operations.

Exercises: Documentation site

These exercises build on previous exercises in the *Documentation site* suite. They can be carried out individually, with some preparations, or in sequence with the previous exercises. The exercises require using the concepts described part A and B in this book, as well as concepts from the Rules and Flag chapters.

Video recordings of the suggested solutions to these exercises can be found at nodeone.se/learn-drupal.

COMMENT NOTIFICATIONS

As site member, I would like to be notified when my content receives a comment. This is important since it helps me being aware of and respond to feedback.

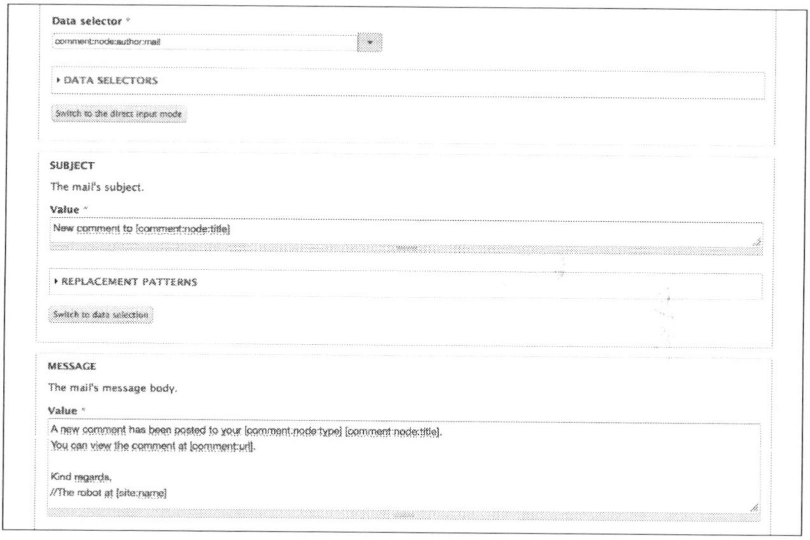

FIGURE 12.15 An example of how a comment notification may look.

How to demo

1 Log in to the site. Verify that the user account has an e-mail you can access.
2 Create a documentation page.
3 Log out and log in as another user. Post a comment to the new documentation page.
4 Verify that a notification is sent node author, with a link to the comment.
5 Log out and log in as the first user again. Post a reply to the comment.
6 Verify that no notification is sent to the user when commenting her own content.

Required preparations

The site should have a documentation page content type, as provided by the first exercise in this suite.

Suggested solution

1 Create a new reaction rule with the name *comment notification*. Have it react on the event *after saving a new comment*. (See *configuring reaction rules* in this chapter.)
2 Add a condition *data comparison*, and use data selection to compare *comment:author* with *comment:node:author*. Check the *negate* option, to have this condition return true if the two objects are different. (See *managing conditions* in this chapter.)
3 Add an action *send mail*. Set the *to* field to *comment:node:author:mail* (using data selection), the subject to *new comment on [comment:node:title]* and make sure to include the *[comment:url]* replacement pattern in the message to have a link to the comment. Leave the from field empty to use the site default e-mail address.

Comments

- This feature could be extended by using a checkbox field on the user page, where each user may select if she wants comment notifications or not.

REMINDERS FOR INACTIVE USERS

As site owner, I would like members to get reminder e-mails if they have not logged in for a month. This is important since it helps catching some users who otherwise would leave the site permanently.

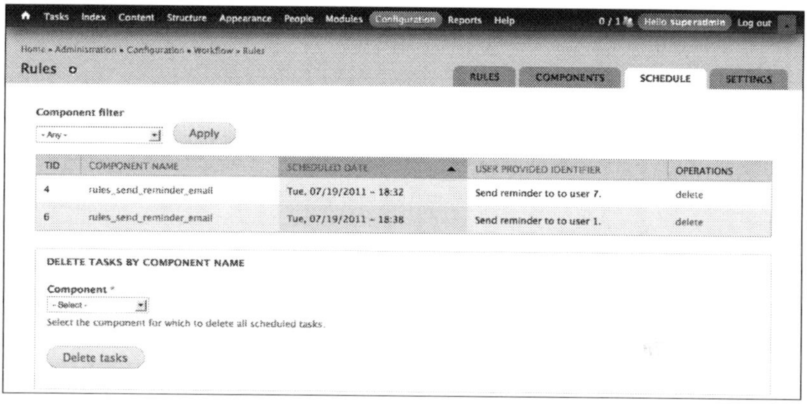

FIGURE 12.16 An example of how scheduled reminders may look in the Rules interface.

How to demo

1   Log in to the site as administrator.
2   Go to admin/config/workflow/rules/schedule and verify that a reminder e-mail has been scheduled to be sent out to the administrator in one month.
3   Log out and log in again.
4   Check that the scheduled time for the reminder has been pushed forward by a minute or so.

Required preparations

• A standard Drupal installation.

Suggested solution

1 Go to the components tab in Rules and add a new *action set*. Give it the name *send reminder e-mail*. Have the action set receive a user object as parameter, with the label *account*. (See *rules components* in this chapter.)

2 In the action set, add the action *send mail*, with *[account:mail]* as the recipient. Use replacement patterns to include the user name in the sent message. (See *managing actions* in this chapter.)

3 At the Rules overview page, add a new reaction rule *schedule reminder e-mail*, triggering on the event *user has logged in*. (See *configuring reaction rules* in this chapter.)

4 In the reaction rule, add the action *schedule component evaluation*. Select the *send reminder e-mail* component. Set *+1 month* as scheduled evaluation date, *send reminder to to user [account:uid]* as identifier, and select the logged in user to send as parameter to the action set. (See *scheduling actions with Rules Scheduler* in this chapter.)

Comments

- If the client wants repeated reminders, this can be achieved by having the action set *scheduling itself* in (say) another two months. When repeating e-mails, it is important to allow users to opt-out and turn off the notifications.

Exercises: News site

These exercises build on previous exercises in the *news site* suite. They can be carried out individually, with some preparations, or in sequence with the previous exercises. The exercises require using the concepts described part A and B in this book, as well as concepts from the Rules and Flag chapters.

UNPUBLISH COMMENTS AT THE THIRD SPAM FLAG

As site editor, I would like comments receiving at least three independent spam flags to be unpublished. This is important since it reduces the manual work needed to keep the site tidy.

How to demo

1 Log in to the site as writer.
2 Post a comment to an article, and mark it as spam. (Create an article first, if necessary.)
3 Log out and log in as editor. Mark the comment as spam again.
4 In a separate browser, as anonymous visitor, mark the comment as spam again. Reload the page to verify that the comment is now unpublished.

Required preparations

- The site should have a news article content type, as provided by the first exercise in this suite.
- The site should have the comment spam flags, as described in the exercises in the Flag chapter.

Comments

- At the time of writing, there is a bug preventing Rules from accessing the number of flags on a comment.
- If there is a flag *approved comments* used by editors to approve comments that some visitors classify as spam – as described in an exercise in the previous chapter – it would make sense to extend this user story to *never* automatically unpublish comments flagged as approved.

REPEATED REMINDERS FOR UNPUBLISHED ARTICLES

As writer, I would like to be reminded if I leave any of my unpublished articles left untouched for more than three days. After the first reminder, I would like repeated reminders every week. This is important since I sometimes forget about my unfinished articles.

How to demo

1 Log in to the site as writer.
2 Create a news article and save it in an unpublished state.
3 In another browser, log in as administrator. Visit admin/config/work-flow/rules/schedule and verify that an e-mail reminder for the created node, to the writer, is scheduled in three days' time.
4 As writer, edit the unpublished article and save it – still in an unpublished state.
5 As administrator, verify that the scheduled reminder time has been pushed forward a minute or so.
6 As writer, again, edit the unpublished article and save it in a published state.
7 As administrator, verify that the scheduled reminder is deleted.
8 Optionally: Create another unpublished article and wait for the reminder e-mail to be sent. This may take some time. As administrator, verify that a new reminder is scheduled to be sent in a week. (To speed up the process you may change the initial delay to one second, and then run cron manually.)

Required preparations

• The site should have a news article content type, as provided by the first exercise in this suite.

Comments

The quick-minded reader may want to add some more Rules logic to this feature – deleting the scheduled reminder if the corresponding article is deleted. This would be tidy, but actually not necessary: If a scheduled task fails loading the required objects – which would be the case if the article is no longer present – it will be cancelled. (Thus, there is also no need to cancel reminders if the writer's user account is removed.)

Basic Page manager and Panels configuration

The *Page manager* and *Panels* modules used to be one and the same project, originally created as an alternative to Drupal's block system. A simplified description of the two modules is:

- *Page manager* is a tool for defining new, arbitrary paths on your Drupal site, and configuring how that page should look and work. It is possible not only to define new paths, but also to override some of the paths defined by other modules. One important part of the Page manager functionality is to collect and send of *contexts* – contextual information that may affect the page.
- *Panels* is a tool for splitting the main content on a Drupal site into several regions, and defining what content each region should contain.

It is possible to use Panels without Page manager, but you will lose most of the points of using Panels. It is also possible to use Page manager without using Panels, but there are few other modules that may provide page content to Page manager – which is necessary for Page manager to be useful.

This chapter presents only the aspects of Page manager and Panels that are relevant for information structure on your Drupal site.

Installation

Page manager is a part of the *Chaos tools suite* project – hosting a number of interesting modules. The *Panels* project also contains a number of modules, of which Panels is one. This book only covers the *Page manager, Views content panes* and *Panels* modules.

The modules are installed and enabled according to the usual procedure.

> TIP
>
> The name *Chaos tools suite* stems from the original author of the project – Earl Miles – who at drupal.org uses the nick name *merlinofchaos*. Apart from Page manager and Panels, he is also the original author of the Views module, and is one of the most appreciated contributors to the Drupal module ecosystem. Hat's off for Merlin!

Managing custom pages

Page manager could be compared to a traffic cop on your website. When a page handled by Page manager on your site is requested, Page manager collects the necessary information, checks which module is responsible for the page content, and calls that module together will all the information it requires. It is worth noting that the actual content it provided by other modules – Page manager only routes the request.

At the toolbar, *structure, pages* is an overview of all the paths handled by Page manager, along with links for editing the pages. (See figure 13.1.) Pages handled by Page manager are called *custom pages*. Above the list is a link *add custom page*.

> HOW CAN THIS BE USED?
>
> Two common use cases for Panels and Page manager in combination, are customized front pages and extended administration pages.

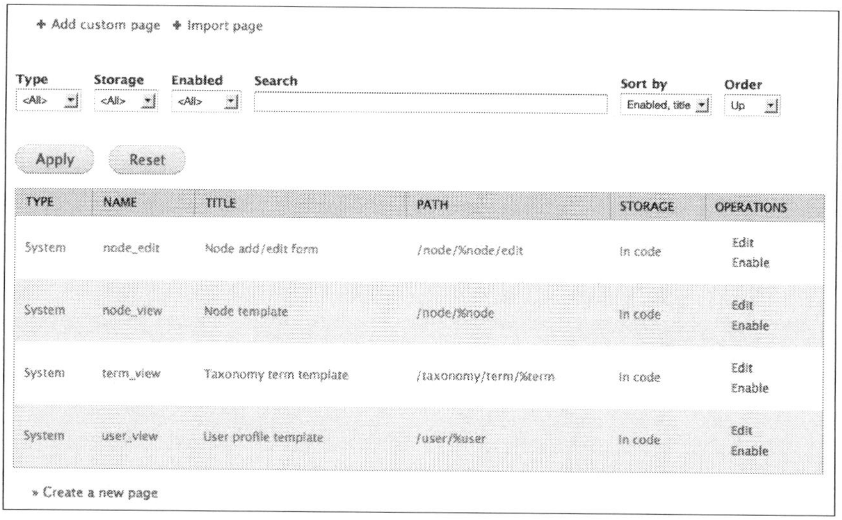

✦ Add custom page	✦ Import page					

Type	Storage	Enabled	Search		Sort by	Order
`<All> ▾`	`<All> ▾`	`<All> ▾`			`Enabled, title ▾`	`Up ▾`

Apply   Reset

TYPE	NAME	TITLE	PATH	STORAGE	OPERATIONS
System	node_edit	Node add/edit form	/node/%node/edit	In code	Edit Enable
System	node_view	Node template	/node/%node	In code	Edit Enable
System	term_view	Taxonomy term template	/taxonomy/term/%term	In code	Edit Enable
System	user_view	User profile template	/user/%user	In code	Edit Enable

» Create a new page

FIGURE 13.1 The overview page for Page manager lists all custom pages on your site.

> **TIP**
>
> Page manager allows you to override a number of paths defined by other modules – in a standard Drupal installation node view, node edit, user view and taxonomy term lists. These overridden pages are managed almost identically to other, manually defined, custom pages – the differences are pointed out below.

BASIC DATA FOR CUSTOM PAGES

The process of creating new custom pages with Page manager is divided into several steps. The first is to provide some basic data for the custom page. (See figure 13.2.)

- Administrative title: This is the name of the custom page, as used on administration pages. You will get an automatically suggested machine name.
- Administratitve description: It is a good habit to always provide your Drupal configuration with descriptions when possible – which holds for custom pages as well.

- Path: This is the path on which the custom page will be displayed. You can set dynamic parts of the path by using the placeholder *%keyword* (required part) or *!keyword* (optional part) as parts in the path. See the section about argument settings for details.
- Make this your site home page: If this option is set, the site settings will be updated to make this custom page the front page.
- Variant type: This option decides how the content of the custom page should be provided. Page manager provides the option *HTTP response code* (see separate section), while the *Panel* option – not surprisingly – is provided by the Panels module. This setting cannot be changed once the the page is saved.

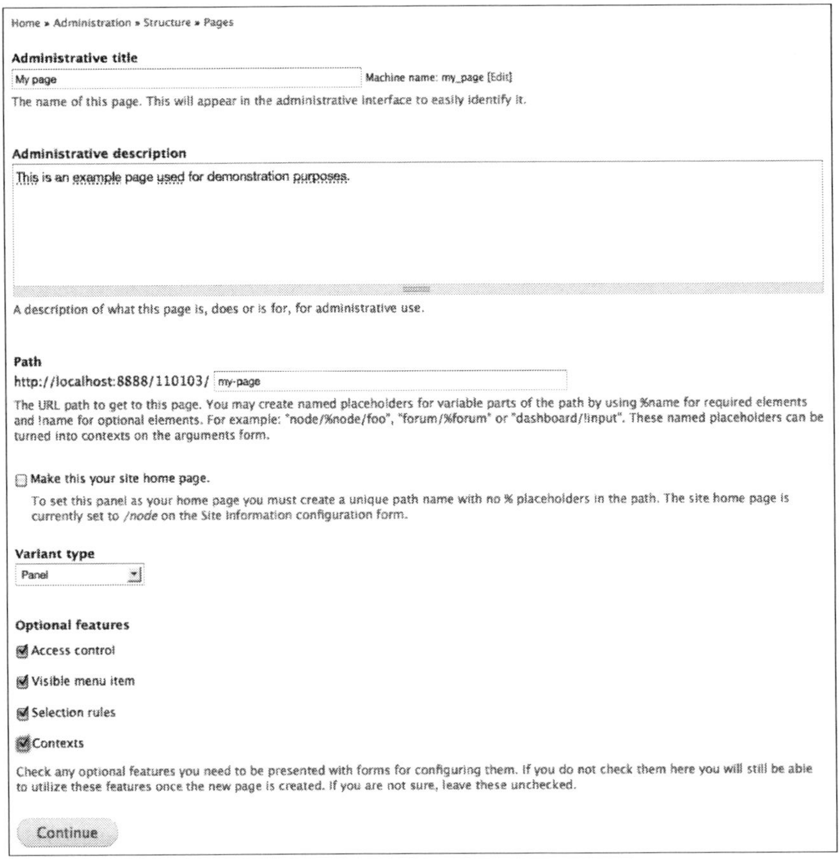

FIGURE 13.2 The first step of creating a new custom page is to set some basic data. Some of the basic data cannot be changed once the page is saved.

- Optional features: If any of these settings are checked (*access control, visible menu item, selection rules, contexts*), their respective settings pages will be included in the wizard for creating the custom page. You can edit and change the settings after creating and saving the page, too. See separate sections for details about how these settings work.

ARGUMENT SETTINGS

If the custom page path includes optional or required keywords (*!keyword* or *%keyword*, respectively), Page manager can use the values provided in the path to load *contextual objects* – see figure 13.3. (See separate section for details about how to utilize these objects.) A click on the *change* button at *context assigned* opens a dialogue where you can specify how Page manager should interpret the provided path argument. In most cases, the path arguments are numeric IDs used to load the corresponding node, user or taxonomy term, but other options are available, too. You are also provided an opportunity to give an administrative name (*context identifier*) for the object loaded from the path argument.

If you for some reason wouldn't like to load any contextual object with the path argument, choose *no context assigned*.

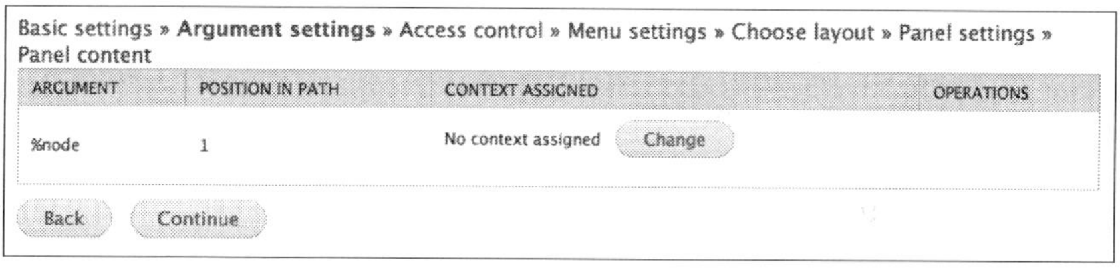

Basic settings » **Argument settings** » Access control » Menu settings » Choose layout » Panel settings » Panel content

ARGUMENT	POSITION IN PATH	CONTEXT ASSIGNED	OPERATIONS
%node	1	No context assigned Change	

Back   Continue

FIGURE 13.3 If the custom page path contains dynamic parts – arguments – Page manager may use the provided values to load data.

HOW CAN THIS BE USED?

Keywords in a path *user/%account/message/%friend* can be used to load two separate user accounts – with IDs corresponding to *%account* and *%friend*. These could then be used to (with Views) list nodes written by %account and addressed to %friend. The keyword in the path *replies/%comment* could be used to load the comment with ID %comment, and (with Views) list all comments posted as a reply to that comment.

ACCESS CONTROL

The *access control* settings allows you to set up conditions that must be met to make the custom page accessible. This could for example be that the acting user is logged in, that the content being viewed is of a particular type, or that the acting user has permission to edit the viewed node. Which conditions can be used depend on the available contextual objects – if there are two user objects available, for example, the array of conditions will include *user: compare.*

A select list will show you which types of conditions are available, and any existing conditions can be edited by clicking the corresponding gear button – and erased by clicking the button with a cross on it. (See figure 13.4.)

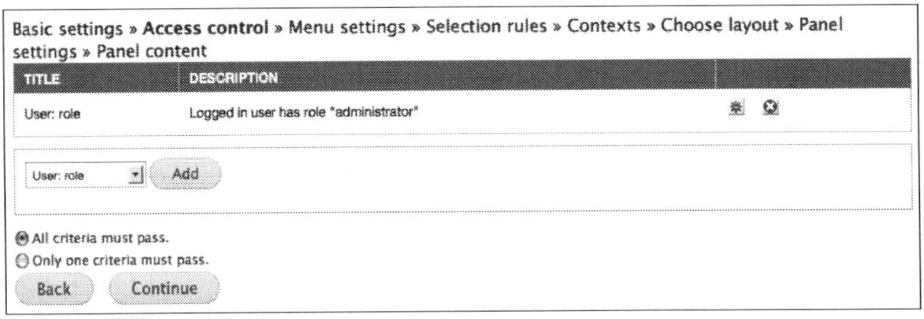

FIGURE 13.4 Access control decides when a custom page as a whole should be visible.

HOW CAN THIS BE USED?

A custom page with the path *admin/content/comments/spam* could have access settings only letting users allowed to administer comments to reach the page. A custom page with the path *node/%node/comments* could have access settings only making the page accessible only if the viewed node is an article.

TIP

Links leading to pages that you are not allowed to visit will normally not be displayed. This is a feature making it possible to use access rules to make custom pages appear as tabs only on nodes of selected types.

> **TIP**
>
> Access control for nodes, users and terms are set by their respective modules, and the access settings in Page manager are skipped. The acting user will always be available as an object when configuring access control.

> **TIP**
>
> The acting user will always be available as an object when configuring access control.

MENU ITEMS

The available menu settings in Page manager are close to identical with the ones found in Views (see figure 13.5) – see the description in the second Views chapter for details. Page manager has one more option for menu items, though – *local action*. Local actions are similar to tabs, but are (in a standard installation) displayed with a plus sign and a link right above the

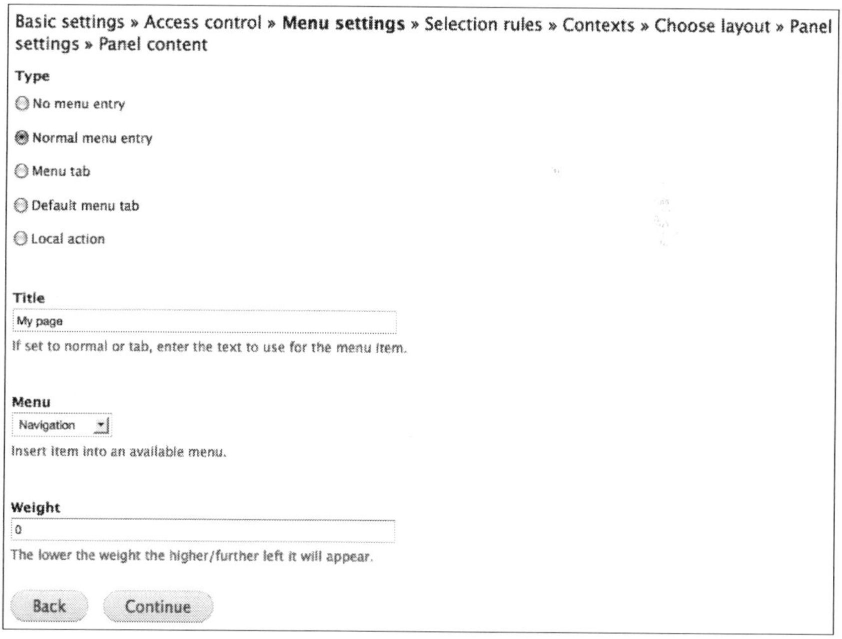

Basic settings » Access control » **Menu settings** » Selection rules » Contexts » Choose layout » Panel settings » Panel content

Type
- ⊙ No menu entry
- ⊛ Normal menu entry
- ⊙ Menu tab
- ⊙ Default menu tab
- ⊙ Local action

Title

My page

If set to normal or tab, enter the text to use for the menu item.

Menu

Navigation ▾

Insert item into an available menu.

Weight

0

The lower the weight the higher/further left it will appear.

Back   Continue

FIGURE 13.5 The menu settings for custom pages are very similar to the menu settings in Views.

main content. Also, while Drupal requires two menu tabs for displaying them, even solo local actions will be rendered.

> **HOW CAN THIS BE USED?**
>
> A custom page with the path *admin/content/comments/spam* can be displayed as a menu tab on the administration page for comments. A custom page with the path *user/%account/comments* can be displayed as a menu tab on user pages.

SELECTION RULES AND VARIANTS

Page manager allows you to create multiple *variants* for one single path. When a custom page is called, Page manager goes through the stack of variants for that custom page, and uses the first one that has fulfilled *selection rules*. One common way of utilizing this is to have separate variants for different node types, all used on the custom page *node/%node*.

Selection rules are configured in the same way as access control, and are just like the access control dependent on the available contextual objects.

> **HOW CAN THIS BE USED?**
>
> The custom page for node display, node/%node, could have a variant called only if a basic page is being displayed. A custom page used as site front page could have separate variants loaded for administrators and other users.

> **TIP**
>
> If no selection rule is fulfilled, Page manager will send back control of the path to Drupal. Drupal will then try to use any default behavior for the path – which works for paths defined by other modules – or fall back to a 404 response (page not found).

CONTEXTUAL OBJECTS

The settings for contextual objects (*contexts*) is, at least in an information structure perspective, the most important and most intersting part of Page manager. These settings allow you to gather information from other parts of the website, making it available to modify the page's behavior and content.

Contextual objects are added in two different ways (see figure 13.6):

- By manual selection, for example a specific user or node. You may also use this to add *the acting user* as a contextual object.
- By relationships to existing contextual objects – such as the vocabulary for a loaded taxonomy term, or the author of a given node. This is the most common way of adding contextual objects.

A third way of adding contextual objects is the argument settings – loaded by dynamic parts of the path of the custom page. These are configured at the *arguments* settings – see the section above for details.

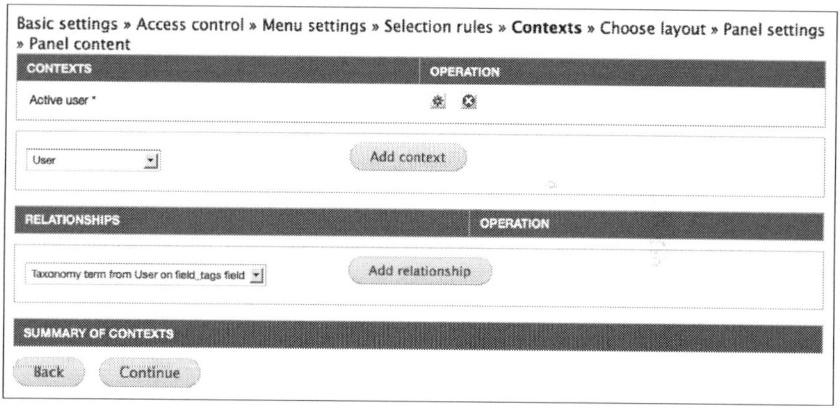

FIGURE 13.6 Contextual objects are one of the most important functionalities in Page manager. The settings allow you to load data from your website, making it available for the custom page.

A custom page displaying a node could load the node author as contextual object, thereby providing more options for use and show data related to the author. On a site with a vocabulary *section*, used to categorize articles, a custom page for article display could load the viewed article's section as a contextual object, then load the top parent term – and finally (with Views) list more articles in the same top-level section.

Panels configuration

Since Page manager and Panels integrate tightly, it is difficult to note where the border between them is. If you configure a custom page step by step, the border is here! Below is a description of the final steps for configuring a custom page getting its content from Panels – if you are creating another type of custom page (such as *HTTP response code*), you won't see these settings.

LAYOUT

One of the points of Panels is to allow you as administrator to split the main content into different regions. How this is done is determined by the panel's *layout*. Panels comes with a number of layouts, grouped by their number of columns. (See figure 13.7.)

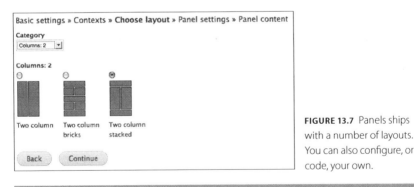

FIGURE 13.7 Panels ships with a number of layouts. You can also configure, or code, your own.

The *flexible* layout allows you to build your own layout by pointing and clicking. The tool is rather complex – but far from impossible to understand – and is not described further in this book.

BASIC SETTINGS FOR THE PANEL

On the next configuration page, you are prompted to set some basic data for the panel. (See figure 13.8.)

- Administrative title: This is the name of the variant constituted by this panel.
- Disable Drupal blocks/regions: This option stops any regular blocks from being displayed in your theme's regions, making the panel alone responsible for all the content on the page. This option may be useful on a front page.
- Renderer: In a default installation only the *standard* option is available. With the *Panels In-Place Editor* module enabled you will have another option – but it is not described here.
- CSS ID: Any string entered here will be used as CCS ID for the panel, making it easier to modify the presentation of this specific page.
- CSS code: Any CSS code entered here will be used with the panel. There are several reasons to put CSS in your theme instead of in your Drupal database – use this setting only if you have good reasons.

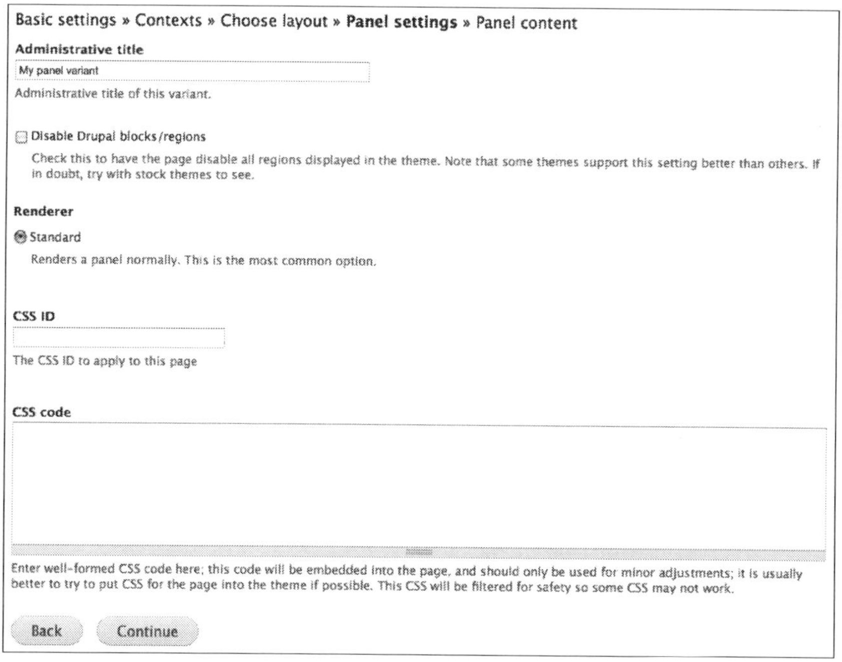

Basic settings » Contexts » Choose layout » **Panel settings** » Panel content

Administrative title

My panel variant

Administrative title of this variant.

☐ Disable Drupal blocks/regions

Check this to have the page disable all regions displayed in the theme. Note that some themes support this setting better than others. If in doubt, try with stock themes to see.

Renderer

◉ Standard

Renders a panel normally. This is the most common option.

CSS ID

The CSS ID to apply to this page

CSS code

Enter well-formed CSS code here; this code will be embedded into the page, and should only be used for minor adjustments; it is usually better to try to put CSS for the page into the theme if possible. This CSS will be filtered for safety so some CSS may not work.

[Back] [Continue]

FIGURE 13.8 Basic settings for the panel mainly concern the presentation of the panel.

PANEL CONTENT

The last step of configuration is to add actual content to the regions in the panel. (See figure 13.9.) This is done by clicking the gear for the relevant region and select *add content*. In the resulting dialogue you may select among available *panes* – pieces of content that can be placed in the panel. The panes are grouped into categories, in order to make them a bit easier to overview. (See figure 13.10.)

Which panes are available depends on the contextual objects available on the custom page, but some examples are:

- Block: All blocks on the website are available as panes.
- Page elements: Elements like tabs, the site name and the breadcrumbs can be used as panes.
- Node: If a node is available as context, different parts of the node and its related information may be used as individual panes – such as node title, the comment form or attached files.
- Entities: Most entities – such as users or taxonomy terms – can be embedded as panes, in a view mode you select.
- Entity tokens: Tokens built from entity data are automatically available as panes.
- Fields: All fields for the available contextual objects can be used as content panes.
- Existing nodes on the website can be added as separate panes, even without being available as contextual objects. This is done by the *existing node* option, in the lower-left corner of the dialogue.
- You can also add custom-written content as panes. This is done by the *new custom content* in the lower-left corner of the dialogue.

Each type of pane may have its own settings, or no settings at all. (See figure 13.11 for an example.) The pane settings are not described further in this book.

On the page for adding panel content, you may also set the title for the custom page. The title will be used both in the rendered HTML page, and as HTML title (displayed in the browser header). You may either set the title manually, let the title be inherited from one of the embedded panes, or have no title at all. A manually entered title may use *substitutions* – the Page manager term for tokens – to allow dynamic titles.

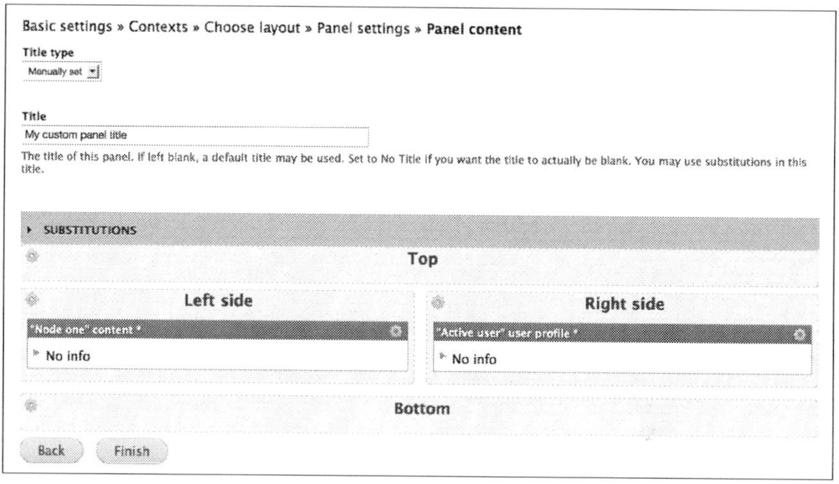

FIGURE 13.9 The last step of configuring a panel is to add content to the panel regions.

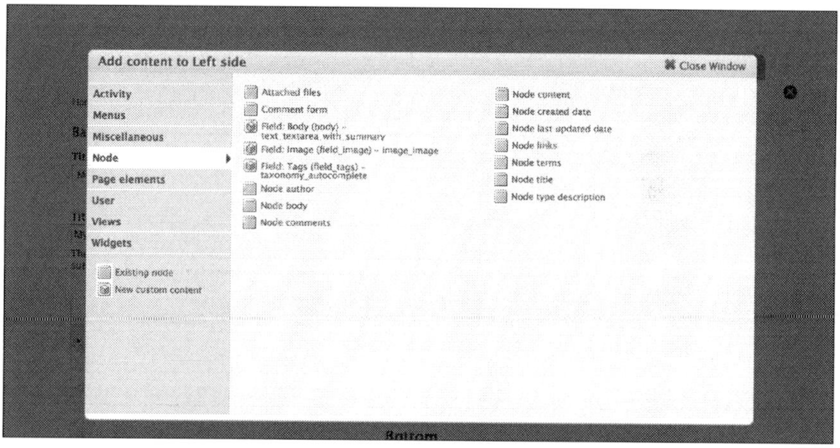

FIGURE 13.10 The available panes are divided into categories to make them easier to browse.

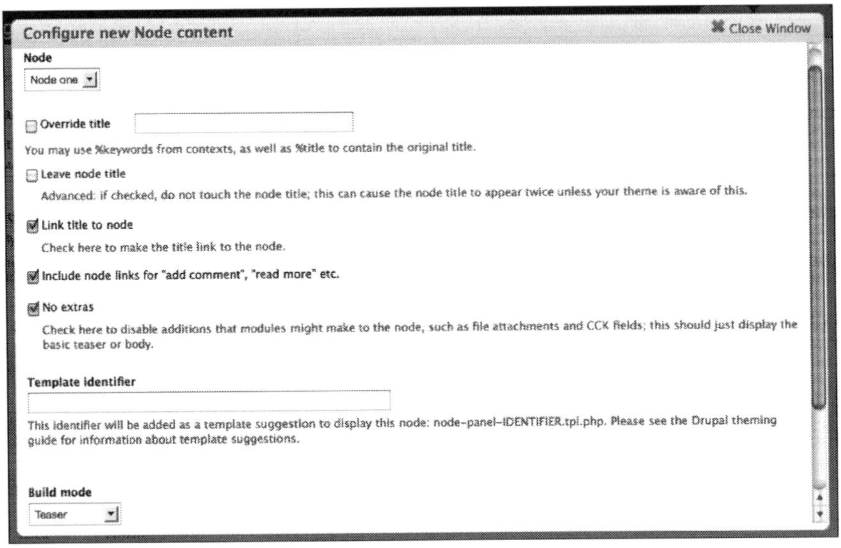

FIGURE 13.11 Each pane may have further settings – which may be specific to this type of pane.

HOW CAN THIS BE USED?

A custom page for articles may have separate panes for displaying title, body, image, tags and the comment form – distributed independently of each other. A custom page with the path *user/%accout/comments* could have the title set to *comments by %account:name.*

EDITING PANES

There are several ways of configuring and tweaking existing panes:

- The pane-specific settings can be changed by clicking the gear on the pane and selecting *settings* (or *edit* for some types of panes).
- One particularly useful setting is *visibility settings*, also accessibly through the gear menu. It allows you to use the same types of conditions used for access control and selection rules, to determine when the pane should be visible or hidden.
- Panes may be deleted by the *remove* option in the gear menu. They can also be temporarily disabled by the *disable this pane* option – then re-enabled with the option *enable this pane*.

- You can set CSS IDs and CSS classes for each pane by the *CSS properties* option, found in the gear menu.
- If the panel inherits its title from a pane, there is also an option in the gear menu for selecting this pane as the one used for setting the title.
- You may move panes between regions by clicking and dragging in the title list of each pane.

HOW CAN THIS BE USED?

A pane displaying the comment form can be displayed only if the acting user is allowed to post comments. A custom page displaying both the acting user's recent content, and the recent content by the author of a currently viewed node, can hide one of these lists if the acting user *is* the node author.

Editing custom pages and variants

When all the steps for creating a custom page eventually are over, you are brought to an overview of the custom page. (See figure 13.12.) It contains a number of tabs on the left side, while the main part of the page is occupied by the settings for the selected tab. You may switch between the tabs to edit any of the settings described above, except the variant types (such as *panel* or *HTTP response code*) – which cannot be changed.

At the overview page you will also find links to clone, export, delete and temporarily disable each variant – and the same settings are also available for the custom page as a whole. You will also find a link to add more variants to the custom page, and – since Page manager will use the first variant with matching selection rules – there is also a *reorder variants* link.

HOW CAN THIS BE USED?

A variant without any selection rules on the *node/%node* custom page may be placed at the bottom of the variant list, to be used if no other variant fits. A variant used to display articles may be cloned and then freely edited, to create a variant used for displaying basic pages.

FIGURE 13.12 The overview of a custom page allows you to switch between all its variants, and edit virtually all settings within them.

> **TIP**
>
> There is a difference between updating and saving a custom page. Just like in Views, it is a good habit to save the settings at least once to not risk losing them all when leaving the configuration.

Configuring HTTP response code pages

The procedure of adding and editing an *HTTP response code* custom page is short and easy when compared to creating panels. These types of variants, too, may have selection rules and contextual objects – but the main configuration only consists of a variant name and the response code used on this path. (See figure 13.13.)

There are three options for response codes: *404 page not found, 403 access denied* and *301 redirect*. The redirect option allows you to enter a path to which the user should be redirected. You may enter internal as well as external paths, and you may use tokens provided by contextual objects.

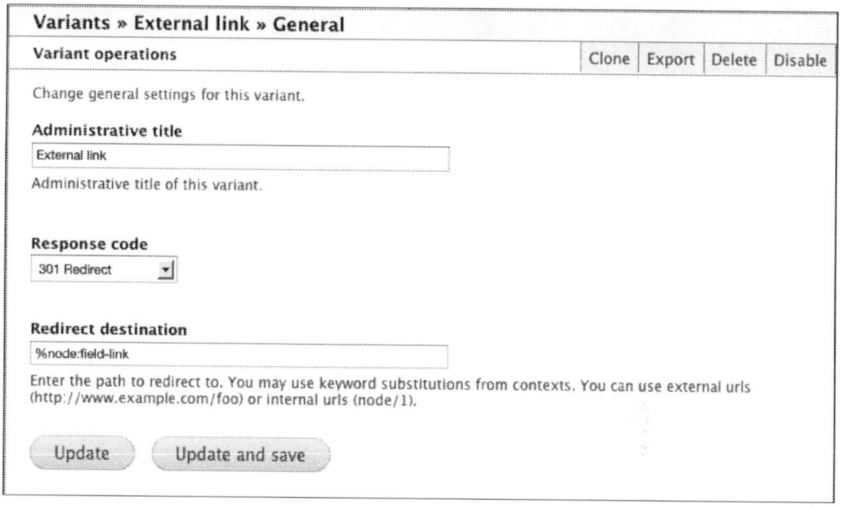

```
Variants » External link » General
```

Variant operations		Clone	Export	Delete	Disable

Change general settings for this variant.

Administrative title

```
External link
```

Administrative title of this variant.

Response code

```
301 Redirect    ▾
```

Redirect destination

```
%node:field-link
```

Enter the path to redirect to. You may use keyword substitutions from contexts. You can use external urls (http://www.example.com/foo) or internal urls (node/1).

(Update)   (Update and save)

FIGURE 13.13 The settings for custom pages of the HTTP response code type all fit within one page. Sweet.

HOW CAN THIS BE USED?

A website using nodes to build a catalogue of external web pages of interest for visitors, may use a redirect variant to send off any visitor clicking on a node to the site it links to. The same site may have another variant also checking if the acting user is allowed to edit the node, and if so redirect to the edit page instead.

TIP

When links are built, Drupal normally checks if the acting user is allowed to visit the target page. If the resulting page is a redirect, Drupal will only check if the redirect is accessible – not the page it ends with. Thus, you may end up displaying links leading to *access denied* pages if using redirects too vigorously.

> **TIP**
>
> At the time of writing, the only module providing variant types – except Panels and Page manager – is *Contextual Administration*. It is used to build customized administration pages, for example to create new nodes with node references pre-populated, account creation pages where roles are set and hidden, or placing an *add term* page in a section of the site where the terms actually are used. Your site administrators will be happier if you learn to use it well.

Views content panes

In the last section of the last chapter in this book (save the appendices), it is only fair to reward the devoted reader with one of the most powerful, flexible and fun tools for building information structure – *Views content panes*.

Views content panes is a module included in the Chaos tools suite project, and it is an excellent bridge between Page manager/Panels and Views. The module provides a new Views display type, *content pane*. Displays of this type can be inserted as panes in a panel, and makes it possible to set parts of the view configuration – not least contextual filters – from the panel.

The two most important factors making this display type powerful are:
- You can control exactly how values for your contextual filters are fed to the view, and what kind of data must be available in order to call the view. This means that you can completely ignore the clunkly (and frankly speaking quite hacky) options for creating default values for contextual filters – which is not only comfortable for you as Drupal developer, but also makes your views more secure and reliable.
- You can adjust quite a few settings for the view, for every panel you embed it in. In one panel you may use the acting user for building a contextual filter value and display ten results, and in another panel use a node author for the contextual filter and display three results. This decreases the need for separate displays and makes it easier to reuse your configuration – which in turn makes the site easier to understand, deleop and maintain.

USING VIEWS CONTENT PANES

When working with Views while the Views content pane module is enabled, you can add displays of the type *content pane*. These have a few display-specific settings, found in the *pane settings* group (see fiture 13.14):

- Admin title: This is the name used to represent the pane in the list of available content panes (in Panels).
- Admin desc: This is a closer description of the pane, shown as a tooltip in the list of available content panes (in Panels).
- Category: This is the category where the pane will be placed, also in the list of available content panes.
- Link to view: This option creates a link from the pane's title to any page display configured for the view (or to any path override).
- Use panel path: When a view is dependent on a path – such as for exposed filters displayed in blocks – this option will make the view use the path where the view is embedded.
- Argument input: This is the setting that more than any other makes this display type powerful. You may set how any contextual filter values should be collected from the panel where the view is embedded. You may set each contextual filter input separately – see below for details about the options.
- Allow settings: This setting allows you to override some of the view configuration at each embedding of the view pane. These settings will be available in the configuration for the pane – see separate section for details about the options.

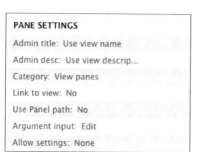

FIGURE 13.14 The Content pane display type has a number of display specific settings. The most interesting ones are *argument input* and *allow settings*.

The *admin title* option is particularly useful when a view has two different content pane displays – since they by default inherits the view name, and thus would be difficult to tell apart when working in Panels. The *category* option is particularly useful when creating a number of displays relating to the same features on a website, for example allowing to group them in a *photo gallery* category in Panels.

Input of contextual filter values in Views content panes

The *argument input* setting at the *pane settings* group has a number of options. (See figure 13.15.)

- No argument: This option collects no contextual filter value from the panel.
- Argument wildcard: This option will have the contextual filter return all results.
- From context: This is the most used setting, and makes it possible to use information from contextual objects in the panel to build filter values. In a remarkably long list you can select (1) which type of contextual object should be required when embedding the view, and (2) which data should be collected from the contextual object. Each filter input can also be checked as *context is optional*, making it possible to embed the view even if the specified type contextual object is not available in the panel. One of the most common options is to require a node object, and collect its ID as contextual filter value.
- From panel argument: If the panel's custom page has any path arguments, these may be used as contextual filter values in the view. Using *from context* will normally provide higher flexibility and precision.
- Fixed: This is used to provide a static, manually entered value for the contextual filter.
- Input on pane config: This allows you as administrator to manually enter a filter value in the pane configuration dialogue. At the time of writing it is not possible to use tokens in this configuration, but this feature is expected soon.

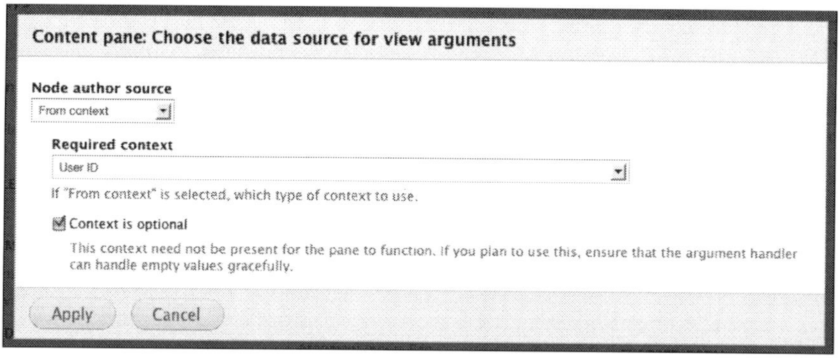

Content pane: Choose the data source for view arguments

Node author source

From context

Required context

User ID

If "From context" is selected, which type of context to use.

☑ Context is optional

This context need not be present for the pane to function. If you plan to use this, ensure that the argument handler can handle empty values gracefully.

Apply   Cancel

FIGURE 13.15 The *argument input* setting allows the display to fetch contextual filter values from contextual objects on a custom page.

HOW CAN THIS BE USED?

A display listing most recent content written by a (with contextual filters) specified user, could fetch filter value *from context* to be sure that the provided value always is a valid user ID. A display listing articles tagged with a (with contextual filters) specified term could be embedded on a node display page where a tag is loaded as a contextual object – to display similar articles – as well as on a taxonomy term page.

Override view settings with content panes

With Views, you normally need to create separate displays to achieve even minimal changes in how the view is displayed and used. With the content pane display, you may override a number of settings in the configuration dialogue displayed in panels every time you embed the view – significantly decreasing the need of different displays. (See figure 13.16.) The settings you may override are:

- Use pager: This allows overriding the pager settings in the view.
- Items per page: This allows overriding the number of results displayed per page.
- Pager offset: This allows overriding the offset for the view, skipping the first few results.
- Link to view: This allows overriding the option to link the pane title to any page display (or path override).

- Path override: This allows manually setting a new base path for the view, to use instead of any page display. This is useful when using exposed settings in a view content pane.
- Title override: This is the most common setting, and allows manually overriding the view title.
- Use exposed widgets form as pane configuration: This setting embeds any exposed settings as part of the pane configuration dialogue, instead of displaying them to the end user.
- Fields override: This option allows you as administrator to select which view fields should be included or excluded from display.

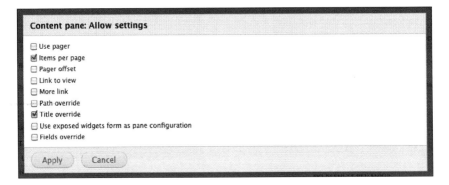

FIGURE 13.16 The *allow settings* options makes it possible to override parts of the view configuration from the panels where the view is embedded.

HOW CAN THIS BE USED?

A display listing content created by a (with contextual filters) specified user may – with the *title override* option – be given the title *my content* in a panel showing the acting user's content. A comment list with filters on publishing day exposed can be embedded three times on the same panel page in order to – with the setting *use exposed widges form as pane configuration* – display comments written today, yesterday and the day before that.

TIP

The Views content panes module also provides a display type called *context*. It can be loaded as a context in custom pages, with two effects. The first is that individual elements from the view – such as the pager, exposed settings or selected rows – may be outputted as panes. The second is that the view results may be loaded as new contextual objects. The latter function allows strange and wonderful things to happen.

Exercises: Documentation site

These exercises build on previous exercises in the *Documentation site* suite. They can be carried out individually, with some preparations, or in sequence with the previous exercises. The exercises require using the concepts described part A and B in this book, as well as this chapter.

Video recordings of the suggested solutions to these exercises can be found at nodeone.se/learn-drupal.

EASILY UPDATE YOUR OWN COLLECTIONS

As site member viewing my own documentation collections, I would like to have the edit form for the collection available in a separate column. This is important since I almost always want to change the content of a collection when I visit my collection pages, and this feature would save me a click on the edit tab.

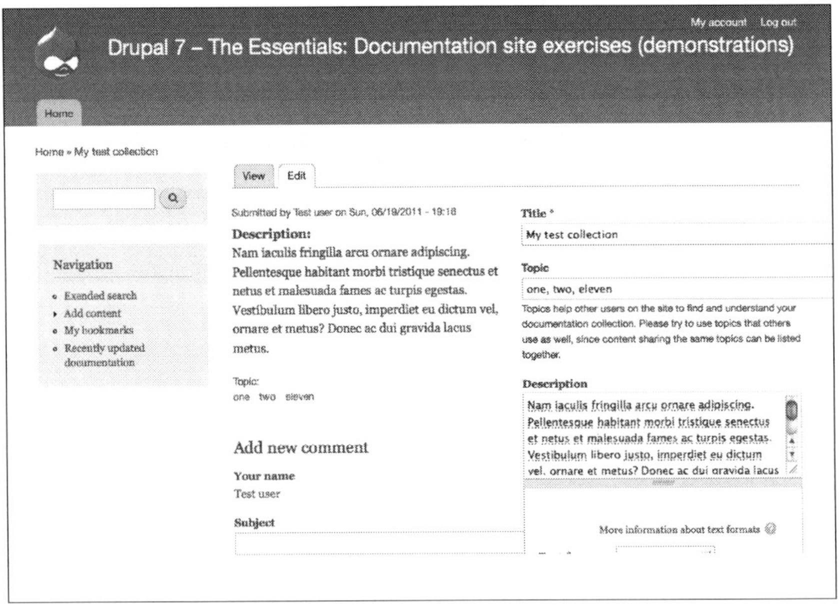

FIGURE 13.17 An example of how the documentation collection pages may look.

How to demo

1 Log in to the site with an account different from user 1. (Create an account if necessary.)
2 Create a collection.
3 When visiting the collection page, verify that you end up at a page displaying both the collection content and the edit form for the collection in separate columns.
4 Log out. With a user account allowed to view and edit the collection, but different from the collection author, visit the collection page. (You could use the user 1 account.)
5 Verify that the collection is displayed without any editing form.

Required preparations

• The site should have the documentation page and collection content types, as provided by the first exercises in this suite.

Suggested solution

1 Go to the overview page for Page manager. Enable the *node/%node/edit* page and add a new variant with the name *editing own collection*. Make it a *panel* variant, and check that you want to add both selection rules and contexts. (See *managing custom pages* in this chapter.)
2 As selection rule, add *node: type* and verify that the node being edited as a documentation collection. (See *selection rules and variants*.)
3 In the context configuration, add the node author as a context by selecting *user from node (on node.node_author)* in the list for adding relationships. Call the new context object *collection author*. (See *contextual objects*.)
4 In the panel layout configuration, select a two column layout. In the basic panel settings, just leave all settings to default values. (See *layout* and *basic settings for the panel*.)

5   In the panel content configuration, add *node content* to the left column. Set all options to mimic the full node display. (See *panel content*.)

6   In the right column, add the *general form* pane. (See *panel content*.)

7   Let the custom page inherit the title from one of the panes. Edit both panes to override their titles with an empty text, as to not duplicate titles on the page. (See *panel content*.)

8   Update and save the custom page. Now, with all context objects available, revisit the *selection rules* tab and add the *criteria user: compare* to verify that the logged in user is the same as the collection author. (See *selection rules and variants*.)

9   In the Page manager overview, enable and edit the *node/%node* custom page.

10 Add a new variant with the name *redirect for editing own collections*. Make it a *HTTP response code* variant, and check that you want to add both selection rules and contexts. (See *managing custom pages*.)

11 Add the same selection rules and contexts as in the previous custom page – using the redirect only on collections, and adding the collection author as context.

12 As response code, choose *301 redirect* with the target *node/%node:nid/ edit*. Update and save the custom page. (See *configuring HTTP redirect response code pages*.)

13 Edit the selection rules again, and add the criteria that the logged in user must be the same as the collection author.

Comments

- There are several possible approaches to this user story. The suggested solution redirects to the edit page. A more natural approach would probably be to embed the edit form on the view page, but at the time of writing a bug makes this impossible.

- In the redirect variant, it would make sense to also add the selection rule *node: accessible* to verify that the logged in user has access to edit the collection. Even if this is the case with the current site configuration, it may change in the future.

VIEW DOCUMENTATION PAGES IN COLLECTION CONTEXT

As site builder, I would like to be able to know which collection is currently active – if any – when a user views a documentation page. I want this implemented by being able to display documentation pages at URLs on the form *node/[collection-nid]/[docspage-nid]*. This is important since it allows further enhancements on the site, displaying documentation pages within the context of a collection. *(Note that this not a real user story, as it doesn't provide any value to end users of the site. It should rather be a development task within a user story.)*

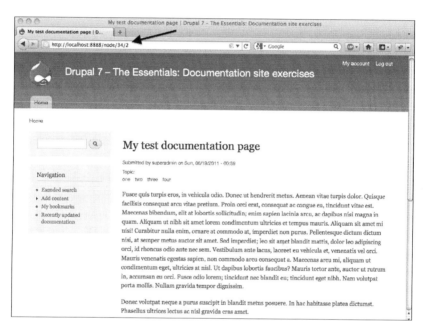

FIGURE 13.18 An example of how documentation pages may be viewed – note the URL in the browser.

How to demo

1   Log in to the site.
2   Create a documentation page. Remember its node ID.
3   Create a documentation collection, including the new documentation page. Remember its node ID.

4   Manually enter the URL on the form *node/[collection-nid]/[docspage-nid]*. Verify that the documentation page is displayed.

5   Alter the URL and replace the documentation page node ID with a string or a number not corresponding to a documentation page node ID. Verify that you are given a "404 page not found" response.

6   Alter the URL to replace the collection node ID with a string or a number not corresponding to a collection node ID. Verify that you are given a "404 page not found" response.

Required preparations

- The site should have a news article content type, as provided by the first exercise in this suite.

Suggested solution

1   Go to the Page manager overview and add a new custom page. Call it *documentation page within a collection*, give it the path *node/%collection/%docspage* and check that you want to have selection rules. Make it a *panel* variant. (See *managing custom pages* in this chapter.)

2   In the argument configuration, set both *%collection* and *%docspage* to be interpreted as node IDs, and give them the labels *collection* and *documentation page*. (See *argument settings*.)

3   In the selection rules configuration, add conditions to check that the collection and documentation page correspond to the expected node types. (See *selection rules and variants*.)

4   Chose the single column layout. Leave the basic panel configuration as it is. (See *panels configuration*.)

5   In the panel content, add *node content* and have the settings mimic a standard node display. Override the title with an empty string, and instead let the panel variant as a whole display the title, inherited from the pane. (See *panel content*.)

Comments

- If there is access control on the documentation collection, it makes sense to also disallow viewing documentation pages within that context. It also makes sense to add access control on the documentation page, to assure that the acting user may view it. (Page manager won't display nodes that a user isn't allowed to access, but explicitly verifying the access makes it possible to have custom reactions.)
- It would definitely make sense to verify that the viewed documentation page actually is included in the active collection. However, this requires conditions not natively supported by CTools. If installing the *Rules Bonus Pack* module, Page manager may use Rules components to check conditions – drastically increasing the possibilities for access control.
- To make the viewer more aware of the collection she is browsing, a custom pane could be added above the documentation page, saying *You are currently browsing the %collection:title collection.*

SELECT LIST FOR NAVIGATING COLLECTIONS

As site visitor viewing a documentation collection, I would like to easily switch between different documentation pages in the collection. I would like to do this using a select list at the top of the page, containing all the pages in the collection. I would like the same select list available when viewing the collection itself. This is important since it helps me view the individual pages without having to refer to the collection all the time.

How to demo

1 Log in to the site.
2 Create a documentation collection, linking to at least two documentation pages. (Create documentation pages first, if necessary.)
3 At the documentation collection, verify that there is a select list with the included documentation pages.
4 When selecting a page in the list, verify that you are presented with the relevant page and that the list is still present.

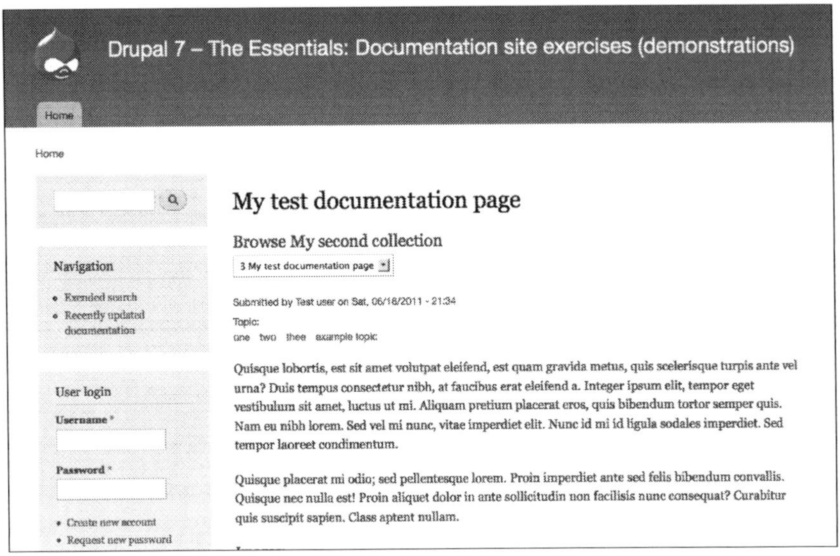

FIGURE 13.19 An example of how the finished documentation page may look.

Required preparations

- The site should have the documentation page and collection content types, as provided by the first exercises in this suite.
- The site should be able to display documentation pages in the context of a collection, as described in the previous exercise.

Suggested solution

1 Create a new node view with the name *collection navigation*. No content type restriction is needed, no sorting, and no displays. (See *creating new views* in the Views basics chapter.)

2 Add a contextual filter *content: nid*, to filter out the active collection. Set title override to *browse %1* and also verify that it is an ID for a collection node. (See *configuring contextual filters* in the advanced Views configuration chapter.)

3 Add a relationship, join in the documentation pages included in the collection. Make sure to include all deltas. (See *adding relationships* in the advanced Views configuration chapter.)

4 Add a view field *content: nid*. Exclude the field, and make sure it has no label. (See *adding view fields* in Views basics chapter.)

5 Add another view field *content: nid*. Use the relationship to the documentation pages, to get the node ID for the page instead of the collection. Enable rewriting, and change the field content to *node/[nid]/[nid_1]* – the path used for viewing documentation pages in a collection context. Exclude the field. (See *rewriting view fields* in the advanced Views configuration chapter.)

6 Add a view field *global: view result counter*. Remove any label. (See *adding view fields*.)

7 Edit the title field included by default. Have use the relationship to the documentation pages. Also reorder the fields to have the title last. (See *utilizing relationships in configuration* in the advanced Views configuration chapter.)

8 Change the view style to *jump menu*. Use the page node ID field as path. (See *view formats* in the Views basics chapter.)

9 Add a *content pane* display to the view. Change the *argument input* settings to *from context*, fetching a content ID from a node available as context. (See *input of contextual filter values in views content panes*, in this chapter.)

10 Set an administrative title, description and category of the display, so it will be easy to understand its functions when embedding it in a panel. (See *using views content panes* in this chapter.)

11 In the overview for Page manager, edit the custom page for displaying a documentation page in the context of a collection. Add the new view at the top of the page, using the collection as filter value for the view. (See *panel content* in this chapter.)

12 At the custom page for *node/%node*, add a new variant called *documentation collections*. Use selection rules to only use this variant when viewing collections. (See *selection rules and variants* in this chapter.)

13 In the collection page, add the collection navigation view pane and the node content of the collection. Make sure that the panel inherits the title from the node content. (See *panel content*.)

Comments

- In this exercise it is actually possible to use a standard views block instead of a views content pane – simply because the function for loading the currently viewed node as contextual filter value is fooled by the URL being similar to a collection page. (This won't be the case in the next exercise.)
- The numbering of the pages is a bonus, not asked for in the user story.
- In the jump menu configuration, there is an option *select the current contextual filter value*. This is an inaccurate description for using the current path as default value in the list – if it matches any of the options. Checking this box will make the select list navigation more natural, since it displays the currently viewed page when possible.
- It may be a good idea to include the collection navigation at the bottom of the documentation pages as well – it seems reasonable that most people are interested in reading the next page when they are done with the current.

THIS DOCUMENTATION PAGE ALSO APPEARS IN...

As site visitor viewing a documentation page, I would like a list of all collections that include this page. If I am already browsing a collection, I only want other collections to be listed. This is important since it may help me find and use other collections, learning more about how to use the topics I am studying.

How to demo

1 Make sure there are at least three documentation pages available.
2 Make sure that there are at least two documentation collections, and that there is at least one page they both refer to, and that they both have at least one page not referred to by another collection.

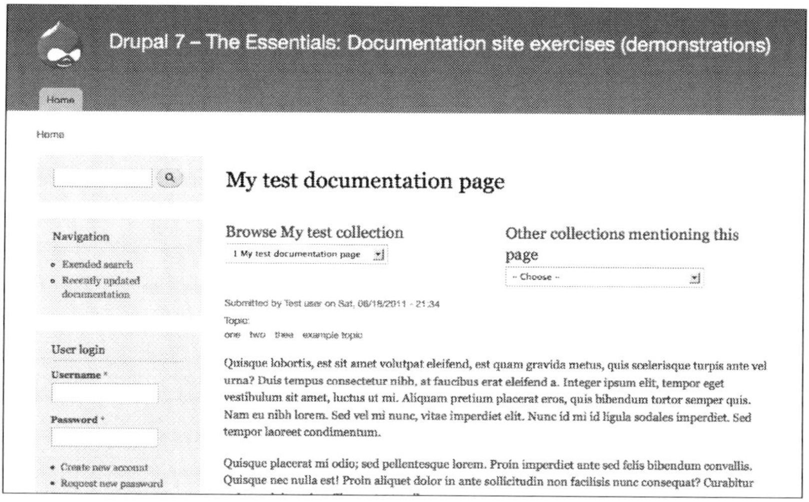

FIGURE 13.20 An example of how a list of collections may look, when viewing a documentation page.

3 Outside any collection context, view a documentation page included in more than one collection. Verify that there are links to the collections available on the documentation page.

4 Verify that the links lead to the documentation page viewed *in the context of the selected collection.*

5 Verify that any currently active selection is not present in the list of collections referring to the viewed page.

Required preparations

- The site should have the documentation page and collection content types, as provided by the first exercises in this suite.
- The site should be able to display documentation pages in the context of a collection, as described in the previous two exercises.

Suggested solution

1. Create a new node view, named *collections mentioning the viewed page*. No sorting, filtering or displays are necessary at the quick-wizard page. (See *creating new views* in the Views basics chapter.)

2. Add a contextual filter on the node reference field – filtering out all collections with a given value in their documentation page references. Verify that the contextual filter value is a node ID for a documentation page. Set the title override to *collections mentioning this page*. (See *configuring contextual filters* in the advanced Views configuration chapter.)

3. Add another contextual filter on *content: nid*. Select *Display all results for the specified field* as the action to take when no filter value is present. (See *managing missing filter values* in the advanced Views configuration chapter.)

4. Validate that the (second) filter value is a collection node ID. Set the title override to *other collections mentioning this page*. In the *more* settings, check the *exclude* option. (See *configuring contextual filters* in the advanced Views configuration chapter.)

5. In the pager settings, set the view to display all results. (See *pager* in the Views basics chapter.)

6. Add a view field *content: nid*. Exclude the field, and use the rewrite options to change it to *node/[nid]/!1* – matching the path for viewing documentation pages in the context of a collection. (See *rewriting view fields* in the advanced Views configuration chapter.)

7. Edit the title view field provided by default and disable the link option. (See *editing view fields* in the Views basics chapter.)

8. Set the view format to *jump menu*. Use the rewritten node ID field as path. (See *view formats* in the Views basics chapter.)

9. Add a *content pane* display. Set administrative title, description and category in a way that makes it easy to understand the pane in Panels. (See *views content pane* in this chapter.)

10. Set the *argument input* to from context for both contextual filters, and fetch *content ID* from a node object. Make the second contextual filter value *optional*. (See *input of contextual filter values in views content panes*, in this chapter.)

11 At the Page manager overview and the *node/%node* page, add a new variant for documentation pages. Have it display the viewed page and also the view pane with collections mentioning the page. Use the viewed page as the first contextual filter input, while leaving the second empty. (See *panel content* in this chapter.)

12 At the custom page displaying documentation pages in the context of a collection, also add the view pane. Use the page for the first contextual filter value, and the collection for the second one. (See *panel content*.)

Comments

- The user story doesn't tell how the collections should be listed – jump menu is one of several options. A plain HTML list would also work.
- It could make sense to add a *no results behavior* to the view, saying *there are no (other) collections referring to this page*. However, it would be difficult to vary the the text depending on the page being viewed in the context of a collection or not – the *(other)* would be nice to exclude if there truly are no collections referring to the page.

Exercises: News site

These exercises build on previous exercises in the *news site* suite. They can be carried out individually, with some preparations, or in sequence with the previous exercises. The exercises require using the concepts described part A and B in this book, as well as this chapter.

REDIRECT FACT BOXES TO ARTICLE PAGES

As site owner, I would like to prevent visitors from accidentally viewing fact boxes directly on their node pages. This is important since fact boxes are always a part of articles, and should never be viewed out of context. (Also, the content pages for fact boxes are not styled properly.)

How to demo

1   Log in to the site as writer.
2   Create an article, and then create a fact box relating to the article. Copy the URL to the fact box page.
3   Log out. As anonymous visitor, visit the page for the fact box (by pasting the URL).
4   Verify that you are redirected to the article page.

Required preparations

- The site should have a news article and fact box content types, as provided by the first exercises in this suite.

Comments

- This is a rather simple case when fact boxes relate to the articles, since it makes it easy to access the relevant node ID. If the reference was put on the articles – relating to any number of fact boxes – it would still be possible to achieve this functionality, but it would (most likely) require using the fascinating *context* display style in views and then loading the first result of the view as a context in Page manager.

ALTERNATIVE FACT BOX REDIRECTS FOR WRITERS

As writer, I would not like to be redirected to the article page when viewing a fact box, but rather the fact box edit page. This is important since I should be able to edit the content of fact boxes.

How to demo

1   Log in to the site as writer.
2   Create an article, and then create a fact box relating to the article.
3   When saving the fact box, verify that you are end up at the edit page for the fact box rather than the view page.

4   Manually truncate the URL of the fact box edit page to "node/NID" rather than "node/NID/edit". Verify that you are still redirected to the edit page.

Required preparations

- The site should have a news article content type, as provided by the first exercise in this suite.

SECTION LISTS FOR TOP SECTIONS ONLY

As site owner, I would like to redirect site visitors viewing taxonomy term lists for any sub section to the list for the corresponding top-level section. This is important since maintaining all the sub section lists takes up too much time for the editors, and the time is better spent improving the top-level section lists.

How to demo

1   Log in to the site as writer.
2   Create an article (Alpha), placing it in the *world* section.
3   Create another article (Beta), placing it in the *Europe* sub section.
4   Log out. As anonymous visitor, visit article Beta and click on its section link *Europe*. Verify that you end up on the taxonomy term list for *world*.
5   Verify that articles in world sub sections are also included in the list, by verifying that Beta is listed.

Required preparations

- The site should have a news article content type, as provided by the first exercise in this suite.
- The site should have a section vocabulary, as described in the exercise in the taxonomy chapter.

ARTICLE VIEW WITH TOP-LEVEL SECTION ARTICLE LIST

As site visitor reading a news article, I would like to have more articles in the top-level section of the viewed article displayed at the bottom of the page. This is important since it helps me find more content I am interested in reading.

How to demo

1 Log in to the site as writer.
2 Create an article (Alpha) and place it in the top-level section *world*.
3 Create another article (Beta), also in the *world* section.
4 Create a third article (Gamma) and place it in the sub section *Europe*.
5 Create a fourth article (Delta) and place it in the top-level section *science*.
6 Log out. As anonymous visitor, view the Gamma article. Verify that Alpha and Beta are listed below Gamma. Verify that Delta is not listed.
7 View the Alpha article. Verify that the currently viewed article is excluded from the list below Alpha – only Beta should be present. Verify that Delta is not listed.

Required preparations

- The site should have a news article content type, as provided by the first exercise in this suite.
- The site should have the section vocabulary, as described by the exercise in the taxonomy chapter.

Comments

- This result is very similar to the exercise redirecting visitors to top-level taxonomy term lists. One difference is that this list only includes articles *directly* marked with the top-level term – sub sections are not included. This would be possible to do using the "depth" settings for contextual filters on taxonomy terms (in Views), but it would also lead to heavy data-base queries. An alternative approach is to use Rules to populate another taxonomy on the news articles with the top-level section, and then run a contextual filter against that field. It would mean duplicated data, which generally should be avoided, but also a lighter query.

ARTICLE VIEW WITH SAME-LEVEL AND TOP-LEVEL SECTION LISTS

As site visitor reading a news article, I would like to have more articles in the top-level section of the viewed article displayed below the article, and also a list with articles in the same sub section as the viewed article. If the article is in a top-level section, there should only be one list present. This is important since it helps me find more content I am interested in reading, without having me browse through duplicated lists.

How to demo

1   Log in to the site as writer.
2   Create an article (Alpha) and place it in the top-level section *world*.
3   Create another article (Beta) and place it, too, in *world*.
4   Create a third article (Gamma) and place it in the sub section *Europe*.
5   Create a fourth article (Delta) and place it, too, in *Europe*.
6   Log out. As anonymous visitor, view the Gamma article. Verify that Alpha and Beta are listed below Gamma. Verify that Delta is listed in a separate list (while Gamma, as the currently viewed article, is excluded).
7   View the Alpha article. Verify that Beta is listed below the article (while Alpha, as the currently viewed article, is excluded). Verify that there is only one list of articles present.

Required preparations

- The site should have a news article content type, as provided by the first exercise in this suite.
- The site should have a section vocabulary, as described in the exercises in the taxonomy chapter.

SECTION EDITOR PRESENTATION

As site owner, I would like to have section editors' presented with photo and contact information along with all articles within my top-level section. This is important since it increases the trust our readers to have for our news, if they feel that they can contact the responsible editor – thereby increasing our revenue possibilities.

How to demo

1   Log in to the site as administrator.
2   Edit a user account ("Alice"), adding the top-level section *world* to it.
3   Edit another user account ("Bob"), adding the top-level section *science*.
4   Log out. As anonymous visitor, view an article in the Europe sub section. (Create one if necessary.) Verify that Alice's image and e-mail address is displayed. Verify that Bob's presentation is not present.

Required preparations

- The site should have a news article content type, as provided by the first exercise in this suite.
- The site should have a section vocabulary present, and applied to both news articles and user accounts, as described in the exercises in the taxonomy chapter.

Appendix 1:
Installation and code base management

INSTALLING DRUPAL

Technical requirements for installing Drupal

Drupal is written in PHP and uses a database to store much of the information being handled on your site. The most common platform for running Drupal is a so-called LAMP stack – Linux, Apache, MySQL, PHP – but Drupal will run on any platform that can run PHP and has a database usable by Drupal. You can, for example, run Drupal on Windows of Mac platforms.

Drupal 7 runs all database queries through an abstraction layer – PHP Data Objects (PDO) – which theoretically allows Drupal to run on a wide variety of databases. To work in practice, though, you need drivers to manage the interpretation necessary between Drupal and PDO. This limits your options of databases to use, but all the most common databases already have drivers ready to use with Drupal. At time of writing there is support for MySQL (and compatible databases, such as MySQLi and MariaDB), PostgreSQL, SQLite, MS SQL, Oracle databases and the non-relational database MongoDB.

A clean install of Drupal 7 requires that PHP can use about 32 MB of memory, but a full website will most likely require much more. The exact memory requirements depends on how a site is set up (and optimized), but a Drupal developer with the *php memory limit* setting at 128 MB will rarely or never need to care about the site's memory.

Installing Drupal

You install Drupal by the following steps:

1   Dowload Drupal and put it on a server.
2   Make two adjustments to Drupal's file system.

3 Provide Drupal with the login information for your database.

4 Set a few basic settings for your site – such as information for the first user account.

These steps are described in more detail below.

Download the Drupal codebase

You will find the latest version of Drupal at drupal.org. There is a big green button *get started with Drupal*, providing you with some easy-to-use links to get started, but there is also a link directly to *Drupal core* on the site's front page. (See figure A1.1.)

The downloaded file package is either a zip or a tar.gz archive, depending on which download link you use. Regardless of its format, the archive should be extracted with a suitable tool, and its content should be moved to the web folder on the server you're using.

Drupal won't care if you place all the files in a sub folder to your server's web folder instead of putting them directly in the web root – the only thing affected is the path used for accessing your site.

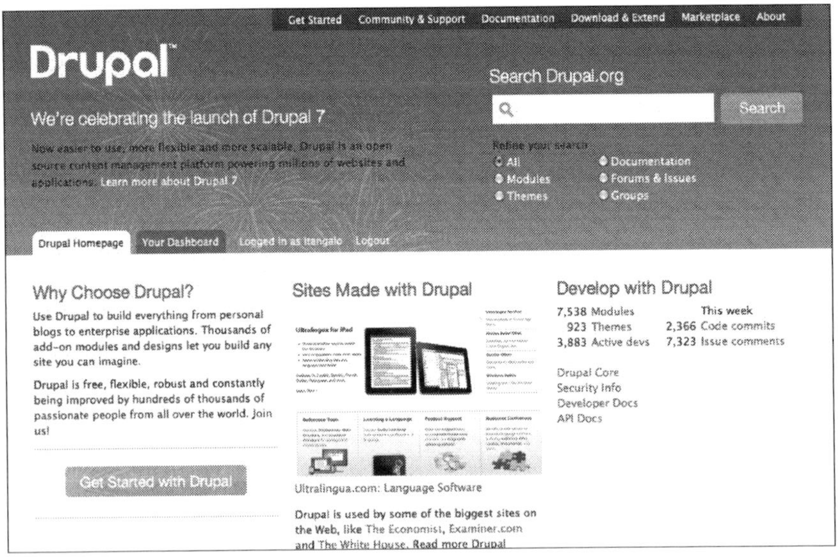

FIGURE A1.1 You can download Drupal from drupal.org – the get started with Drupal button is a good start.

TIP

If you're using a web hosting service, you will probably need an *ftp client* to connect to upload files. A good and free ftp client is *FileZilla*, downloadable from http://filezilla-project.org/. You will need login information, provided by your web hosting service.

Make two changes to the file system

Before the actual installation can start, you will (on most servers) need two make two adjustments to the file system – to assure that Drupal is able to write files to two places. The required steps are:

1   In Drupal's root folder there is a subfolder sites, containing a subfolder *default*. Within it is a file named *default.settings.php*. You should copy this and give the resulting file the name settings.php (placed in the same folder). Note that the file should be copied, and not renamed – Drupal requires the original file as well.

2   In the same foler (*sites/default*), you should create a subfolder named *files*.

3   The file and folder you have created should both be writable for Drupal – meaning that they should be writable for your server. These are the only places Drupal requires write access (except a temporary folder that should be outside the web folder and usually are inherited from your server settings without you having to even think about it).

TIP

If you're using an ftp client, you can change the write access for files and folders by right-clicking on them and choosing any option similar to *properties* or *file attributes*. How the settings appear depends on your ftp client, but you should be able to find a setting for *group write access*. Check that option.

Installation through the web interface

When the file structure is in place, you will do the actual Drupal installation by visiting your soon-to-be website. The server will find Drupal's index.php file, and if no database environment is available, Drupal will run the installation wizard. The steps in the wizard are:

1   Select an installation profile. Drupal core contains the *Standard* and *Minimal* profiles. (See figure A1.2.) The standard profile contains a number of commonly used settings, while the minimal profile is as bare as it gets. There are a number of other installation profiles available at drupal.org, for example for building news sites or project management sites. The examples in this book all build on the standard profile.

2   Choose language. By default only English is available, but if you (or the installation profile) have downloaded additional language packs, Drupal will recognize them and offer alternatives on this screen. (See figure A1.3.) You can add new languages while building your site, as well as during the installation.

3   When language settings are complete, Drupal will check that all requirements are met – such as the file and folder described in the previous section are writable. If anything is wrong, and Drupal can't fix it by itself, you will get an error message along with notes about how to fix the problem.

4   Database configuration. This includes selecting the type of database and entering information necessary to access the database – database name, username and any password. (See figure A1.4.) If you use a web hosting service only providing you with a single database, you may separate different installations by using a *table prefix* – short text added before all database tables created by Drupal (such as *site1_*).

5   When the database settings have been entered, Drupal will run the actual installation. This means that Drupal will be busy in a minute or so – displaying the different steps in the installation process as entertainment.

6   Configure site. When the installation is complete, you will be asked for basic site information – such as site name and time zone settings. (See figure A1.5.) You should also enter information for the first user account on the site. This account will be granted all permissions on the site, and should only be used during development and system updates. (It should not, for example, be a personal account used to post content to the site.)

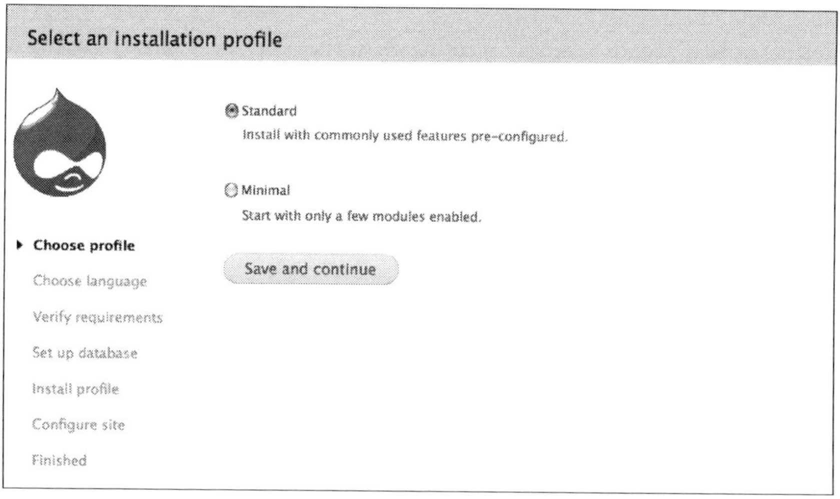

Select an installation profile

◉ Standard
Install with commonly used features pre-configured.

○ Minimal
Start with only a few modules enabled.

▶ **Choose profile**

Choose language

Verify requirements

Set up database

Install profile

Configure site

Finished

Save and continue

FIGURE A1.2 Professional Drupal developers tend to like the minimal installation profile. Others tend to like the standard profile.

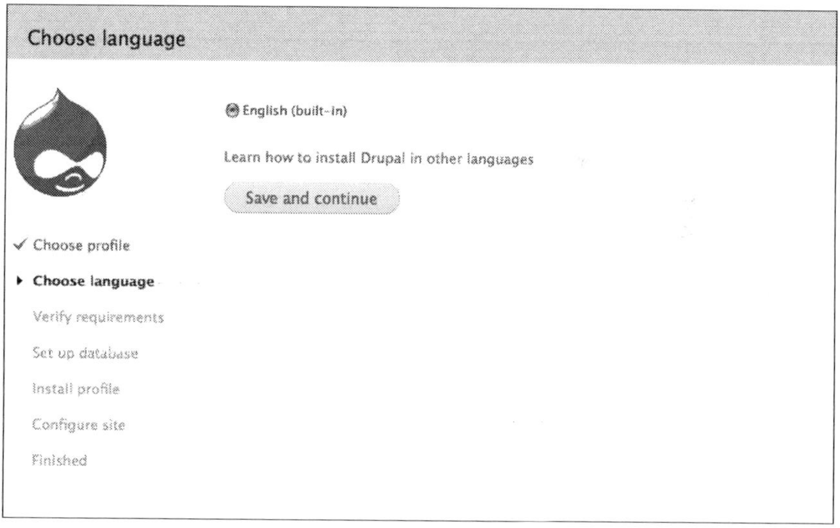

Choose language

◉ English (built-in)

Learn how to install Drupal in other languages

Save and continue

✓ Choose profile

▶ **Choose language**

Verify requirements

Set up database

Install profile

Configure site

Finished

FIGURE A1.3 By adding more languages you can use Drupal in non-English even during the installation.

279

7   When all these settings are made, your installation is complete. (See figure A1.6.) You can now start all the fun experimenting with Drupal!

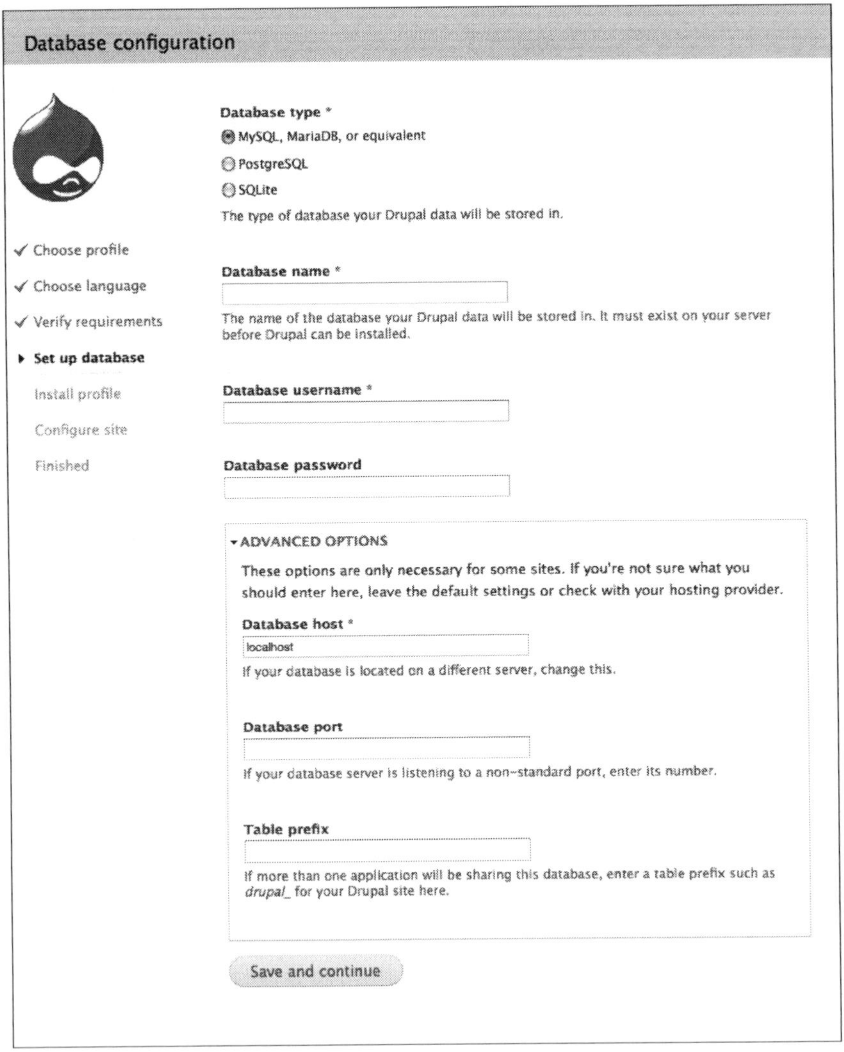

Database configuration

MySQL Drupal logo

Database type *
- ◉ MySQL, MariaDB, or equivalent
- ○ PostgreSQL
- ○ SQLite

The type of database your Drupal data will be stored in.

✓ Choose profile

✓ Choose language

✓ Verify requirements

▶ **Set up database**

Install profile

Configure site

Finished

Database name *

The name of the database your Drupal data will be stored in. It must exist on your server before Drupal can be installed.

Database username *

Database password

▾ ADVANCED OPTIONS

These options are only necessary for some sites. If you're not sure what you should enter here, leave the default settings or check with your hosting provider.

Database host *

localhost

If your database is located on a different server, change this.

Database port

If your database server is listening to a non-standard port, enter its number.

Table prefix

If more than one application will be sharing this database, enter a table prefix such as *drupal_* for your Drupal site here.

(Save and continue)

FIGURE A1.4 Drupal needs database login information to work properly.

Configure site

SITE INFORMATION

Site name *
Learn Drupal 7

Site e-mail address *
johan.falk@nodeone.se
Automated e-mails, such as registration information, will be sent from this address. Use an address ending in your site's domain to help prevent these e-mails from being flagged as spam.

✓ Choose profile
✓ Choose language
✓ Verify requirements
✓ Set up database
✓ Install profile
▶ **Configure site**
  Finished

SITE MAINTENANCE ACCOUNT

Username *
superadmin
Spaces are allowed; punctuation is not allowed except for periods, hyphens, and underscores.

E-mail address *
johan.falk@nodeone.se

Password *
••••••••   Password strength: **Strong**

Confirm password *
••••••••   Passwords match: yes

To make your password stronger:
  • Add lowercase letters

SERVER SETTINGS

Default country
Sweden
Select the default country for the site.

Default time zone
Europe/Stockholm: Wednesday, February 23, 2011 - 15:15 +0100
By default, dates in this site will be displayed in the chosen time zone.

UPDATE NOTIFICATIONS

☑ Check for updates automatically

☑ Receive e-mail notifications

The system will notify you when updates and important security releases are available for installed components. Anonymous information about your site is sent to Drupal.org.

Save and continue

FIGURE A1.5 The last step is entering some basic site information, including information for user account 1.

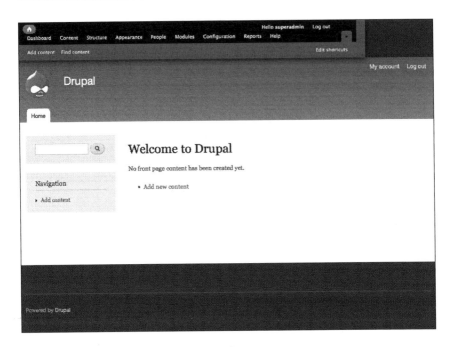

FIGURE A1.6 A new Drupal website, fresh from the installation process.

Alternative ways of installing Drupal

People who have used Drupal a lot, or very little, sometimes use other methods for installing Drupal. Many experienced Drupal developers use the script collection *Drush* to automate downloading and installing Drupal – and there are even tools available for automating Drush, creating new Drupal sites in assembly-line stype. (Anyone fascinated by this should check out the *Ægir* project at http://groups.drupal.org/aegir-hosting-system.)

New Drupalists sometimes prefer prepared single-click installations, where as much as possible is pre-configured. These installations normally require that the automated installer knows the server configuration – which is why these are offered by some web host providers, but not in the default Drupal installer. Another way for an installer to know the server setup is to install a server while installing Drupal.

One example of hosted one-click installers is found at WebEnabled (http://webenabled.com/). An example of installer including both Drupal and a server to run it on is Acquia Drupal (downloaded at http://acquia. com/downloads).

MODULES

What makes Drupal powerful is only partly the functions included in a standard installation. The real power lies in the possibility to extend and customize these functions by using *modules* – plugin programs altering the behaviour of your Drupal site.

This chapter summarizes how you find, assess, install and also update modules.

Modules are found at drupal.org

Since Drupal is open source software, anyone may create their own modules, and may in general do a lot of things to the Drupal codebase. When looking at Drupal's development – as well as many other phenomena – you will soon see that cooperation works better than each and everyone working on their own. One of the ways to facilitate cooperation in the Drupal world is the possibility to create project pages for modules at drupal.org, Drupal's main hub.

The project pages contain information about module features, documentation links, and issue queues for giving feedback to module maintainers, report bugs, submit patches, and a lot of other stuff. Having a single site for contributed modules – *contrib modules* in Drupal lingo – has an important and positive effect on the Drupal community, since it helps Drupalistas to cooperate even more.

> **TIP**
>
> Modules only constitute one of the project types available at drupal.org. There are also themes, installation profiles, documentation and translations. Drupal core itself is run as a project on drupal.org, using the project name *drupal*.

> **TIP**
>
> Technically, what you download from drupal.org is a *project*, while the items you enable in the module list are *modules* – a project may contain many modules. Most Drupalistas, though, call module projects as simply *modules*.

Finding modules

- Use the search box at drupal.org and limit your search to modules.
- Visit the *download & extend* link at drupal.org to browse lists of popular modules. You can also go directly to http://drupal.org/project/Modules.
- Ask around in any of the available forums, to get experienced Drupal developers' opinions about which modules match your requirements. You will find links to web forums and other ways of contact at http://drupal.org/getting-involved (including live chats). Wise people learn from others' experiences.
- Use your favorite search engine to search the internet.

Assessing modules

Learning to recognize good modules is a skill that takes time to master. A good start is, once you found a module you think match your requirements, to check these criteria:

- Make sure that the module works with Drupal 7 (or the Drupal version you are using). On the module's project page is a list of all versions you can download – the Drupal 7 versions have version number starting with 7.x (such as 7.2).

- At the project page is also a header *project information*. It is a good sign if *maintenance status* is *actively maintained* and *development status* is *under active development*. It is also good if *reported installs* is as high as possible – consider anything less than a thousand reported installs a warning.
- The information about the latest release of the module – also found on the project page – could provide further information. A high version number indicates that the module has been around for a while and should be more mature. If, on the other hand, it was more than six months since a new release was published, there is a risk that this module is not very actively maintained. Modules available in (only) beta, alpha or dev versions should normally only be used on experimental sites.
- In contrast to the naïve reaction, a large number of issues reported on the project page is a good sign – it means that a lot of people use the module and cares about its future. It is usually a bad sign, though, if more than 10–20 percent of the reported bugs are open.
- Modules offering general solutions are in most cases to prefer over those that solve very specific problems. This is probably the most difficult factor when assessing modules, since it is far from obvious what you can do with the most general modules. Lucky you, to have this book to help you!
- Finally, you can of course also install the module and try it out. The more rigorous you are with other ways of assessing modules, the more time you can spend on trying out and learning the modules with the highest potential.

Installing modules

The easiest way of installing modules usually looks like this:

1 You find the module at drupal.org and copy the link to the module's archive file (in the *tar.gz* format).
2 You go to the module list on your Drupal site (modules in the toolbar) and click the link *install new module* found at the top of the page.

3 You paste the link to the archive of the module, and hit the *install* button. If Drupal asks for login information for your server, you enter these.

4 To get back to the module list, you follow the link for enabling the newly installed modules.

5 You check the modules you want to enable, and save the settings. (See figure A1.7.)

6 Done!

However, this does not always work. In these cases, the most common installation procedure is this:

- You carry out step 1–4 in the previous list, but fail when you try to enable the module, can't find any administration page for changing the module settings, or you simply won't get the module to work.
- You return to the module's project page at drupal.org and read the installation instructions, and/or notes about how the module works. You may even check out the README or INSTALL text files for the module.
- You find any additional steps you need to carry out before you can start using the module. These could be:
  o The module depend another module, and can't be enabled until you have downloaded that module too.
  o The module depends on an external library, which must be downloaded manually.
  o The module is an API module, without any user interface of its own (and only useful when combined with other modules).
  o The module connects to a third-party service, and requires API keys from that service before you can use it properly.
- You carry out the required additional steps.
- Done!

> **TIP**
>
> You can also add modules manually in the Drupal file structure, which for example is useful when writing your own modules. Contributed modules should be placed in the sites/all/modules folder (and **not** in the root folder modules, used for Drupal core modules). Custom-written modules are usually placed in the *sites/default/modules* folder.

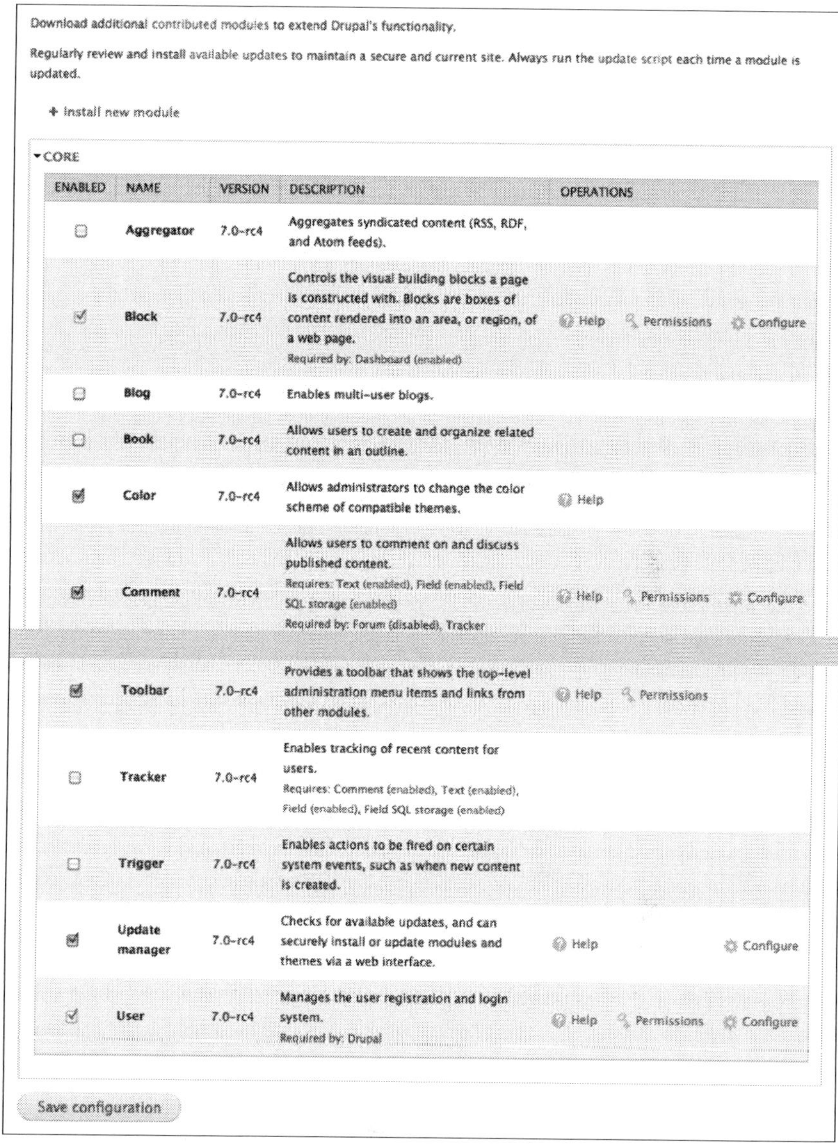

Download additional contributed modules to extend Drupal's functionality.

Regularly review and install available updates to maintain a secure and current site. Always run the update script each time a module is updated.

+ Install new module

▼ CORE

ENABLED	NAME	VERSION	DESCRIPTION	OPERATIONS
☐	**Aggregator**	7.0-rc4	Aggregates syndicated content (RSS, RDF, and Atom feeds).	
☑	**Block**	7.0-rc4	Controls the visual building blocks a page is constructed with. Blocks are boxes of content rendered into an area, or region, of a web page. Required by: Dashboard (enabled)	🔵 Help 🔍 Permissions ⚙ Configure
☐	**Blog**	7.0-rc4	Enables multi-user blogs.	
☐	**Book**	7.0-rc4	Allows users to create and organize related content in an outline.	
☑	**Color**	7.0-rc4	Allows administrators to change the color scheme of compatible themes.	🔵 Help
☑	**Comment**	7.0-rc4	Allows users to comment on and discuss published content. Requires: Text (enabled), Field (enabled), Field SQL storage (enabled) Required by: Forum (disabled), Tracker	🔵 Help 🔍 Permissions ⚙ Configure
☑	**Toolbar**	7.0-rc4	Provides a toolbar that shows the top-level administration menu items and links from other modules.	🔵 Help 🔍 Permissions
☐	**Tracker**	7.0-rc4	Enables tracking of recent content for users. Requires: Comment (enabled), Text (enabled), Field (enabled), Field SQL storage (enabled)	
☐	**Trigger**	7.0-rc4	Enables actions to be fired on certain system events, such as when new content is created.	
☑	**Update manager**	7.0-rc4	Checks for available updates, and can securely install or update modules and themes via a web interface.	🔵 Help ⚙ Configure
☑	**User**	7.0-rc4	Manages the user registration and login system. Required by: Drupal	🔵 Help 🔍 Permissions ⚙ Configure

(Save configuration)

FIGURE A1.7 The module list is used to enable and disable modules. There is also a link for adding new modules.

> **TIP**
>
> Experienced Drupalistas often use the tool Drush ("Drupal shell") to download modules. Check out the project page for Drush at drupal.org for more information.

Uninstalling modules

You should disable and uninstall modules that you don't need. It is done in the following way:

- You *disable* modules by deselecting the relevant check boxes in the module list, and then saving the settings. This turns off any functionality provided by the module, but won't delete any data – if you enable the module again, everything is restored.
- Modules are *uninstalled* at the uninstall tab found at the module list. Uninstalling a module removes any data saved by the module.

There are some benefits of removing unnecessary module folders from your file structure – the biggest benefit being that you won't confuse other developers with modules that are neither used nor enabled. You cannot remove the files using Drupal's web interface, but must manually go into your Drupal files and remove the module's folder at *sites/all/modules*. You should always uninstall a module before removing its folder.

Updating modules

As you will notice after building your first Drupal site, there are frequently module updates published. The procedure for installing module updates is:

1. Log in as user 1, or another account with permission to perform system updates.
2. Put the site in *maintenance mode*, an option found from the toolbar, *configuration, maintenance mode*. This prevents visitors from affecting your database while you're performing the updates.
3. Make a backup of your entire database, and preferably also the file structure of your website. (You should at least backup the folder of the module you're updating.)

4 Download the updated module and replace the relevant module folder.

5 Visit *update.php* in the root folder of your site – there is a link available at the module list. The page will display a summary of the steps desribed above – review these and then click continue to get a list of any update scripts that need to be run in order to convert now old data in the database. Click *apply pending updates* to run them. (If no available updates are displayed, it means that you are already done!)

6 Make sure that the website works as it should, and then take it out of maintenance mode.

> **TIP**
>
> If you find the procedure above time-wasting, or even outright boring, you are recommended to check out the Drush project – allowing you to apply updates with a single command in a terminal.

Modules in Drupal core

A standard Drupal installation contains almost 50 modules. Some of these are enabled in the standard installation profile, and some modules are so important for Drupal that you can't turn them off.

All core modules are described briefly in the list below.

Disabled modules in the standard installation profile

- Aggregator: This module allows your website to read RSS feeds from other websites and publish their content in blocks and separate pages. It is possible to use aggregator data in Views.
- Blog: This module provides a node type and some functionality for managing blogs on your website. You can build more powerful and flexible blogs using fields and Views.
- Book: This module allows you to order nodes in a tree structure, and also provides forward/backward/up links at nodes included in a tree structure. The feature can be useful when writing documentation.
- Contact: This module creates a simple contact form on your website, and also per-user contact forms.

- Content translation: See the chapter about Drupal in more than one language for details.
- Forum: This module provides functionalities for simple discussion forums. You can build more flexible forums using fields and Views.
- Locale: See the chapter about Drupal in a non-English language for details.
- OpenID: This module allows users to log in using OpenID technology, which for example means that authentication can be managed by another website. See http://openid.net/ for more information about OpenID.
- PHP Filter: This module provides a text format parsing and executing PHP code in the entered text. Using PHP in this way is a bad habit and will create massive security risks if put into the wrong hands.
- Poll: This module provides a node type for simple polls on your site.
- Statistics: This module provides site traffic statistics by counting visits to each node page. Statistics data can be used in Views. This module is not recommended on larger websites, since it may cause performance problems.
- Syslog: This module logs activities on your site in the syslog standards, which for example means that you can be notified if severe errors would occur.
- Testing: This module provides a number of automated tests for functions provided by Drupal core, as well as a testing framework for contributed modules. Automated testing should be a part of all professional software development.
- Tracker: This module provides lists to track the most recent activity for users, or the website as a whole. You can create more flexible lists with Views.
- Trigger: This module allows you to configure simple reactions when selected events occur on your website. You can create more flexible reactions using the Rules module.

Enabled non-required modules in the standard installation profile

- Block: This module is responsible for block rendering in Drupal.
- Color: This module allows you to customize the color scheme used in the default Bartik theme as well as in some other themes.

- Comment: This module provides the standard commenting functionality in Drupal.
- Contextual links: This module provides the gear links with some handy links, visible when hovering over blocks and some other elements on your site.
- Dashboard: This module provides simple functions for building an administration dashboard using blocks.
- Database logging: This module logs different types of events to your website's database.
- Field UI: This module provides the user interface for changing entity field settings. It can usually be turned off on live sites.
- File: This module provides an entity field for storing files.
- Help: This module provides simple help pages on your site.
- Image: This module provides an entity field for managing images.
- List: This module provides entity fields for lists.
- Menu: This module is responsible for displaying menus, as well as the administrative interface for managing menus.
- Number: This module provides entity fields for numbers.
- Options: This module provides some widgets for entity fields.
- Overlay: This module allows administrative pages to be displayed in a layer rendered on top of your public website.
- Path: This module provides URL alias functions for your website.
- RDF: This module provides your site with RDFa metadata about the elements displayed on a page. This may be useful for screen-readers as well as search engine robots.
- Search: This modules provides tools for searching content on your site.
- Shortcut: This module allows you to create sets of shortcut links, as well as links for adding and removing shortcuts.
- Taxonomy: This module provides taxonomy term entities, and the functionalities for managing these.
- Text: This module provides entity fields for text.
- Toolbar: This module provides the administrative toolbar, displayed at the top of a standard Drupal installation.
- Update manager: This module makes regular checks to see if there are any updates available to Drupal core or contributed modules and themes.

Required modules

- Field: This module is responsible for basic management of entity fields.
- Field SQL storage: This module allows entity field data to be stored in SQL type databases.
- Filter: This module provides the text formats applied to user input, and the filters the formats consist of.
- Node: This module provides the node entity, and related functions.
- System: This module provides many of the most basic functions in Drupal, as well as some of the site settings.
- User: This module provides the user entity, as well as the login and permission system.

Exporting configuration to code

One of the great advantages of Drupal, compared to other frameworks used to build websites, is how quickly you can build new functions on your site. This is to a large extent explained by the fact that 90 percent of all functions can be provided by clicking and configuring modules, rather than writing code. In that light, it may seem strange that Drupal's community is putting a lot of effort into finding a good way for converting the configuration on a Drupal site into code – to export the configuration.

There are several reasons to why so many are interested in saving configuration as code. One of the reasons is that it is easy to reuse functions that you have built – if you spent a day at clicking around in Drupal to build a photo gallery, you probably don't want to spend another day repeating this configuration the next time you want to build a similar gallery. If you could export your configuration, and move the exported code to your new site, you could have the gallery set up in five minutes instead! Indeed, that would be useful.

But the most important motivation for exporting configuration into code is not that it could be copied. It is that it could be *version controlled*.

Professional software development have for many years been using *version control systems* as a part of the standard tools. These are tools used to record a certain state of the code being built, allowing you to view – and revert to – the code in different stages from the development. Version control systems could be compared to the saving functions in large computer games, allowing you to save your progress between every level (or right in the middle of it). If things go bad or you spent a lot of resources just to hit a dead end – which is hopefully more common in games than in development – you can return to these save points and start over.

Modern version control systems don't only allow developers to save the code they are working on themselves, but can also merge your own work with that of others – even if you should be writing code within the same file. This means that you could be working with a specific feature in a project, while your colleagues are working with several other features, and you could still share your progress with each other.

Version control has become such a natural part of software development that no professional coder would like to take on a project without version controlling her code. It allows you to keep track of the files you're working with and, maybe even more importantly, to transfer a recorded state of the code to test servers, staging servers and live servers. If, for some reason, it would turn out that the latest updates on the live server – despite all testing – have severe bugs, you can always revert to the previous version of the live code. You have *saved*.

Today there are many good systems for version control of code. The problem, though, is that configuration you make in Drupal is saved in the database – and there are no good ways of version controlling database content.

In the old days, this has lead to Drupal developers being forced to do point-and-click changes on the actual live site rather than a development copy of it. Even if you have done this over and over again on a test environment, something may go wrong. Maybe you make a mistake when you click. Maybe there are differences between the live and test server you didn't know about. Maybe someone else has been fiddling with the settings on the live Drupal site, without telling you. If you don't have version control, there is a risk that you can't undo your changes. There is no saved state to return to. No ctrl + z.

This is not the way it should be.

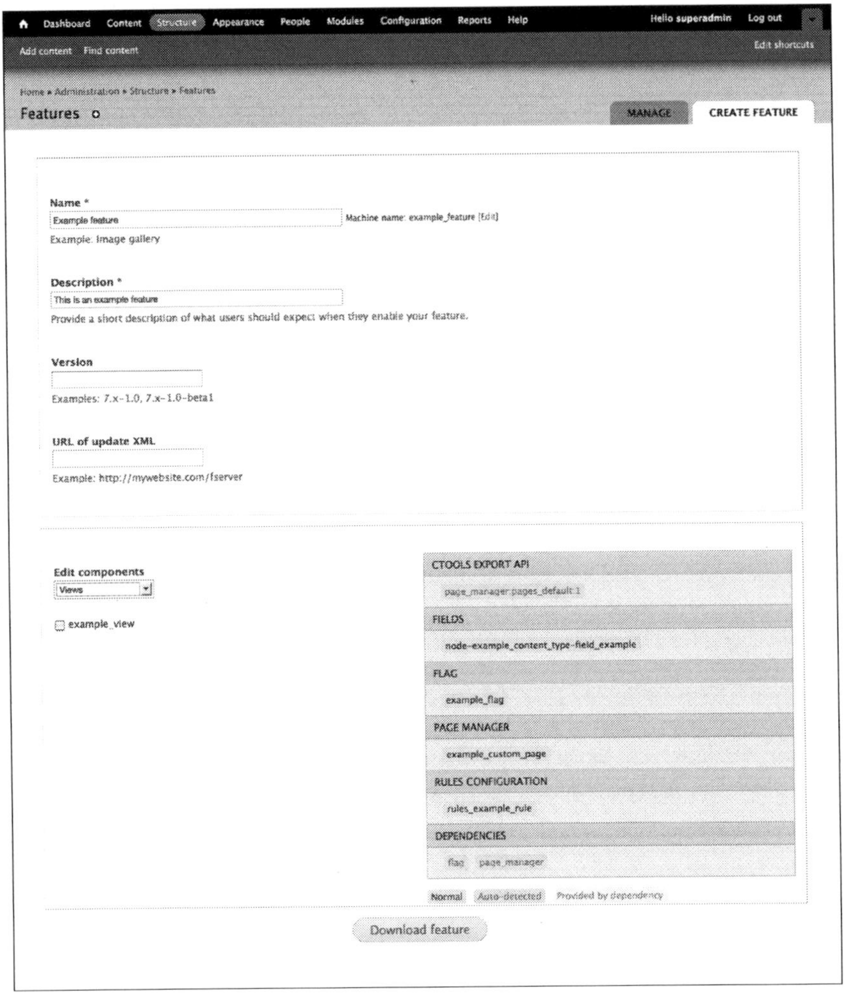

FIGUR A1.8 The Features module allows you to export selected part of your Drupal configuration, and save this configuration as a mini module.

Features

The method for exporting configuration that has become de facto standard in the Drupal community is based on a module called *Features*. Features allows you to select *components* of your site configuration that you want to export, and saves all the related settings into a mini module. (See figure

A1.8.) The module can be used on the site where the configuration was originally made, or any other site where you want to reuse the same settings. When the mini module is enabled, install scripts will run and replicate the configuration for the components you selected to export – node types, entity fields, views, flags, rules and custom pages.

The mini module consists of a number of small files, which can be treated as any other files – which means that they can be version controlled. You can save, update, move between different environments, and revert if you need to.

The Features module has some functions making it particularly useful:

- If any component provided by a mini module are changed by manual configuration, Features will notice and mark the component as *overridden*.
- In combination with the *Diff* module, you may review the overrides of each mini module.
- You may revert each component individually to the state defined by the mini module.
- If the overrides reflect improvements you want to keep, you can let Features recreate the mini module, giving you some new files that you can track in your version control system.

TIP

Features integrates well with the tool Drush, mentioned several times in this book.

TIP

The mini modules created by the Features module are, too, called features. In online documentation, these features are usually written with a small f, while the Features module has a capital F. Feel free to suggest a different naming convetion.

Strongarm and update hooks

Features has solved many of the problems that used to block version control of Drupal configuration. But some problems are still left.

In order for Features to be able to export configuration, the corresponding module must save its settings in a way that Features can recognize. Practically all larger modles support Features, but many smaller modules don't. If you want to version control all configuration in a project, this forces you to either spend a sizable amount of time to improve a number of modules – or to find other solutions.

In particular there are a number of settings in Drupal core that are not natively recognized by Features. To solve this, the Strongarm module was written, acting as a bridge between Features and settings stored in the Drupal variable table. Since many small modules have so few settings that the chose to store them in the variable table as well, rather than creating their own tables, Strongarm will be able to pick up these settings too and tell Features about them.

Still, the Features + Strongarm combination will usually not give you 100 percent exported configuration. If you want this – which you should always strive to – you will sometimes be forced to custom-code so called *update hooks*. These are functions being executed when you update modules (or Drupal core) from one version to another. Your custom update hooks should be written to perform the last database changes which otherwise would have required manual clicking – finally providing you with a fully automated workflow for updating site configuration.

Elaboration: Using Features efficiently

It takes time and training to use Features efficiently, and you are encouraged to start using Features to export configuration early on to get this training. Here are a few tips.

- The best way of assuring that Features has captured all the settings you want to export is to install your features (mini modules) on a clean Drupal site. On the site used to build the features, non-exported settings in your database may trick you to believe that everything is exported.

- Divide your site configuration into several different features. This makes it easier for several developers to work in a single project – working on separate features – and it also makes it possible to enable and disable each feature individually on the resulting site. You can also reuse selected features on other sites more easily.

- When dividing site configuration into separate features, you want the lines between the features to be as clear as possible to avoid conflicts. Usually this means that different sections or functionality on the site is kept in separate features – for example building a *blog* feature and a *news* feature – but you could also break configuration up further, such as *blog creation/management* and *blog display*. In general, many and small features are better than few and large.

- You will get features that depend on other features. Marking any required features as *dependencies* when building a new feature may save you future problems.

- A lot of small modules store their configuration in the variable table. All these variables are available as Strongarm components when creating features – check this list if module settings don't show up as separate component groups.

- You will probably find it useful to have a *core* feature including all the basic settings for a site, such as permission roles and site front page. This feature could, if necessary, be treated as a standard module and used for including any custom update hooks.

- Exporting individual menu items with Features is sometimes problematic, since menu items can be defined by (say) a custom page and then overridden by the Menu module. If you want to export manually created menu items in the same menu as menu items provided by modules, you will most likely end up with overridden features that cannot be reverted. This can be solved by removing the menu items defined in (say) custom pages, and adding the corresponding menu links manually in the menu interface.

- Drupal block settings cannot be exported with Features, even when using Strongarm. Three modules that helps in exporting block-like configuration are Panels, Context and Boxes.

TIP

The work for improving configuration export in Drupal is ongoing. At time of writing, there is a dedicated project for improving this for Drupal 8 – where the current approach is to by default store *all* configuration in code. Features is the de facto standard for Drupal 6, and so far also for Drupal 7, but it is possible that the work for Drupal 8 will provide new and better configuration management even for Drupal 7. Anyone interested in this progress should join the discussion group at http://groups.drupal.org/build-systems-change-management.

THEMES

At a large scale, Drupal does three things happen when a page on your website is requested. The first is that Drupal checks which files and libraries are necessary to collect the information on the page – and how much of the information the requesting user is allowed to access. The second is to actually collect all the information, which usually involves quite a bit of querying and poking in the database. The third and last step is to take the big, naked array of collected data and dress it up with different templates and HTML tags to make it presentable in a web browser.

The last step is called Drupal's *theme layer,* and is governed by your site's *theme.* The theme layer is separated from the rest of the data management – meaning that one and the same website may have its look and feel completely changed without having to change the content a bit. For anyone skilled in HTML, CSS, JavaScript and other languages used to present digital content, it also means the possibility to do an extreme makeover of Drupal's presentation.

> **TIP**
>
> Most Drupal themes outputs (X)HTML, but nothing in Drupal forces the content to be presented as a web page. A theme could for example present content as spoken text, or as XML files processed by other applications.

Changing the theme of your website

At the toolbar, *appearance,* you will find a list of all themes available on your Drupal site. (See fiture A1.9.) In a standard Drupal installation you will find four themes:

FIGUR A1.9 The themes overview page allows you to select which theme should be used on your site.

- Bartik: This is the standard theme, used for non-administration pages.
- Seven: This is the theme by default used on administration pages.
- Garland: This is the default theme used in Drupal 6, ported to Drupal 7 as an alternative to Bartik.
- Stark: This is a stripped-down theme that could be used as a *base theme* (see separate section).

Each theme has a *set default* link, used to set which theme should be used on non-administration pages. Just below the themes list is an option to select which theme should be used on administration pages.

The page for selecting theme has a tab *settings,* used to change a number of theme settings. The theme settings usually include options to turn on and off page elements – such as site name or *main links* – and the option to change logo or shortcut icon for your site.

Each theme enabled on your site will have its own sub tab, where you can change settings individually, and themes may also add new settings to this page. The Bartik theme, for example, allows changing color settings on your site using the *Color* module. (See figure A1.10.)

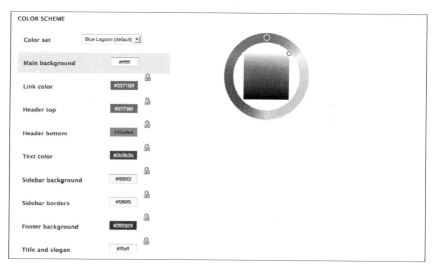

FIGUR A1.10 Each theme may have its own particular settings. The core theme Bartik allows changing color scheme.

> **TIP**
>
> If more than one theme is enabled, users with appropriate permissions may themselves choose which theme to use. This may be useful to offer a high-contrast theme to users with visual impairments.

Installing contributed themes

Developing themes for Drupal is an art in itself, and will not be covered in this book. Luckily, you don't have to write your own theme to be ably to vary the look and feel of you Drupal site – there are plenty of contributed themes to download and use. (At the time of writing, six months after Drupal 7.0 was launched, 169 themes are available.)

You will find contributed themes at the same place as contributed modules – at drupal.org, and the tab *download & extend*. Themes are, just as modules, installed in one of two ways:

- By using the link *install new theme* found at the theme overview page, and pasting a link to the theme archive at drupal.org – in parallel to how modules are installed.
- By manually downloading and extracting the theme, and placing it in the folder *sites/all/themes* in your Drupal installation. (**Not** the root folder *themes*, used for core themes.)

When this is done, then new theme will be available in the themes overview list and may be used in the same way as other themes.

Base themes and writing your own themes

For small websites is is often enough to use a contributed theme – perhaps with a tweak here and there – but in professional web development few clients would accept having a site that looks as hundreds or thousands of other Drupal sites.

The art of writing new themes will not be covered in this book, but there is room for two tips for anyone hungry to develop a theme of her own:

- Instead of building a new theme from scratch, you should use a *base theme* – a theme written to be extended and built upon. Using a base theme will spare you a lot of work in resetting parts of Drupal's standard markup, and you will also get good support for older versions of Internet Explorer (which have a tendency to make web sites in general look broken). With a good base theme, at least 80% of your theming work can be accomplished by just writing CSS.

- Instead of hacking and changing your base theme, you should create a *sub theme*, including only the things separating your theme from the base theme. This allows you to update the base theme when necessary, without jeopardizing your own work.

> **TIP**
>
> The *Stark* theme, included in Drupal core, is an example of a base theme – and more base themes can be found on drupal.org. One good base theme when learning to theme is the *Zen* theme, the most popular of all Drupal themes. Next to Stark in the theme overview is a link to more information about how to create your own theme.

Appendix 2:
Language management in Drupal

DRUPAL IN A NON-ENGLISH LANGUAGE

Drupal has good support for creating websites using other languages than English. This chapter presents how to switch the user interface from English to another language – see the *multilingual Drupal sites* chapter for information about how to have several languages present on a site.

In this example, Swedish will be used as the non-English language.

Installing contributed translations

When using Drupal in some other language than (US) English, the contributed translations are an invaluable asset – providing translations of thousands and thousands of expressions and strings.

Installing contributed translations with Localization update

While writing this book, the module *Localization update* was published. The module drastically simplifies the process of installing new languages – automatically downloading and installing from Drupal's central translation repository. It can also notify you when there are updated translations available, allowing you to update your site.

With Localization update, the language installation process is as simple as this:

- Install the Localization update module, according to the same procedures as with other modules. This will require you enabling the *Locale* module, used to allow translation of the user interface.
- Go to the toolbar, *configuration, languages* and click on the link *add language.* (See figure A2.1.)

307

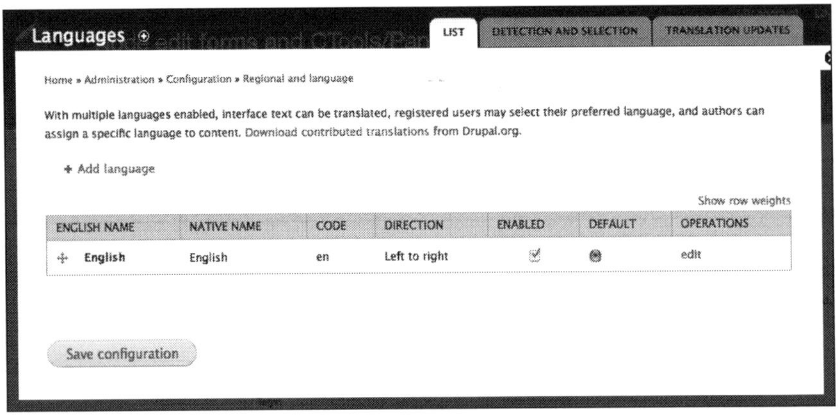

FIGURE A2.1 The language overview page, including the link for adding new languages.

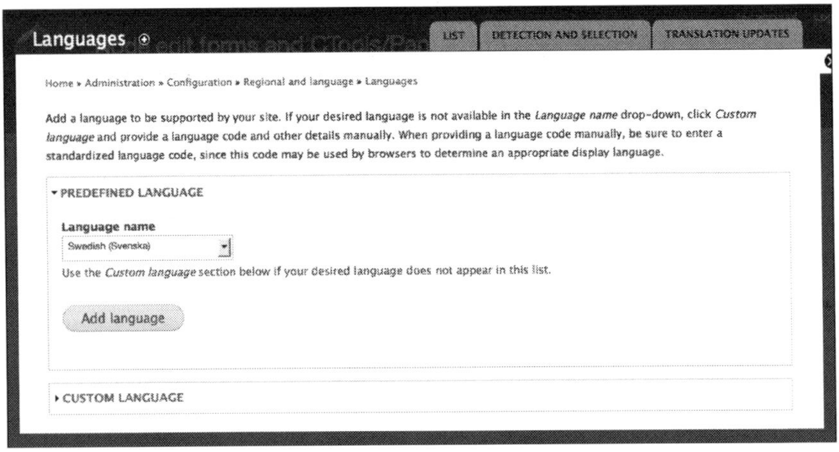

FIGURE A2.2 Drupal has a large number of pre-defined languages, most of which have contributed translations.

FIGURE A2.3 Localization update will fetch available translations for Drupal core as well as for contributed modules. You will appreciate this step in particular if you have previously installed translations manually.

- Select which contributed translation you want to add. (See figure A2.2.)
- Click the *add language* button and wait for Localization update to download and install the translations for Drupal core and any contributed modules you have enabled. (See figure A2.3.)
- When the import is done, you will be redirected to the language overview page, where you can select the new language as the default language on your Drupal site. This will make Drupal display administration links, description texts and other parts of the user interface in the chosen language rather than English. (See figures A2.4 and A2.5.) Easy as that!

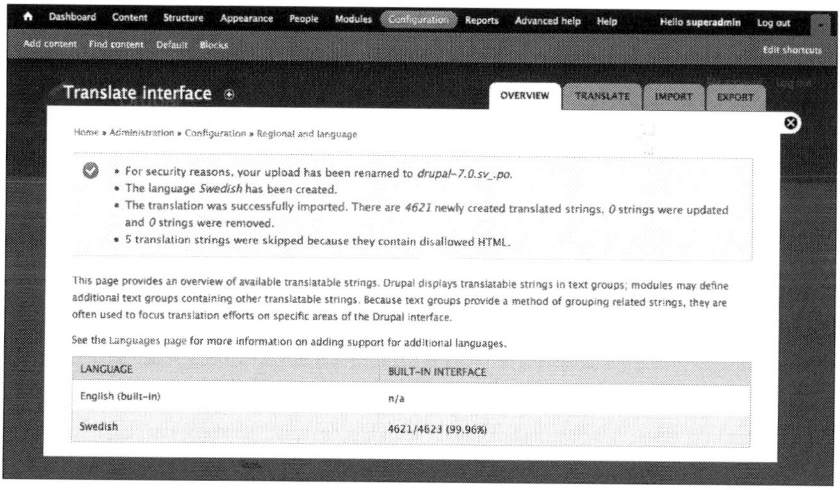

FIGURE A2.4 The language overview page, now with Swedish freshly installed.

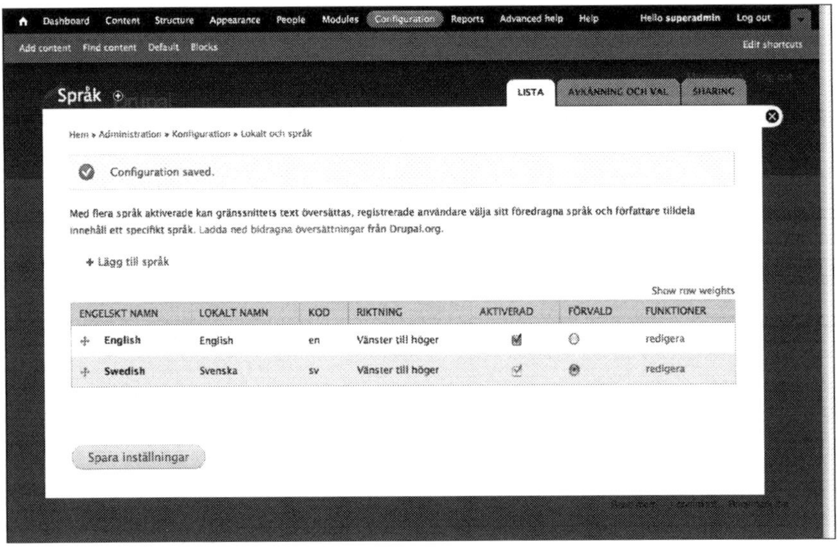

FIGURE A2.5 The language overview page – now with Swedish set as default language.

Adding or editing translations

Since Drupal and its contributed modules are in a state of constant development, you will most likely find parts of your interface that are not yet translated. You may also discover translations that you would like to change to make them fit better with the terminology used on your site.

Drupal has built-in tools to translate strings in the interface right on your website. You find the tools in the toolbar, *configuration, translate interface* and finally the tab *translate*. The resulting page contains a search function to find text strings – verbatim expressions – on your site. (See figure A2.6.) Each search result has a link for creating/editing its translation – clink on the link to set the translation to whatever you like!

If you don't find the text string you want to translate, it if probably because one of the following factors:

- Drupal has not yet loaded the text string – only strings that have been displayed are recognized by Drupal and available for translation. Visit a page where the string is displayed, and try searching again.

- You have set small or capitalized letters differently from how the string is stored – the search function is pretty picky about this. Check your spelling and search again.
- You're *trying to find a string that contains a variable, such as* Hello admin. Try searching again, excluding any parts that you suspect are variable. (*Hello admin* is actually stored as *Hello @username *, to allow translations of even variable phrases.)
- The string you want to translate is not a part of Drupal's own interface, but the configuration – such as the content of a block or a node. Configured strings need special tools to become translatable – see the chapter about multilingual Drupal sites.
- The string you want to translate is not passed through Drupal's translation function. Since all interface text should be passed through the translation function, you have found a bug – and the module maintainer will probably be happy if you report this at the module's issue queue.

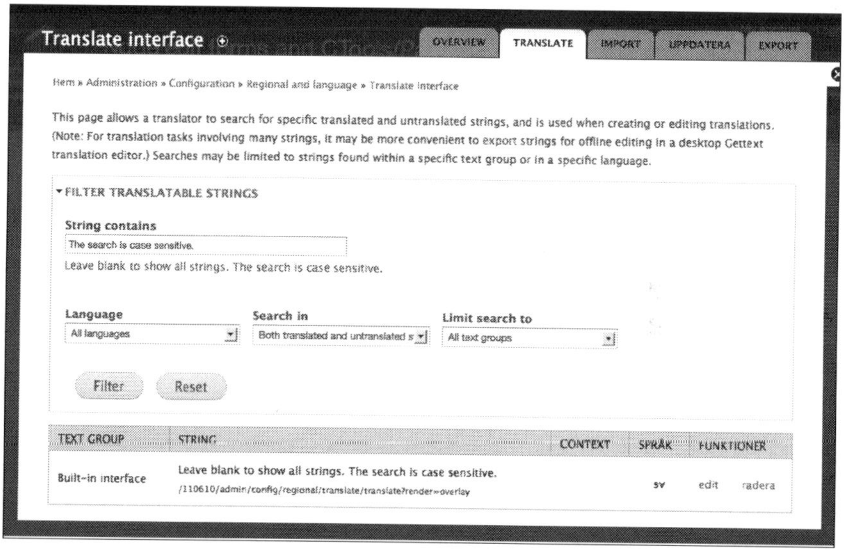

FIGURE A2.6 Drupal has a built-in tool for allowing site administrators to set or update translations.

When translating strings that include variables, you should make sure that the variables are included even in the translated string – or Drupal won't be able to vary the string content correctly. The string *Hello <strong> @username</strong>*, for example, should be translated to *Hej <strong> @username</strong>* in Swedish.

When changing translations, you should be aware of the fact that new translations (in most cases) will be used at all places where the English original phrase turns up. Changing the string Save, for example, will affect nearly all forms on your website.

Translating with Localization client

The *Localization client* module provides a number of tools useful when making more extensive translation work. The two most important are:

- Pop up boxes used to search text strings and creating translations, available on every page when a non-English language is selected.
- Functions to contribute translations to Drupal's translation repository at localize.drupal.org. (See the toolbar, *configuration, languages* and the *sharing* tab.) If you do this, you should also consider getting involved in your local translation team – visit localize.drupal.org for more information.

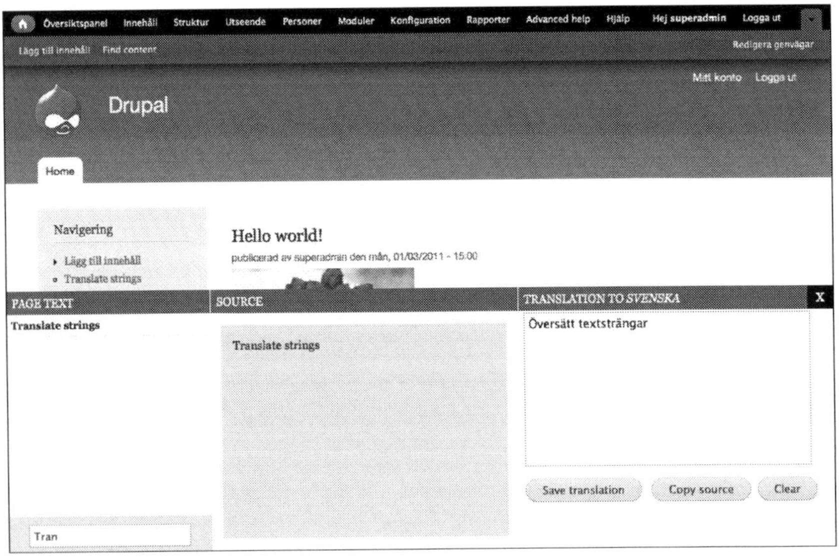

FIGURE A2.7 The Localization client module is a good tool if you need to translate large parts of your website, rather than just a few strings.

The Localization client features are not described in detail in this book.

Installing translation updates

The Localization update module not only allows you to import contributed translations, but also to fetch and apply translation updates when they become available.

By default, you have to check for updates manually. This can be changed by going to the *translation updates* tab found at the toolbar, *configuration, languages*. The configuration page also allows you to determine how locally changed translations should be treated – either keeping them on new updates (default), or overwriting them if their remote translations have changed.

You may check for translations updates manually by visiting the *update* tab in the toolbar, *configuration, translate interface.*

MULTILINGUAL DRUPAL SITES

Building a website that should be able to present content in more than one language requires a fair amount of planning. What content types should be available in more than one language? Should the nodes be translated, or should each node be created for one language at a time – independently of each other? How should taxonomy terms be handles? Menus? Is it enough to have administration pages in one language only? Should labels for entity fields be translated, too? Which views should display all content, and which should be language-sensitive?

This chapter describes the basics in managing Drupal content in more than one language, and gives some advice about where to find information about more advanced multilingual options.

Translating nodes

The first and most important things to translate are the nodes on a website – and for many websites it is enough if a handful nodes are translated to more than one language.

To allow translations of nodes you have to enable the *Content translation* module (included in Drupal core) – and to use it to any effect you must also have more than one language available on your site. (See the previous chapter for details about how to add languages.)

With Content translation enabled you will find a few new settings available for each node type – see the toolbar, *structure, content types* and the *edit* link for each node type. Under the *publishing options*, a setting *multilingual support* is now available with the following options (see figure A2.8):

- Disabled: This will give nodes of this type the default site language.
- Enabled: This provides a language selector for each node of this type. (This option is available as soon as the Locale module is enabled.)
- Enabled, with translation: This option not only allow you to make nodes language-specific, but also to translate nodes into other languages.

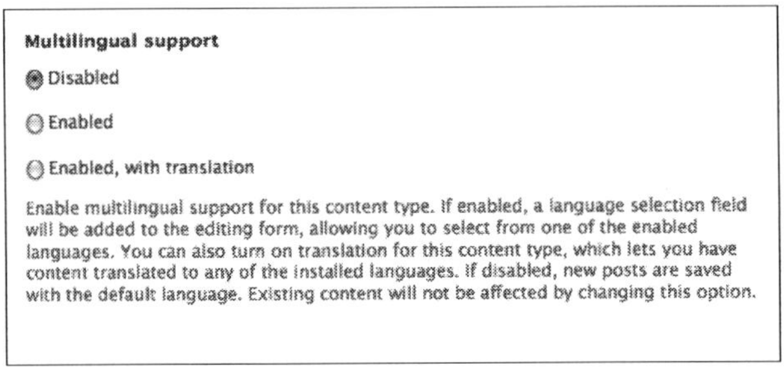

Multilingual support

⦿ Disabled

◯ Enabled

◯ Enabled, with translation

Enable multilingual support for this content type. If enabled, a language selection field will be added to the editing form, allowing you to select from one of the enabled languages. You can also turn on translation for this content type, which lets you have content translated to any of the installed languages. If disabled, new posts are saved with the default language. Existing content will not be affected by changing this option.

FIGURE A2.8 The Content translation module allows handling nodes in more than one language.

> **TIP**
>
> Changing language settings for a node type doesn't affect any existing nodes. Normally you want to set the language options for node types before content is created.

Editing nodes with language support enabled

When creating or editing nodes with language support enabled, there is a new field available – *language*. This option allows selecting the language used for the node, or selecting *language neutral*.

At nodes with translation functionality enabled, site administrators will see a new tab – *translate*. It leads to a page listing all available translations of the node, and offering links to create new translations. (See figure A2.9.) In the list of translations, one of the nodes are marked as *source* – this is used as the original text for the other nodes, and its content will be copied into node forms when creating translations.

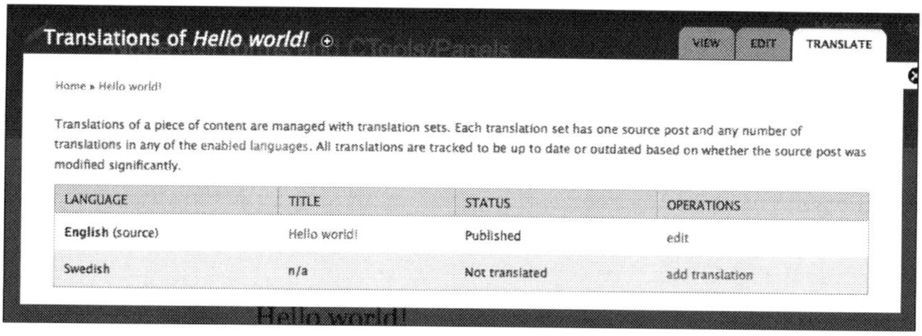

FIGURE A2.9 Translatable nodes have a new tab, used to overview or create translations.

With translatable nodes come a few new functions that help site visitors and administrators.

- Each node has links leading to any existing translations. (See figure A2.10.)
- When editing source nodes, there is an option *flag translations as outdated* available in the *translation settings* fieldset. (See figure A2.11.) If checked, all translations will have a corresponding checkbox *this translation needs to be updated* checked.

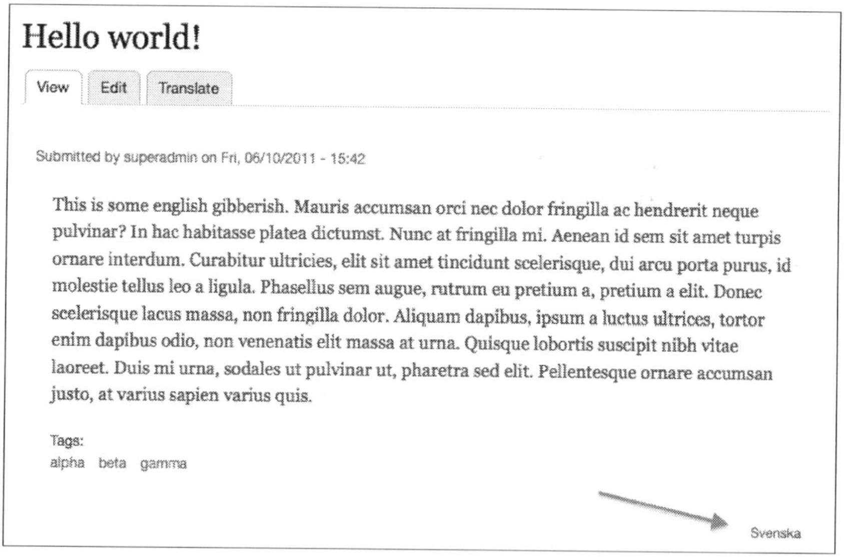

FIGURE A2.10 Nodes with translations get links to each translation.

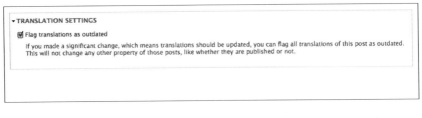

FIGURE 12.1 When editing a source node, all its translations may be marked as outdated.

- The content overview page (*content* in the toolbar) has a new filter option for status – *outdated translation* – making it easier to find content that needs to be updated.

Language selection

With more than one language available on your site, there is of course also the question about which language should be displayed. Drupal has several ways of selecting this:

- By domain name or path prefixes for each language, such as en.example. com and sv.example.com, or example.com/en/node/1 and example.com/ sv/node/2.
- By a parameter in the request or session, such as example. com?language=en.
- By detecting language settings in the visitor's browser.
- By reading the language settings in a logged-in user's account.

You may select which of these options should be used, and how they should be prioritized, by visiting the *detection and selection* at the toolbar, *configuration, languages*. Which prefix should be used for each language can be changed at the language overview page, by following the *edit* link for each language

More tools for multilingual sites

On most sites, you will get very far by having the interface in one single language and some information pages translated into several languages.

> **TIP**
>
> The Locale module provides the block *language switcher*, with convenient links for switching between different language versions of the same page (where available). You must enable language detection by prefix to use this block.

But on some sites, this is not enough. The starting point for making truly multilingual sites is the *Internationalization* module. This module offers, among other things:

- Multilingual options for taxonomy terms and vocabularies, similar to those previously described for nodes.
- Multilingual options for menus.
- Translatable blocks, and block visibility settings based on language.

The project page for Internationalization contains a number of useful links for anyone who wants to read more about multilingual issues, and also lists for more modules extending the multilingual capabilities of Drupal..

> **TIP**
>
> At the time of writing, the *Entity translation* module is being developed. It builds on Drupal core's translation capabilities, but also provides a user interface for translating fields rather than entire entities.

13264757R00185

Made in the USA
Lexington, KY
22 January 2012